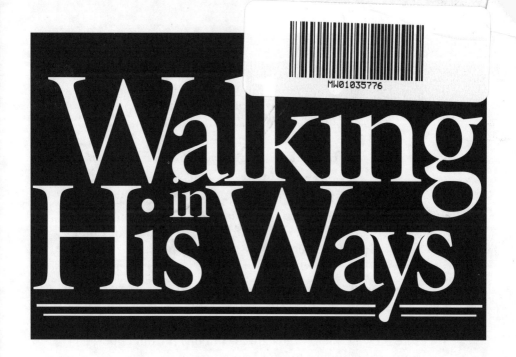

Walking in His Ways

*"Thus saith the Lord of hosts,
If thou wilt walk in my ways . . . I will give thee
places to walk among these who stand by."*
—Zechariah 3:7

GREG HINNANT

CREATION
HOUSE
PRESS

WALKING IN HIS WAYS by Greg Hinnant
Published by Creation House Press
A part of Strang Communications Company
600 Rinehart Road
Lake Mary, Florida 32746
www.creationhouse.com

Scriptures marked Weymouth's New Testament
in Modern Speech.

Words that are set off by vertical lines are words in the New
Scofield Reference Bible that differ from the authorized King
James Version. These differences are slight, but the reader who is
very familiar with the King James Version would notice them.

Scripture quotations marked NIV are from the Holy Bible, New
International Version. Copyright © 1973, 1978, 1984,
International Bible Society. Used by permission.

Greg Hinnant
P. O. Box 788
High Point, N.C. 27261

Library of Congress Catalog Card Number: 00-108955
International Standard Book Number: 0-88419-758-1

2 3 4 5 6 7 VERSA 8 7 6 5 4 3 2
Printed in the United States of America

This book is dedicated
to my mother,
Edna L. Hinnant,
who for so many years blessed my life
with unconditional love, unswerving devotion and
unceasing encouragement to pursue the call of God.
And to my very dearest ones, my children,
Samuel,
Sarah,
John
and Joseph,
to whom, I pray, God's grace will enable
me to give the same Christ-like love,
devotion and encouragement
for many years to come.

Acknowledgments

I would like to acknowledge, with deepest thanks, the extraordinarily faithful ministry associates with whom the Lord has blessed me. Their ceaseless, selfless service to this ministry for Christ's sake—in gifts, prayers, labors and fellowship—has made this book, and indeed this teaching ministry to the body of Christ, possible. For so generously blessing others, may the Lord generously bless...

Alice W. Bosworth

Jean Brock

John J. McHugh, Jr.

Virginia G. McHugh

Kathleen E. McHugh

Phyllis H. McNeill

Mary Ann Mowery

Evelyn A. Ward

I am also grateful to Dr. Judson Cornwall, who, periodically over the last few years, has helped me with unselfish assistance, prudent counsel, fatherly love, the kindness of a friend and the able tutelage of a literary and ministerial mentor.

Contents

FOREWORD

In this day of "easy believism," where all an inquirer is asked to do is "accept Jesus," it is refreshing to find among us a minister of grace who feels that acceptance is merely an initial step into discipleship. This was Paul's concept of conversion. He affirmed, "When someone becomes a Christian he becomes a brand new person inside. He is not the same any more. A new life has begun!" (2 Cor. 5:17, TLB). This demands something more than lip confession—it is a life conversion. It is not merely a one-time action; it is a life commitment. Like a newborn infant, we must grow up.

When Jesus was here on the earth, His call was not for acceptance, but for followers. He didn't seem to teach a sinner's prayer; He taught walking out of the old life into the new. His effect upon converts was a radical change in lifestyle. It is highly unlikely that Jesus Christ has changed His requirements. He still wants us to walk out of the world system into the kingdom of God.

Perhaps converts in today's generation would move from their self-centered lifestyles if they knew how to do so. Through the prophet Isaiah, God promised us, "Although the Lord gives you the bread of adversity and the water of affliction, your teachers will be hidden no more; with your own eyes you will see them. Whether you turn to the right or to the left, your ears will hear a voice behind you, saying, 'This is the way; walk in it'" (Isa. 30:20–21, NIV).

We may have many more persons willing to walk in the ways of God than know the ways of God. After all, the Scriptures tell us, "He made known his ways to Moses, his deeds to the people of Israel" (Ps. 103:7, NIV). Persons who have made a commitment to walk out of their personal Egypt may know what God has done for them, but often they lack understanding of how to walk with God. They need a Moses— a teacher—who will point them into the ways of God.

Greg Hinnant is such a teacher. I personally know him to be a faithful student of God's Word and a capable exposi-tor of that Word. In this book, he gives us twenty-four paths, or ways, God has asked us to walk as believers. These ways are neither complex nor complicated, but they are commanded. Like the multiple lanes of a freeway, they are all headed the same direction. Reverend Hinnant gives an accurate road map, points out the signposts, and shows us how one way leads into another until finally we stand in the presence of Almighty God in the great heaven He has prepared for us. It is a lifetime adventure of "Victory in Jesus."

—JUDSON CORNWALL

PREFACE

C hristianity is both a relationship and a way of life. By grace, through faith, the believer suddenly enters into a personal relationship with God through Jesus Christ and, out of that relationship, embraces life anew. While becoming a Christian is an instantaneous miracle, living as a Christian is a continuing educational process. It is all about learning a new way of life. But what exactly is a "way?"

Literally, a way is a selected route of travel, a corridor or channel of passage from one location to another. It is a path trodden, a road taken. Spiritually, a way is a *manner of living*. To the Christian, then, a way is a set of habits formed, a lifestyle developed, a spiritual road followed—from here to eternity. The Bible's repeated use of the term way is noteworthy.

Most significant is Jesus' declaration, "I am the way" (John 14:6). He also likened the lifestyle of His truest followers to a straight and narrow way. (See Matthew 7:14.) Appropriately, then, the Christian lifestyle, and the church itself, were at first known as simply the "way" (Acts 19:9). The writer to the Hebrews resounded this keynote, characterizing Christianity in general and Christian worship in particular as "a new and living way" (Heb. 10:20). Moses prayed,

Walking in His Ways

"Show me now thy way" (Exod. 33:13); and, as if to inform the reader of God's response, the psalmist declares, "He made known his ways unto Moses" (Ps. 103:7). Note the deliberate change here from the singular (way) to the plural (ways). Why is this?

It is because the way of the Lord is multifaceted. As a long automobile journey (way) is comprised of many shorter highways (ways) linked together, so the way of true Christianity is comprised of many smaller ways of biblical discipleship, each linked sequentially to the next. Hence, it is a way of ways. To know God's general way, we must know the more specific ways of God.

So David prayed, "Show me thy ways, O Lord; teach me thy paths" (Ps. 25:4); and the Spirit answered, "The meek will he teach his way" (25:9). Paul exhorted the Corinthians to walk in the ways of God, which he had incorporated into his lifestyle, sending Timothy to teach them "my ways which are in Christ, as I teach everywhere in every church" (1 Cor. 4:17). God cited ignorance of the ways of God as the chief reason Moses' generation failed to do His will: ". . . they have not known my ways" (Heb. 3:10). Through Zechariah He challenges us to rise above our failures, promising to open doors of service to all who walk in His ways:

> Thus saith the Lord of hosts, If thou wilt walk in my ways...I will give thee places to walk among these who stand by.
>
> —ZECHARIAH 3:7

Will we answer God's challenge? To walk in God's ways, of course, we must know them.

The following messages set forth the ways of Christian discipleship, from spiritual infancy to spiritual maturity. Throughout the Christian era, no one has ever left a significant mark upon the church without walking in these ways. Let us, then, learn them and learn them well, that we may walk in them . . . until He comes, in whom all the ways of God terminate.

—GREG HINNANT

Chapter One

The Way of
Devotion

"When thou saidst, Seek ye my face, my heart said unto thee, Thy face, Lord, will I seek."

—PSALM 27:8

To glorify God, we must serve Him acceptably. To serve God acceptably, we must know Him deeply. To know God deeply, we must seek Him diligently. To seek God diligently, we must learn the lifestyle of devotion.

Let us, then, go to the top of the mount . . .

GO TO THE
TOP OF THE MOUNT

"And Moses went up into the mount . . ."

—EXODUS 24:15

Chiefly, the Christian life is about knowing God in an ever-increasing measure. It is the beginning of eternal life in time. Jesus revealed this when He said, "And this is life eternal, that they might know thee, the only true God, and Jesus Christ, whom thou hast sent" (John 17:3). Inflamed with loving gratitude, the apostle Paul gave up everything to know the Lord who saved him: "Yea doubtless, and I count all things but loss...that I may know him..." (Phil. 3:8, 10). Sadly, many born-again ones do not share Paul's passion. For while all true Christians are equally related to God, all are not equally knowledgeable of Him.

We know the Lord only as much as we seek Him. And the Bible reveals repeatedly that seeking God is an "if" matter:

> *If* thou seek him, he will be found by thee.
> —1 CHRONICLES 28:9, EMPHASIS ADDED

> *If* thou seekest her as silver, and searchest for her as for hidden treasures; then shalt thou . . . find the knowledge of God.
> —PROVERBS 2:4–5, EMPHASIS ADDED

1

> And ye shall seek me, and find me, *when [if]* ye shall
> search for me with all your heart.
> —JEREMIAH 29:13, EMPHASIS ADDED

Steadfast seekers eventually acquire a full and deep understanding of their God, while the uninterested remain unacquainted with and unsure of Him. Or, to put it simply, the more we seek God, the more we know Him. We see this portrayed in the Israelites' experiences with God at Mount Sinai.

All the Israelites who came out of Egypt were equally related to Jehovah, but not all knew Him in the same degree. Exodus 24 reveals that among the company of the redeemed there existed three distinct levels of intimacy with God. The congregation, the seventy elders and Moses each represent a different depth of the knowledge of God.

THE CONGREGATION

Encamped on the plain at the base of Mount Sinai, the people of Israel experienced God at a distance. (See Exodus 24:3–8.) When earlier He had appeared on the Mount and, amid an awesome display of light, smoke and blaring trumpet blasts, delivered His Ten Commandments, the people fled in mortal terror. Rather than draw near to their Savior, they drew back and stood afar off: "And God spoke all these words...And all the people saw the thunderings, and the lightnings...and when the people saw it, *they moved, and stood afar off*" (Exodus 20:1, 18, emphasis added).

And afar off they remained. Never did they fellowship with the Lord. Never did they speak with Him face to face. Never did they sit in hushed wonder and concentrate on His unique beauty. Never did they spend long hours bathing in His cleansing, transformative presence. They saw the fire and the cloud brooding atop Sinai and wondered at the glory that made Moses' face shine, but they never drew near to know the source of these miracles for themselves. Always, they heard from God indirectly, never personally. After declaring His Decalogue, God never again spoke to the people; He spoke to Moses and Moses spoke to the people. And it was their desire that it remain that way: "And they said unto Moses, Speak thou with us, and we will hear; but let not God speak with us . . ." (v. 19).

Therefore, the congregation's knowledge of the Holy One was entirely secondhand. It was impersonal, distant, limited, shallow. Though redeemed from Egypt, they remained largely ignorant of the One who had redeemed them.

THE SEVENTY ELDERS

The seventy elders of Israel went farther in the quest to know God. Unlike the people, they at least began to seek their Savior, spending some time—albeit a little in close, personal fellowship with Him. In the company of Moses, Aaron, his sons and Joshua, Israel's elders climbed the lower slopes of Sinai, where they held a communion supper with God on the side of the mount. (See Exodus 24:9–11.) There they beheld the same glory Moses beheld at the burning bush. The inspired record reads, "Then went up Moses, and Aaron, Nadab, and Abihu, and seventy of the elders of Israel; and *they saw the God of Israel...they saw God, and did eat and drink*" (Exod. 24:9–11, emphasis added). But this communion, though personal, was brief. Apparently, it lasted only a few hours. The Lord then returned to the top of Sinai and called Moses to come up to Him (24:12–13), leaving the elders on the sides of mount (24:14).

These seventy, then, knew God more deeply than the people. The reason is simple: They sought Him more. Rather than drawing back, they drew near. Rather than looking away, they looked on, their eyes beholding the indescribable beauty of the Lord. Rather than fleeing from the cloud, they spent time basking in the presence of the King of glory and communing with Him over a meal. Their knowledge of the Holy One, therefore, was direct. It was firsthand, clear, personal. But even so, it was limited. The seventy elders were not nearly as intimate with God as Moses.

MOSES

Of all the Israelites, only Moses spent an extended period of time alone with God. (See Exodus 24:12–18.) While the people encamped in the plain and the elders abode on the sides of the mount, Moses made the long, arduous climb to the top of the mount alone: "And Moses went into the midst of the cloud, and got up into the mount " (24:18). (Joshua also went to the top of the mount, but only to aide Moses, not to commune face to face with God; compare Exodus 24:13–14 and 32:15–17.)

Moses' spiritual communion was the deepest, and rarest, kind—forty consecutive days and nights, or 960 straight hours in fellowship with the eternal Spirit! (See Exodus 24:18.) Unlike the people's communion, which was nil, or the elders', which was brief, Moses' time in God's presence was *sustained*. Day after day, night after night, week after week, fortnight after fortnight, he soaked in the miraculously creative atmosphere of the Shekinah. At the end of his visit he was a thoroughly remarkable man—a man permeated with God.

Hence, the fruit of his fellowship was remarkable. Out of Moses' prolonged fellowship came Israel's entire knowledge of her God. It was on the mount that Moses received the Ten Commandments, God's will for mankind. It was on the mount that he received the judgments, God's regulations for Israel's social order. It was on the mount that he received the ordinances, God's instructions for His chosen way of worship. And it was on the mount that he received the pattern for the Tabernacle—the "pattern shown to thee in the mount" (Heb. 8:5)—which blessed the sons of Abraham with grand visions of their coming Savior, His church and heaven.

These lofty revelations were the rewards of Moses' lofty fellowship. While the people were content to hear God's voice afar off, and the elders rested in their limited experience with Him, Moses was blessed with an abiding spiritual hunger that kept him ever climbing, ever seeking, ever inquiring, ever meditating, and, consequently, ever finding more of God. This led him into a knowledge of God much deeper than that possessed by his peers. Moses' knowledge of the Most High was not only firsthand, it was intimate, full, rich and overflowing; and all Israel drank from his fount. In his extraordinary sojourn atop Sinai, we see a spiritual lesson too clear to miss: God reveals Himself most to those who seek Him most.

∼

Now all these things happened to the Israelites as illustrations for us. We will find that it is the same with us today as it was with the Jews of Moses' generation. All born-again Christians are equally related to God through faith in Christ, but not all enjoy the same degree of fellowship with Him or possess the same knowledge of the Lord. There are in the churches today three distinct types of believers corresponding to the three kinds of Israelites seen at Sinai—plain, mount, and summit Christians.

PLAIN CHRISTIANS

Some Christians live their entire lifetime at the base of the mount. After being saved in an exalted encounter with Jesus and experiencing a brief period of spiritual zeal, they draw back from their first love for their Savior. Consequently, they follow Him, but only from a distance. They see Him, but only dimly. They are Spirit-born, but not Spirit-filled. They know the Lord, but their knowledge is shallow. Their knowledge of the Word is little more than the Ten Commandments. These hear God's voice, but always from afar—through their pastors' weekly messages, over Christian television or radio, in Christian publications, in Bible study groups or in the lyrics of gospel music.

Never have they experienced the Spirit opening the Word to them in private Bible meditation. Never have they discerned the still, small voice speaking to them through dreams, prophecies or counsel. The reason? Simply, that they have never sought the Lord in a personal way. Their contact with Him is strictly public, never private. It is confined to the meetings and activities of the church. Theirs is a knowledge of God that is entirely secondhand, and they are quite content for it to remain that way. These plain Christians are happy enough to be saved but quietly determined to keep the Savior at arm's length. Seeking God, they reason, is for monks, fanatics and foolish new converts, not sane churchgoers.

It is a dry, dull existence that non-seekers choose for themselves. Never do they hunger for more of God, hence, they never taste and see that the Lord is good. Never do they thirst for living water, hence, they never drink in spiritual refreshment. Never do they yearn to go *up* to new heights of spirituality, faith and power; so, they never rise above their carnal peers. Because they profess to be "Christians," these uninspired residents of the church plain are reported to have spiritual life but are, in fact, spiritually dead. And their spiritual deadness is the fitting reward of their spiritual indolence.

MOUNT CHRISTIANS

Thankfully, many Christians at least make a start at seeking God. As Israel's seventy elders did, they climb part of the way up the mount of holy fellowship. But, sadly, too many of them turn aside and settle for life on the sides of the mount. They talk and feel after the summit-life for a season, only to fall back gradually into a lifestyle distinctly less than the highest. Thus, they abide in the spiritual middle, not on the summit or in the plain but on the sides of the mount; not hot or cold, but spiritually lukewarm.

Unlike plain Christians, these mount Christians have known personal fellowship with the Lord, but only on a limited basis. They have sat at His spiritual table during exalted times of fellowship, nourishing their hearts with the bread of His Word and sipping refreshing truths from His cup of biblical insights, but only occasionally, not daily. They have *visited* His secret place, making known to Him their hearts' desires in times of crises, but have never formed the habit of *dwelling* there. (See Psalm 91:1.) Their fellowship has been sporadic and brief, not sustained. Never have they kept a daily devotional over a long season. Why have these, unlike Moses, failed to come up unto God into the mount and *be there?* (See Exodus 24:12.)

Several hindrances keep them back. Though they have moments of genuine desire, mount Christians lack the self-discipline to daily climb and abide in the high places of spiritual blessing. A plethora of snares bind them to the low places. The cares of this world demand, and get, their thoughts. Good but unimportant interests enter and consume their free time and energy. The lust for material gain first rivals, then usurps their desire to become rich in God. Unspiritual people steal their affections and attention. They become entangled in purely worldly pursuits.

Or, as they begin forming a Word-centered lifestyle, tribulation or persecution arises; so, offended, they turn back to avoid further trials, as many did in Jesus' day: "From that time many of his disciples went back, and walked no more with him" (John 6:66). These often justify their spiritual procrastination, concluding that there is only so much time in the day

6

and God, gracious as He is, will surely be content with His devotional half-hour, or quarter-hour or minute. So they stop short of the top of the mount.

SUMMIT CHRISTIANS

There are yet Christians who, bearing a strong spiritual semblance to Moses, go on to the top of the mount. Refusing to give their hearts to less than the Highest, they set their affections on God: "Because he hath set his love upon me . . ." (Ps. 91:14). Instead of limiting their devotional life, they "follow on to know the Lord" (Hos. 6:3), beyond the multitudes on the plain, beyond other seekers that settle on the sides of the mount, all the way to the summit of the knowledge of God.

These spiritual mountain climbers seek the King and build up His kingdom in their souls *first* every day: "But seek ye *first* the kingdom of God, and his righteousness..." (Matt. 6:33, emphasis added). They have heard the Lord's call to seek Him *early:* "I love those who love me, and those who seek me *early* shall find me" (Prov. 8:17, emphasis added). And they have responded in love to Him, "O God, thou art my God, *early* will I seek thee..." (Ps. 63:1, emphasis added). By study and experience, they have discovered the threefold meaning of the word early:

- In the early hours of the day
- Before other things
- Diligently

So they seek the Lord diligently, with businesslike regularity and steadfastness. So they seek Him before other things, jealously guarding their intimacy with Him by heeding His words before any others and talking to Him before anyone else. So they seek Him in the early hours of the day, when all is quiet and Jesus draws near the temple courts of their souls to teach. Morning by morning, they sit quietly and submissively at His feet, seeking daily bread from His Word. (See Matthew 6:11; Luke 10:38–42.) Even if they should rise late, they insist on at least a brief morning interview with the Lord of the day.

There, in His presence, they make decisions and order changes according to His will, as David did long ago: "Thy servant did meditate in thy statutes...I thought on my ways, and

7

turned my feet unto thy testimonies" (Ps. 119:23, 59). They tell Him all their problems, ask His wisdom and assistance, and thank Him in advance for His unfailing help. (See Philippians 4:6–7.) In sharp contrast to Christians of the plain, summit Christians steadily keep worldly anxieties at a distance and the Lord of peace close by; hence, He works steadily in their behalf, adding all the things they need little by little: ". . . and all these things shall be added unto you" (Matt. 6:33).

As time passes, these conscientious seekers know God ever more deeply. Because of their special love for Him, God gives them special understanding of Himself, His Word, and His plan for their generation, as Jesus promised: "He it is that loveth me...and I will love him, and will manifest myself to him" (John 14:21). As a result, they increase steadily in biblical knowledge, personal understanding and spiritual discernment and, as sons of Issachar, soon know their times and what God's people should do. As their vision grows ever sharper, they discern truth from error, true servants from impostors and the Spirit's ways from the tempter's paths. As Moses did, summit Christians speak to Omnipotence face to face and are noticeably changed by the transformative power of the presence. God will call these for special service. He will lead them in the way He chooses. They shall bear much fruit, bring much glory, reap many rewards and execute the divine plan for our generation.

Friend, you may have a relationship to Jesus Christ, bought and paid for on the cross, but that does not guarantee you will know the Lord. To know Him, you must seek Him. To know Him deeply, you must seek Him diligently. In Exodus 24, God sets your options before you. Which kind of a seeker will you be—plain, mount or summit?

Hear what the Spirit is saying, and make the right choice. Don't stop short in your quest to know God—deeply, fully, brilliantly, overflowingly. Don't be content to follow Jesus at a distance; life on the plain is not God's chosen way for His people. Nor is life on the sides of the mount; limited seekers abide partially satisfied. Life more abundant is found only at the top of the mount. So get going! Begin climbing towards those glorious heights today, this very hour! Go ever onward and upward until you reach the apex of the Christian way. And when you arrive at that lofty spiritual camp, be wise. Never again descend from that standard of fellowship with Jesus. Live on the mount forever. That is, remain in the way of devotion the rest of your days. Or, as the Lord put it in His original charge to Moses, *be there!* "And the Lord said unto Moses, Come up to me into the mount, and *be there…*" (Exod. 24:12, emphasis added).

To do that, you will have to learn the way of self-discipline.

Chapter Two

The Way of
Self-Discipline

"Give diligence to make your calling and election
sure..."

—2 PETER 1:10

Discipline is an essential part of discipleship. A disciple is not
only a learner, but also a disciplined one—one who is orderly,
regular, diligent. An undisciplined learner God will not—He
cannot—use. Upon Christ's disciplined ones His Spirit will
invariably fall, and through them He will remarkably work.
The only lasting discipline is self-discipline, and time management is one of the most practical forms of self-discipline.

We must learn to take and make time for God...

Taking and
Making Time for God

"So teach us to number our days, that we may apply our hearts unto wisdom."

—Psalm 90:12

Time is a very precious and perishable commodity. With mercy toward none and impatience toward all, it steadily slips away, minute by minute, hour by hour, day by day. Even while you take the time to consider this subject, your life, like a mist, is gradually vanishing from the earthly scene: "For what is your life? It is even a vapor that appeareth for a little time, and then vanisheth away" (James 4:14). It was this that was before the psalmist when he prayed, "So teach us to number our days, that we may apply our hearts unto wisdom" (Ps. 90:12).

To "number our days" is to *highly value and wisely use the time God has allotted us.* It is time management pursued and perfected. Our mastery of time is directly related to our ability to glorify God.

If we want our lives to count for God, we must get to know Him. In His high priestly prayer, Jesus voiced this, His heart's desire, "[Oh!] that they might *know thee*, the only true God" (John 17:3, emphasis added). To know God, we must seek Him: "*Seek ye the Lord* while he may be found, call ye upon him while he is near" (Isa. 55:6, emphasis added). To seek Him, we must spend time with Him. We see this clearly in the apostles' calling.

Before the twelve preached and ministered healing and deliverance in Jesus' name, and before they called others to come unto Him, they had to spend time with their divine Master. Extended private fellowship with Jesus—to "be with him"—was the first and most vital phase of their calling. Note Mark's words: "And he |appointed| twelve, that they should *be with him...* " (Mark 3:14, emphasis added).

Truly, there would have been no going forth to work the works of Jesus if the apostles had refused to spend time with Him. Though Jesus called them "that he might send them forth to preach, and to have authority to heal sicknesses, and to cast out demons" (3:14–15), they neither received power nor began preaching on the day Jesus appointed them. In fact, instead of going out, they went in. That is, they "went into an house" (3:19), where they began discharging their sacred duty to spend quality time with Jesus—pondering His Word, asking Him questions, soaking in His Spirit, observing His utter dependence on His Father, learning His ways, wondering at His power and marveling at His compassion.

The apostles' active public ministry—the second and more visible phase of their calling—did not begin until sometime later. Again, note Mark's words: "And he called unto him the twelve, and began to send them forth by two and two, and gave them |authority| over unclean spirits..." (Mark 6:7; See also verses 8–13). So we see that the apostles first formed the habit of spending time with Jesus (a habit they continued thereafter); then, as that time in His presence began transforming them, they began to go forth as His agents, living members of His body, true expressions of His very purpose, message, grace and power. And He was glorified.

We are called to follow the apostles' example. To do so, we also must learn to "be with him" (Mark 3:14). This, our sacred duty, demands our time. Hence, we must take, and at times make, time for Him. And we must do it now. Life is extremely short and Jesus' return is very near; there is simply no time to waste. That is, if we seriously hope to glorify God.

In his insightful book, *The Root of the Righteous*, A.W. Tozer writes:

Probably the most widespread and persistent problem to be found among Christians is the problem of retarded spiritual progress. Why, after years of Christian profession, do so many persons find themselves no farther along than when they first believed?

Tozer concludes that the probable cause of retarded spiritual progress is "failure to give time to the cultivation of the knowledge of God." Then he adds:

> Progress in the Christian life is exactly equal to the growing knowledge we gain of the Triune God in personal experience. And such experience requires a whole life devoted to it and plenty of time spent at the holy task of cultivating God. God can be known satisfactorily only as we devote time to Him...We may as well accept it: there is no short cut to sanctity...A thousand distractions would woo us away from thoughts of God, but if we are wise we will sternly put them from us and make room for the King and take time to entertain Him. Some things may be neglected with but little loss to the spiritual life, but to neglect communion with God is to hurt ourselves where we cannot afford it.

Tozer's observation is a word in season. In this instant age, we tend to look for shorter, easier ways of doing everything. But there is no way to obtain instant spiritual reality. Christian maturity is available only on a pay-as-you-go basis: if we don't pay the price, we don't go on to know God. We cannot press a key, or click on a computer button and have God suddenly create in us a wonderful, well-rounded knowledge of Himself. Abraham could not. It took years of seeking, trusting, waiting and obeying before he fully knew the God who called him. And it was the same with Joseph, Moses and David. Why, even Jesus did not mature in a moment.

Over a thirty-year period, Jesus spent many long hours in private communion with His heavenly Father. Then He went forth "full of grace and truth" (John 1:14). Then He outwitted the tempter time and again and accepted rejection with amazing grace. Then He heard the voice from above, when others only heard thunder. Then He spoke truths that humbled the proud and encouraged the oppressed. Then He walked calmly on stormy waters. Then He perceived His Father's hand in every circumstance and quietly suffered the cruelest injustice rather than fail to do His Father's will.

All this glory sprang from one spiritual well—the time Jesus spent alone with His heavenly Father. Jesus was driven by a passion for His Father's presence. To satisfy it, He mastered the art of time management. This demanded rigorous self-discipline. Morning by morning Jesus rose early to pray and meditate upon Scripture. Often He withdrew Himself from the multitudes, and from the twelve, to restore His soul in the presence of His Father.

Today, the heavenly Father is looking for Christians who are willing to live as Jesus lived: "As he is, so are we in this world" (1 John 4:17). Where are those Christians who love Jesus enough to spend time with Him? Are we among them? Are we being honest with ourselves, and with God, about our use of time?

In *Workman of God*, Oswald Chambers writes:

> Peter said to Ananias, "Thou hast not lied unto men, but unto God." Christian worker, how much time are you giving to prayer, to reading your Bible? "Oh, I am giving all the time I can." Be careful that you are not lying to the Holy Ghost. Pentecostal lying begins in this way, dragging down the intense holiness of God which keeps a man right with God in every detail of his life. Let us examine ourselves the next time we say, "I have not time," or, "I give all the time I can to the study of God's Word," "I give all the time I can to praying." God grant we may be put on the alert on these lines that we may not be found lying to the Holy Ghost. May these words come with warning and with scrutiny and bring our souls face to face with God.

As Solomon observes, "There is...a time to every purpose under the heaven" (Eccl. 3:1). Let us consider, then, the purposes to which we give our time. We take time to eat, sleep and work. We take time for education, entertainment, recreation and relaxation. We take time to visit with family and friends. We take time to examine, buy and sell the material goods needed for life in this world. We take time for births, deaths and marriages. We take time for special events, and national and religious holidays. We take time for church and social activities. But amid all this careful allocation of time, where does God fit in? Where is our time for Him? Where is our window of opportunity to obey Christ's command, "Come unto me," on a daily basis? (Matt. 11:28).

Isn't it unreasonable to take time for everything and everyone but God and yet expect to know God so closely that we possess the faith of Abraham, the wisdom of Joseph, the devotion of David, the insight of Daniel, the courage of Nehemiah and the love of Paul? Certainly it is, for such character traits thrive only in souls that give much time to God.

If we are ever going to spend time with God, now is the time to do so: "Behold, now is the accepted time..." (2 Cor. 6:2). If ever we are going to rise and seek the Lord first morning by morning, now is the time to do so. If we are ever going to study the Bible, now is the time to do so. If we are ever going to "pray without ceasing" (1 Thess. 5:17), now is the time to do so.

If we are ever going to become "approved unto God" (2 Tim. 2:15) and "disciples indeed" (John 8:31), now is the time to give ourselves "wholly" to the process of becoming: "Till I come... give thyself *wholly*...." (1 Tim. 4:13, 15, emphasis added).

Spiritual procrastination—putting off God's plans while we pursue our plans—is a disciple's greatest enemy. It hinders our spiritual growth so effectively that the devil doesn't have to oppose us! He rests while we self-destruct—by wasting our precious, and irrecoverable, time. Many fail to make the best use of their free time.

So often believers have plenty of free time but refuse to use any of it for God. Forgetting that the good is ever the enemy of the best, they commit all their spare moments to good works. Hence, in their lives, worldly busywork usurps spiritual activity and temporal interests crowd out eternal pursuits. Mary "sat at Jesus feet, and heard his word" (Luke 10:39), but these distracted saints, as Martha, hustle about, encumbering themselves from dawn to dusk with activities, activities and more activities. They soon become so entangled with the affairs of this life that they cannot even see, much

15

less run, the race the Lord would set before them.

Consequently, the Christ-life in them is quenched—either worked to death or clubbed to death—by the garden club, the book club, the civic club, the music club, etc. While society may praise them, such lives will at last be reckoned "much ado about nothing" from God's perspective. Why? Because they failed to use their leisure time to seek Him.

Other saints have very little extra time. The demands of job, family and church consume almost all their waking moments. Yet, surprisingly, some of these hear and answer the call to seek the Lord. How do they do it? Where do they find the time to abide with Jesus in the secret place? They don't find it, they *make* it. Because they take Matthew 6:33—"Seek ye first the kingdom of God, and his righteousness"—seriously, they prayerfully rearrange their daily schedules to create windows of opportunity to give time to the Lord. Then something wonderful occurs.

Because they give time to the Lord, He gives them more time to give. In Matthew 25:29, Jesus revealed an amazing spiritual law, that believers who make good use of what they have will be given more: "For unto every one that hath shall be given [more], and he shall have abundance." And, He continues, those who do not use what they have will lose it: "...but from him that hath not [used what he hath] shall be taken away even that which he hath."

Applying this principle to our use of time, we discover that *God gives more time to those who use their time for Him.* When the Lord sees us using our free time to seek Him, He is so pleased that He works wonders in our circumstances to give us more free time—which we may then use to seek Him further. So the more we make time for Him, the more we find new time to take for Him: "...and he shall have abundance." Why does the Lord do this? Because He sees we are numbering our days well and knows He can trust us to value highly and use wisely any additional time to "apply our hearts unto wisdom" (Ps. 90:12); that is, to glorify Him. So He gives us more time that He may ultimately reap more glory.

Conversely, those who consistently misuse their free time and never even think of making time for God, receive the opposite treatment: *God takes time from those who misuse their time.*

Eventually, what little time they have is taken away. Christ said, "From him that hath not [used what he hath] shall be taken away even that which he hath." Apparently, the Lord reasons, why should He help us manage our time if we refuse to use it for His purpose and glory?

Fellow disciple, where are you in regard to time management? Does this way of self-discipline mean anything to you? Are you using or wasting the time God has given you? Whatever your answers, here is one question infinitely more important: Are you willing now to take time to seek the Lord? To do so, you will have to establish new, spiritual priorities. This will likely result in a major disruption of your present lifestyle. It will mean rescheduling your typical workdays, evenings and weekends to create time for God.

As life at the feet of Jesus becomes your new passion, you will find that many formerly important pastimes fade away forever; many of your firsts become lasts and your lasts firsts. Such a personal reformation commands the attention of God, whose eyes run to and fro throughout the whole earth seeking those who willingly take time to know Him, and He will immediately begin revealing Himself to you in a much greater dimension. And, henceforth, you will be marked as an extraordinary Laodicean.

An ordinary "Laodicean," of course, is a Christian who is disappointingly typical of this spiritually lukewarm, and final, period of the Church Age in which we live. In the Book of Revelation (chapters 2–3), Jesus' messages to the seven churches of Asia are more than a historical record. They are also prophetic, giving us an inspired (and, hence, infallible) pattern of the course the church will follow down through the centuries from its beginning at Pentecost to its end at the Rapture.

His last message, which is addressed to the church at Laodicea, reveals the kind of churches and Christians that will prevail in the last days. With indisputably clear language, Jesus depicts a Christian body whose members are infatuated with this present world, zealous for money and material things, given to moral compromise, untested, deceived about their true spiritual state, smugly self-satisfied with their limited Christian experience and, hence, a sickening disappointment to Him (3:16). And the day of which He speaks is the day in

17

which we now live. For proof of this, I would say simply look around you.

Take off your spiritual bifocals (religious pride and wishful thinking) and really examine the spiritual state of things. Honestly consider yourself, your church, your denomination and the interests and teachings popular among Christians today. Then compare your findings with the high ecclesiastical standard set for us in the Book of the Acts. Take your comparison further by putting today's typical Christian faith and commitment alongside that seen during the Roman persecution, Luther's Reformation, Wesley's revivals, Finney's crusades and the original Pentecostal movements of the twentieth century. If you do, you will find that most Christians in this present day have put other things—"all these things do the Gentiles seek" (Matt. 6:32)—before Jesus.

We have sought material things passionately and our Lord indifferently. When confronted with difficult moral decisions, we have generally compromised Jesus' teachings to avoid unpleasant conflicts, criticism and rejection. As a result, our generation has been slow to follow on to know the Lord. We've been born of the Spirit but we've not grown up in the Spirit. And our spiritual procrastination has kept the Lord waiting to bless us with the riches of His Word, His presence and His power: "Therefore will the Lord wait, that he may be gracious unto you . . ." (Isa. 30:18).

But in these last days the Lord will wait no longer. The night is far spent and the day is at hand. Now other things, the temporal interests to which the foolish Laodiceans still hold, will have to wait while God moves on with those who are developing a passion for His presence. So today, if you have free time for the Lord, take it. And if you don't, *make* it.

Then you will be ready to walk in the way of study.

Chapter Three

The Way of
Study

"Study to show thyself approved unto God, a workman that needeth not to be ashamed, rightly dividing the word of truth."

—2 TIMOTHY 2:15

To walk with Christ, we must obey Him. To obey Him, we must know His Word. To know His Word, we must study the Bible. Not speed-read it or scan it lightly, but study it—slowly, thoughtfully, thoroughly, believingly, prayerfully. And this labor of love must not be occasional. It must be regular, systematic, determined.

Every disciple, then, must become a spiritual treasure hunter...

TREASURE HUNTERS

"If thou seekest her [wisdom] as silver, and searchest for
her as for hidden treasures; then shalt thou under
stand...and find the knowledge of God."

—PROVERBS 2:4–5

From ancient times men have engaged in various forms of
treasure hunting. Years have been sacrificed; seas, lands,
and deserts crossed; mountains scaled; ocean depths fath-
omed; caves explored; mines dug; and many other hardships
and dangers faced, all for the purpose of retrieving the hidden
treasures of this world. It was this fever that lured prospectors
by the thousands to California, Colorado and Alaska during
their gold rush days. Why, even the celebrated explorer,
Christopher Columbus, was a kind of treasure hunter. He discovered the Americas while seeking a shorter, safer route to
the East Indies—to obtain its treasured spices.

The usual motive for these extensive searches is obvious.
Once these vast sources of unclaimed riches are found, their
discoverers often live the rest of their days in the luxurious
ease reserved for the rich and powerful. We call it "the good
life."

THE SEARCH FOR THE ATOCHA

In the late 1960s, Mel Fisher, an American treasure hunter,
began investigating the record of the sunken Spanish galleon,
Atocha. This famous treasure ship, heavily laden with a huge

fortune in gold, silver, precious stones and other valuables, sank in 1622 in the stormy waters of the Gulf of Mexico near Key West, Florida. Captivated by the Atocha's reported wealth, Fisher planned and launched his own quest to find it.

The expedition that followed was extremely demanding. Great diligence and persistence were required, for the exhausting search continued sixteen years. This hunt also demanded total commitment, for as time passed Fisher's sacrifices became great. Personally, he lost his son and daughter-in-law, who perished at sea. Financially, the expedition's expenses became astronomical. Psychologically, the stress of searching year after year after year, apparently for nothing, wore heavily on him and his entire crew. At long last, however, on July 20, 1985, they located the Atocha—and Fisher had his treasure! Never before salvaged, the galleon was loaded with treasures worth hundreds of millions of dollars. Weary, but jubilant, Fisher, his crew and his investors each received their share of the fortune. And to this day, I suppose, they are living the good life (see website: shipwrecktreasures.com; October 2000).

In this worldly story there are spiritual truths worthy of our deepest consideration. By conducting a serious, sustained search, requiring great diligence and sacrifice, this treasure hunter obtained vast wealth. That wealth in turn raised his material standard of living. We see, then, that *a man's diligent search led to wealth, and that wealth improved his life.* As it is in the natural, so it is in the spiritual.

The Bible declares that spiritual wealth—the wisdom and knowledge of God—is far more valuable than the most fabulous treasures of this world: "Happy is the man that findeth wisdom...for the merchandise of it is better than the merchandise of silver, and the gain thereof than fine gold. She is more precious than rubies; and all the things thou canst desire are not to be compared unto her" (Prov. 3:13–15). It then urges us to become spiritual treasure hunters: "If thou seekest her [the wisdom and knowledge of God] as silver, and searchest for her as for hidden treasures..." (2:4). The Spirit is saying that we should expend the same kind of effort hunting for God's riches that Mel Fisher put forth searching for the Atocha's treasures.

While some Christians do study to show themselves approved unto God, the plain truth is that many put forth no effort to seek the riches of God's Word. They reserve no time, study no books of the Bible, explore no translations, research no topics, consult no concordances, expend no thought and probe not the rich depths of individual Bible verses and phrases. As a result, they possess only a pittance of the spiritual wealth God has hidden in His Word and never experience the good life He offers. They abide needlessly in spiritual poverty—destitute of the peace of God, deprived of the sense of His presence, hungry for understanding, thirsty for encouragement and insufficiently clothed with confidence in His keeping power. They are easily taken captive by the tempter's wiles, often misled by workers of iniquity and destroyed daily for lack of knowledge. Truly, their spiritual standard of living should be much higher.

SEARCHING OR STROLLING?

There are important differences between a searcher and a stroller. A searcher is serious, not easy-going. He is a businessman, not a vacationer, and therefore eager, not casual or leisurely. He is concentrated, not distracted or inattentive. A stroller, however, is just the opposite. He is unwinding, not focusing. While seeing many things, he *seeks* nothing. He is just out to take in fresh air and enjoy the spontaneous sights and sounds of a leisurely walk.

Now there is nothing wrong with strolling. It's a wonderful way to relax. Everyone needs to go for a stroll occasionally. But God did not promise to disclose the great truths of His Word to strollers. He offers them only to searchers: "If thou seekest her…and searchest for her…Then shalt thou…find…" (Prov. 2:4–5). The issue before us here is largely a matter of attitude. The attitude we take in approaching God through His Word is all-important because it determines what we come away with. What strollers miss, searchers find. What casual readers of Scripture overlook, patient students grasp and revel in.

RICH SOULS IN THE MAKING

Theoretically, treasure hunters are rich men in the making. Because they seek wealth enthusiastically and systematically, eventually they find it. In reality, however, there are no guarantees. Despite the amazing technological strides of the last century, treasure hunting is still at best a risky business. Mel Fisher's success is the exception, not the rule. Most seekers of worldly treasures find frustrations, not fortunes.

Spiritual treasure hunting, however, is a different kind of proposition. There is no element of risk, no chance of loss. Unlike worldly prospectors, all seekers of truth are spiritually rich souls in the making. Every Spirit-filled Christian who humbly and earnestly seeks God's treasures—the priceless, timeless revelations of His Word—finds them. Jesus Himself personally assures us that if we will only seek, we will surely find: "Seek, and ye shall find" (Luke 11:9). And that's not all. The more we seek, the more we find. If we seek much, we find much. And finding, we become rich in the knowledge of God and His ways.

The Lord yearns for every believer in this Laodicean age to become spiritually wealthy: "I counsel thee to buy of me gold...*that thou mayest be rich...*" (Rev. 3:18, emphasis added). Why does He so urge us? Because in our search of the Bible the wealth of knowledge we find enables us to live the good life—the spiritually rich life, the life that is good in God's sight. That life lies in delighting to be near Jesus every moment, pondering His Word, talking to Him, thanking Him, obeying Him, loving Him, pleasing Him. It is this simple, quiet, God-centered lifestyle of "righteousness, and peace, and joy in the Holy |Spirit|" (Rom. 14:17) that alone overcomes the world, our flesh and the devil. The good life is the lifestyle Jesus lived when He sojourned among us; every day He delighted in cultivating His closeness to His Father. But this is not the only reason Jesus wants us to be spiritually rich.

Only the rich have reserves to give others. Philanthropists are invariably wealthy people. The poor cannot give to the poor, for they haven't any resources to spare.

To give, I must have; to give much, I must have much. So it is also in Christ. To give others spiritual treasures, we must first have them. We must be rich in the knowledge of God to have precious gems of truth, emeralds of insight, rubies of understanding, diamonds of interpretation, silver bars of revelation and gold coins of wisdom to share with spiritually needy Christians. And to have such spiritual resources to give away, we must become a committed seeker of spiritual truth.

So Jesus challenges us to become spiritually rich, knowing that those who refuse to search for the riches of the Bible will never find them...nor experience the good life...nor have a wealth of knowledge to give others.

BECOME A SPIRITUAL TREASURE HUNTER!

Consider this: We spend considerable time and effort seeking worldly wealth, which we then use to improve our material standard of living. Should we not also put forth an effort to improve our spiritual life? And shouldn't that effort be greater than our quest for temporal gain? God's truth *is* worth more to us than mammon, isn't it? Then we should begin hunting!

Here is the way to become a spiritual treasure hunter. Determine to salvage all the sunken treasures of the Bible. Stop strolling; brief religious devotional readings will no longer suffice. Start searching; bind yourself to the horns of the altar of serious, orderly Bible study. Then do the following:

- RECEIVE...the fullness of the Holy Spirit, who alone can teach you all things.
- PRAY...asking the heavenly Father to lead you to practical, timely truths.
- BELIEVE...expecting your Father who sees in secret to reward you openly.
- WORK...pondering and recording every truth you find.
- OBEY...doing the word, that you may understand more of it.
- BE DILIGENT...taking or making the time to study daily.
- BE THOROUGH...research passages and truths until you understand them.
- FOCUS...concentrating on the most important truths.
- BE SELECTIVE...refusing to be sidetracked by mere theology, testimony or fiction.

Thus you will dig straight into God's holy mount of knowledge and dive headlong into the great depths of His truth, giving yourself wholly to the Word, the Word, the Word! Let your commitment to your expedition be total—persevere, sacrifice, pay the price of a spiritual treasure hunter.

～

Beloved in Christ, if you do these things, you will never be the same. The precious knowledge you discover, when applied to your life by the illumination of the Spirit, will enable you to enjoy the good life for the rest of your days. And through you many others will be made rich. So make no tarrying. Get "getting": "Get wisdom, get understanding... Wisdom is the principal thing; therefore, get wisdom; and with all thy getting, get understanding" (Prov. 4:5, 7).

And as you find the riches of God's Word, seek also the riches of the way of prayer.

Chapter Four

The Way of
Prayer

"But thou, when thou prayest, enter into thy |room|, and when thou hast shut thy door, pray to thy Father, who is in secret; and thy Father, who seeth in secret, shall reward thee openly."

—MATTHEW 6:6

Relationships begin with, and grow by, conversation. To get to know someone, we must talk to them and let them talk to us.

By prayer, the disciple talks to his heavenly Father in secret. By the answers He sends, the heavenly Father responds, and thus talks, to His child. So the two grow closer. But not all disciples pray with equal effectiveness, for God's promises to answer prayer have conditions attached to them. To receive answers, we must meet those conditions.

As we do so, we learn the secret of power in prayer . . .

THE SECRET
OF POWER IN PRAYER

"And the Lord did according to the word of Moses..."
                                        —EXODUS 8:13

An examination of Moses' prayer life reveals this remark-able fact: God frequently acted according to Moses' words. Consider these references.

When Moses besought the Lord to remove the plague of frogs from the Egyptians, the Lord did "according to the word of Moses" (Exod. 8:13), and the frogs died. When Moses later asked the Lord to remove the plague of flies, again, the Lord did "according to the word of Moses" (8:31), and the flies were removed. At Kadesh-barnea, God informed Moses that He had forgiven the Israelites "according to thy word" (Num. 14:20). In all of these instances, God, in a sense, obeyed a man. The Creator condescended to comply with the will of His creature. Divinity deferred to dust. The Lord listened very carefully to Moses' words and acted accordingly. That's remarkable. That's very remarkable.

What power, what influence, Moses had with God! He was able to walk into the secret place of the Most High, ask for help, and then walk out confidently, knowing that the Lord would do according to his word. That's tremendous power! Any creature whose prayers set the Creator's hands in motion exercises more authority than a head of state. His petitions release more energy than a nuclear explosion. Truly, as James asserts, "the effectual, fervent prayer of a righteous man availeth much" (James 5:16b). So did the prayers of Moses.

The question naturally arises, how did Moses gain such power in prayer? What qualified him for such a privilege? And, more importantly, how may we qualify to pray with equal effectiveness?

MOSES' SECRET

The secret of Moses' prayer-power was his *complete obedience*. He lived daily in a state of surrender to God, not sentimentally, but practically. Everything God told him to do, he did: "Thus did Moses: according to *all* that the Lord commanded him, so did he" (Exod. 40:16, emphasis added)—not only in building the Tabernacle, but in every other matter also. In so doing, he walked in the way of Noah before him: "Thus did Noah; according to *all* that God commanded him, so did he" (Gen. 6:22, emphasis added)—and in the way of Joshua after him: "And so did Joshua; he left nothing undone of *all* that the Lord commanded Moses" (Josh. 11:15, emphasis added).

Consistently, Moses chose life within the borders of the will of God. He feared to stray into the forbidden territory of disobedience, lest he should lose his coveted influence with God. Nothing was more valuable than that. Consequently, because Moses did "according to all that the Lord commanded him," the Lord did "according to the word of Moses." Because Moses hearkened diligently to God's voice, God hearkened diligently to Moses' voice whenever he petitioned heaven. So he reaped what he sowed—and showed us one of the great secrets of answered prayer.

Moses' secret is simply the principle of 1 Samuel 2:30 in action: "Them who honor me I will honor, and [but] they who despise me shall be lightly esteemed." God honors the prayer requests of those who honor His Scriptural commands, but He disregards the petitions of those who disregard them. Clearly, what we sow in obedience, we reap in answers to prayer. If we carry out God's sayings, He carries out our petitions. If we respect His will, He respects our desires. And He does so in the same proportion that we obey. If we ignore His words, He ignores our petitions. If we obey partially, He

30

answers them partially. If we obey fully, He answers us fully. For those who withhold no obedience He withholds no answers. As the psalmist observed, "No good thing will he withhold from them that walk uprightly" (Ps. 84:11).

THE BASIS OF PRAYER

As important as Moses' secret is, it must be remembered that obedience is not the basis of prayer itself. That basis is Christ's redemption.

Only by Jesus' blood may we, as believer-priests, enter into the holiest, the very presence of God, and pour out our hearts before the Lord. Only by the name of Jesus may we pray with authority and confidence. If Jesus' had not sacrificed Himself for us, none of Adam's children could draw near the heavenly Father in the new and living way of prayer. So states the writer to the Hebrews: "Having therefore, brethren, boldness to enter into the holiest by the blood of Jesus, by a new and living way, which he hath consecrated for us, through...his flesh" (Heb. 10:19–20). Christ's obedience, not that of any mere man, has made God's throne room accessible to us. All Christians, whether fully obedient, partially obedient or occasionally obedient, pray on one great foundation—Jesus' finished work of redemption.

THE ESSENTIAL PARTS OF PRAYER

In emphasizing Moses' secret of power in prayer, we do not want to minimize the importance of all the other elements of prayer. They, too, are important.

First, we must always pray according to *God's will*. His Word reveals His general will, and His Spirit reveals His specific will to us as individuals. We may pray with confidence for anything we know to be God's will. (See 1 John 5:14–15.) Jesus also urged us to pray for our hearts' desires (Mark 11:24), so long as they are not contrary to the known will of God.

Furthermore, every time we pray, *faith*, *patience* and *persistence* must be present. We must have faith, believing we receive the petitions we ask when we pray, if we hope to see them answered. If we waver with doubt or openly disbelieve, God cannot answer our petitions, for without faith it is impossible to please Him. (See Hebrews 11:6.) We must be

31

patient, willing to await God's time for our answers. He is working all things together for our good and for the good of others; sometimes He must delay the manifestation of our answer only because He is doing something larger, and far better, than what we asked for. If we are unwilling to await God's time, we cannot receive His blessing. And we must be persistent, like the widow who kept coming to the unjust judge until she received justice. We, too, must pray without ceasing until our desired ends are granted. If we refuse to importune heaven, we will forfeit the answers to many prayers. (See Luke 18:1–8.)

To these elements of prayer, we must add one more: *fasting*. What is fasting? In a word, it is *concentration*. It is a leaving off of one thing to lay hold of another. It is doing without the unnecessary to have the vital. It is setting aside secondary things to better see and grasp priorities. Usually we fast from food and drink, either totally or partially. Total fasting—leaving off all food and drink—should be practiced only as the Lord leads and with sensible preparation and follow-up, so as not to harm our bodies. Partial fasting—leaving off a meal, or food only, or certain kinds of food—may be practiced much more often and with less preparation. But food is not the only thing from which we may fast. Leisure activities, newspapers, television or radio programs, computers, hobbies or anything else that distracts us from the Lord. We must remember that merely leaving off things is not true fasting; only when we also lay hold of God by spending more time in His presence is our fasting acceptable. The benefits of such fasting are enormous.

Fasting clears our minds, enabling us to focus more clearly on the Lord and on our prayer objective. It allows the Spirit to flow through us more freely, resulting in an increased fervency in our spirit. This enables our prayers to bring more of God's power to bear upon the people and situations about which we pray. The net result is that our prayers are more effective. More tangible changes result—more lives are changed, more mountains moved and more souls delivered.

Jesus taught that there are some matters that mere prayer will not resolve; prayer and fasting are necessary to achieve the desired breakthrough. When His disciples failed to exorcise a demon from a young man, and they asked Him why they had failed, He responded, "This kind can come forth by nothing, but by *prayer and fasting*" (Mark 9:29, emphasis added).

All these elements—God's will, faith, patience, persistence, fasting—are necessary if we hope to enjoy the blessings of answered prayer. Yet even when practicing all of them, we may still find our prayers hindered if we forget Moses' secret and fail to obey God as closely as we should.

OLD AND NEW TESTAMENTS AGREE

Many Old Testament references teach the secret to power in prayer. Isaiah proclaimed that by continually walking in disobedience we erect a wall of separation between ourselves and God, thus rendering Him able to hear but unwilling to answer our prayers: "Behold, the Lord's hand is not shortened, that it cannot save; neither his ear heavy, that it cannot hear. But your iniquities have separated between you and your God, and your sins have hidden his face from you, that he will not hear" (Isa. 59:1–2). Jeremiah teaches that our disobedience withholds from us "good things," which obviously include answers to prayers: "Your iniquities...your sins have Iwithheldl good things from you" (Jer. 5:25). The psalmist states the case succinctly: "If I regard iniquity in my heart, the Lord will not hear me" (Ps. 66:18).

To these testimonies, the New Testament adds its enthusiastic amen. Jesus taught that we could freely "ask what ye will"—as long as we were abiding in obedience to His words: *"If ye abide in me, and my words abide in you,* ye shall ask what ye will, and it shall be done unto you" (John 15:7, emphasis added). The apostle John cited obedience as the key to having confidence that our prayers will be answered: "Beloved, if our heart condemn us not, then have we confidence toward God. And whatever we ask, we receive of him, *because we keep his commandments, and do those things that are pleasing in his sight*" (1 John 3:21–22, emphasis added). The man born blind, though yet a spiritual novice, nevertheless spoke by inspiration when he acknowledged that the Lord only hears [that is, *answers*] the prayers of those who do his will: "Now we know God heareth not sinners; but if any man be a worshiper of God, *and doeth his will*, him he heareth" (John 9:31, emphasis added).

All of these inspired writers were convinced that full

obedience makes prayer more effective, and that incomplete obedience, or harbored sin, renders it less effective or unanswerable. And they were not alone in their belief. Consider these examples.

HEZEKIAH'S PRAYER

King Hezekiah recognized the secret to power in prayer. He knew that he could not come boldly to God in time of need without the backing of an obedient life. When suddenly informed that he would soon die, Hezekiah immediately turned to God, begging and reasoning with Him to extend his life. His reasoning was simple. He asked God to honor his request for a longer life because he had honored God by his submission in years past: "Remember now, O Lord, I beseech thee, how I have walked before thee in truth and with a perfect heart, and have done that which is good in thy sight..." (Isa. 38:3).

God's quick and affirmative response shows that He agreed with Hezekiah's reasoning: "I have heard thy prayer, I have seen thy tears; behold, *I will add unto thy days fifteen years* . . ." (38:5, emphasis added). Note that God dealt with Hezekiah exactly as He did with Moses. He did according to the words of Hezekiah, because for years Hezekiah had done according to God's Word. Truly, God was gracious and Hezekiah exercised fervent faith, but neither of these factors tipped the scales of divine judgment in Hezekiah's favor. It was Hezekiah's obedient lifestyle that saved him, his characteristically submissive manner of living before God. Without that, his tearful plea would likely have gone unanswered.

JESUS' PRAYER

In His high-priestly prayer for the church, Jesus used the secret of power in prayer. (See John 17:1–26.) Before presenting His final earthly petitions to His Father, Jesus reminded Him of His complete obedience as a man. His repeated assertions emphasize that there was not one point of current disobedience in His life: "*I have finished* the work which thou gavest me to do...*I have manifested* thy name unto the men whom thou gavest me...*I have given* unto them the words which thou gavest me…While I was with them in the world, *I kept them* in thy name; those that thou gavest me *I have kept*…And now come I to thee…" (17:4, 6, 8, 12, 13, emphasis added).

It was as if He were saying, "Father, I have honored You fully by doing everything You have given me to do. There is nothing lacking in my obedience. Therefore, with this in mind, please honor these requests that I now make for my followers…" Here is a fact that should arrest our attention and awaken us from all presumption: Even Jesus did not take His prayer-privilege for granted! He did not say, "Father, You know that I am Your Son, Your only begotten Son. Therefore, I know You will answer my petitions whether I am fully obedient or not…" There was no such presumption in Him. Clearly, Jesus felt that if His prayers were to be effective, His obedience had to be full; that if His obedience were lacking, His confidence could not be full. And if this was His attitude, should it not also be ours?

~

Beloved, remember all the things that make prayer effective. Pray on the basis of Jesus' shed blood and in the authority of His name. Pray according to God's revealed will. Ask for your heart's desires. Pray in faith, believing the heavenly Father hears you when you pray. Pray patiently, willing to wait for God to manifest His answer in His time and way. Be persistent, determined to pray without ceasing until God's answers arrive. When necessary, fast, leaving off food, drink or any other distractions. But, most importantly, remember Moses' secret: Be fully obedient to God. Obey His Word and submit to the leading of His Spirit. Then the benefits of Moses' secret will be yours.

Henceforth, you will find yourself able to approach your heavenly Father with a new confidence: "Let us, therefore, come boldly unto the throne of grace" (Heb. 4:16). And, after prayer, you will enjoy the fullest possible assurance: "Then have we confidence toward God…because we keep his commandments, and do those things that are pleasing in his sight" (1 John 3:21–22).

You will no longer hope, you will *know* that your heavenly Father has heard you in secret and will reward you openly. To your delight, you will see Him working in your life as He did in Moses' life, according to *your* word—your counsel, your petitions, the requests of your lips will be fulfilled regularly before your eyes! "The Lord hear thee... grant thee according to thine own heart, and fulfill *all thy counsel*... the Lord fulfill *all thy petitions*" (Ps. 20:1, 4–5, emphasis added). "The king shall joy... O Lord... Thou hast given him his heart's desire, and hast not withheld *the request of his lips.* Selah" (Ps. 21:1–2, emphasis added). Thus your prayer life, as Moses', will become remarkable. Very remarkable.

Walking in the secret of power in prayer leads you naturally into the way of obedience.

Chapter Five

The Way of
Obedience

"Hath the Lord as great delight in burnt offerings and sacrifices, as in obeying the voice of the Lord? Behold, to obey is better than sacrifice, and to hearken than the fat of rams."

—1 SAMUEL 15:22

By virtue of his fallen nature, the natural man is an incorrigible rebel that inwardly resents submission to any higher authority, especially God. For the rebelliousness of Adam's children God has only one cure—death and rebirth. When we die with Christ and rise with Him to newness of life, for the first time we feel love for the authority we formerly hated. It is then that we must face, and learn, the great issue of obedience.

And whom we obey thereafter determines our true, and final, master. If we obey only the impulses of our independent will, our gods will be self and the lord of all self-servers, Satan; and Jesus will grieve over us. If we obey the Word of God and the voice of His Spirit, the Lord will be our God, and He will rejoice over us. Nothing pleases God as much as the spirit of obedience.

Let us consider, then, the profound meaning of obedience . . .

THE PROFOUND
MEANING OF OBEDIENCE

"Having confidence in thy obedience I wrote unto
thee…"

—PHILEMON 21

O bedience is arguably the most important topic in the
Bible. For wherever there is salvation, there is grace; by
grace are we saved. And wherever there is grace, there is saving
faith; for faith is the gift of God. And wherever there is faith,
there is obedience; for faith without works (corresponding acts
of believing obedience) is dead. A truly obedient life, then, is
irrefutable evidence of faith, grace, and salvation. What could
be more important than that? The Bible's multitude of references on the topic of obedience certainly betray its immense
importance in God's sight.

To God, every act of human obedience speaks eloquent-
ly. It sends Him a message that is rich with meaning, full of
significance, spiritually profound. Why? Because God understands what many Christians fail to grasp; that is, that obedience is much more than a cold, isolated act mechanically carried out to comply with the letter of God's Word. *It is the
manifest response of our entire being to God.* All of the most basic
Christian attitudes—faith, submission, the fear of God and
love for God—are manifested, and exercised, in every act of
obedience. Disobedience is evidence that at least one of them
is lacking.

Let's consider, then, the attitudes God discerns in every act of obedience.

An Expression of Faith

Obedience is an expression of faith. If we believe God, we obey Him. If we do not obey God, it is because we do not really believe Him. We may say we do, but in reality we do not. If we did, faith would compel us to act upon our belief. So it is with every soul. Our consistent actions reveal our consistent thoughts—and true beliefs—with perfect accuracy. As a man thinketh in his heart, so is he; and so, he acts. Whatever we are doing, we are doing it because of what we believe.

The Christian who consistently turns away from sin believes the New Testament's warnings against sin. The Christian who consistently sins believes the voice of unbelief—that the heavenly Father does not chasten His children and that death is not the wages of sin. The sister who gossips regularly believes she will never reap what her tongue is sowing. The brother who watches his thoughts and quenches wrong attitudes believes that one day he will give account for his thoughts and motives. The brother who diligently brings his problems and needs before God in prayer believes that his heavenly Father, who sees him in secret, will reward him openly. The brother who refuses to separate from worldly activities and ungodly associates believes that there is no danger in worldliness, that evil company will not corrupt his morals.

Christians who draw close to Jesus daily believe that if they abide in the Vine and let His Word abide in them, He will bless them and bear fruit through them; they are convinced He is a "rewarder of them that diligently seek Him" (Heb. 11:6). Those who do not abide in the Vine believe that personal devotion is unnecessary and has no effect on Christian usefulness. The brother who is unconcerned about his usefulness to God in this life, does not believe that Jesus will reward Christians according to their works at the judgment—that obedience and sacrifice will bring rewards and disobedience and negligence will cause their forfeiture. If he did believe this, he could not be indifferent about serving the Lord. Throughout all these examples runs this common thread:

Belief, of whatever kind, commands action; and action, of whatever kind, reveals belief.

A DEMONSTRATION OF SUBMISSION TO JESUS' LORDSHIP

Obedience demonstrates true submission to the lordship of Christ. It is the easiest thing in the world to call Jesus "Lord." Many do so without the slightest intention of actually submitting their lives to the authority of His Word and His Spirit.

The New Testament foretells the coming of a generation of saved but unsubmissive children of God, or "Lord, Lord" Christians:

> And why call ye me, LORD, LORD, and do not the things which I say?
> —LUKE 6:46, EMPHASIS ADDED

> Many will say to me in that day, LORD, LORD, have we not prophesied in thy name?
> —MATTHEW 7:22, EMPHASIS ADDED

> Afterward came also the other virgins, saying, LORD, LORD open to us...
> —MATTHEW 25:11, EMPHASIS ADDED; (SEE LUKE 13:25.)

I believe ours is that generation. In this Laodicean era (see chapter 2, page 17), the mass-marketing of Jesus has cheapened the gospel. Multitudes now take Christ's authority lightly, mistaking the profession of His lordship for the reality of it. They give religious lip service to Jesus, proclaiming openly that He is Lord, yet they refuse to do His will when it requires anything unpleasant. Thus, they confess Him with their words, yet deny Him with their deeds. They offer Him the honor of praise, but not the honor of obedience. They sing of His cross, yet reject their crosses. They hear the Word constantly, but consistently refuse to do it. These "Lord, Lord" types deceive themselves, for Jesus taught this sobering truth: Those who deny His lordship will be denied residence in the eternal city. Clearly, He asserted that what we do, not what we say, determines our eternal status in New Jerusalem: "Not every one that *saith* unto me, Lord, Lord, shall enter into the kingdom of heaven, but he that *doeth* the will of my Father, who is in heaven" (Matt. 7:21, emphasis added).

Despite the prevalence of these hearers only, God still has His doers of the Word.

By practicing God's Word in their actual living, obedient ones submit to Jesus' supreme authority and make Him—the living expression of the written Word—their Lord in the truest and most practical sense. Obedience to Christ's words expresses real inward submissiveness toward Him. Continuance in this obedience establishes that He is our Lord and we are His disciples: "If ye continue in my word, then are ye my disciples indeed" (John 8:31). An internal spiritual coup then follows. Self, our most-present antichrist, is deposed and banished to outer darkness and we enthrone Jesus as king of our soul. Thereafter, we bow the knees of our will and do many things we would not...because they are *His* will. This is one revolution the eyes of the Lord delight to see. We haven't merely said Jesus is Lord, we've made Him Lord.

Proof That We Fear the Lord

Obeying the Lord proves that we fear Him. For wherever the fear of the Lord is, there is obedience; and wherever disobedience prevails, there is no fear of the Lord.

Totally unlike the spirit of fear—which torments souls with the fear of man, the fear of catastrophe, the fear of failure, the fear of the future, etc.—the fear of the Lord is a holy fear that brings deep peace and security: "In the fear of the Lord is strong confidence . . . " (Prov. 14:26). In every way it is to be desired. It is an attitude of heart that deeply respects God's awesome power and His unfailing promises—and warnings. In fact, succinctly, the fear of God is *faith in God's warnings*. One simply believes God's promises to punish just as one believes His promises to bless. The fear of the Lord believes in God's unrivaled, unlimited and, hence, irresistible power, that none can stay His hand or overrule His will. It also understands that God is not only loving, but holy, true and just; so, He will not condone sin, He cannot lie and He is perfectly fair in all His judgments.

Furthermore, those who fear the Lord realize that God is no respecter of persons. Consequently, everything He says, whether a promise to bless or a threat to punish, is equally true and applicable to all His creatures without exception.

Invariably, this attitude produces prompt obedience. Consider these examples.

When God informed Noah of the coming flood and ordered him to build an ark, he obeyed promptly: "Noah, being warned of God of things not seen as yet, moved with fear, prepared an ark to the saving of his house..." (Heb. 11:7).

When God ordered Abraham to offer up Isaac (Gen. 22:1–19), Abraham obeyed promptly, beginning his journey early the next morning: "And Abraham rose up early in the morning, and saddled his ass...and went unto the place of which God had told him" (22:3). And for three days he went steadily forward with God's plan (22:3–10). In his prompt and unwavering obedience God perceived the fear of the Lord, for the angel of the Lord, speaking for God, told Abraham, "Lay not thine hand upon the lad...*for now I know that thou fearest God*, seeing thou hast not withheld thy son..." (Gen. 22:12, emphasis added). Thus, the father of faith set an example for the ages for all who fear the Lord.

Like Noah and Abraham, Christians who fear the Lord keep His Word promptly. Whenever God speaks to our hearts, holy fear creates within us a healthy sense of urgency that constrains us to respond to His behest at the first opportunity. Intuitively, we feel that we should act *now*, that procrastination, which is disobedience, will bring sure divine chastisement. To avoid wrath, therefore, we hear, we fear and we act. Said Joseph, "This do [now!], and live; for I fear God" (Gen. 42:18). In every such act of prompt obedience, heaven sees the fear of the Lord.

PROOF THAT WE LOVE GOD

Our obedience to God proves that we love Him. In the divine mind, obedience is always equated with love. Wherever there is love, there is obedience. Jesus obeyed His Father because He loved Him. So strong was His desire to please His Father that He delighted to do His will: "I do always those things that please him" (John 8:29). "I delight to do thy will, O my God" (Ps. 40:8). To Jesus, obedience was not a matter of necessity or duty, it was an opportunity to express His love for His Father. His deeds of obedience were acts of pure passion. And as He lived, so He taught.

In John's Gospel, Jesus asserts three times that those who

love Him, obey Him: "If ye love me, keep my commandments ...He that hath my commandments and keepeth them, he it is that loveth me...If a man love me, he will keep my words..." (John 14:15, 21, 23). Clearly, Jesus measures our love for Him by our obedience to His words. If we obey His words, we love Him; if we refuse to keep His words, we do not love Him.

Now love, like faith, is a gift of God. Scripture reveals that the love of God is shed abroad in our hearts by the Holy Spirit the moment we receive Him. (See Romans 5:5.) We show this overruling preference for God in many ways—by seeking Him, serving Him, worshiping Him and obeying Him—but the most important of these is obedience. Without it, all other expressions of love for God become hypocritical, pharisaic, fraudulent. God accepts no devotion, service or worship from disobedient ones. Truly, then, our life of obedience—voluntarily rendered, gladly maintained and joyfully finished—is the greatest love gift we can render to the One who first loved us. Always, when God sees obedience, He sees love. By every act of obedience we further "set," or permanently fix, our love upon Him: "Because he hath set his love upon me..." (Ps. 91:14).

Misunderstood in Our Time

Due to the emphases of modern theology, the topic of obedience has been generally misunderstood in our times. In many Christian schools of thought, we grossly overemphasize God's grace, de-emphasize His wrath and ignore altogether the vital issue of obedience. Obedience is considered an obsolete doctrine, a dreadful duty the Jews could not discharge and Christians are not expected to fulfill. The further down this "mal-theology" trickles—from theologian to pastor to layperson—the more errant it becomes, and the worse are its effects on ordinary believers. Many brothers and sisters go so far in misunderstanding obedience that they equate it with spiritual immaturity, even bondage. The enlightened are free to disobey with impunity, because, whatever their sin, grace will automatically cover it. Meanwhile the archaic notion that God desires obedience causes ignorant Christians to constrict themselves needlessly. Thus, are many taught and, thus, they believe.

But precisely the opposite is true. Obedience is neither a

44

burden nor a shackle, it is the most liberating activity on earth. The disciple who obeys his Lord grows freer, more mature, more discerning and more fruitful by the hour. Every act of obedience liberates him yet more from the deadly control of the author of rebellion. It strengthens and enlarges his faith, sharpens his spiritual discernment and increases his capacity to know and be used of God.

But the Christian who twists precious biblical truths to excuse his rebellious spirit will never come to know Him who humbled Himself by becoming obedient unto death, even the painful, humiliating death of the cross; nor will he accept His invitation to share His yoke of obedience and receive the heart-rest and joy that is found only in that blessed harness. Despite his clever reasonings and claims of spiritual maturity, that Christian will decrease, not grow, in spiritual stature. And eventually, if he persists, he will totally unfit himself for the Master's use. He will abide not in liberty but in confusion and bondage, and the shackles will grow tighter every time he disobeys.

No Substitutes for Obedience

Many Christians err by offering religious compensation. Religious compensation is anything we do for God hoping to make up for our refusal to obey Him. It is a religious substitute, some unrequested good deed that we offer the Lord in lieu of the simple obedience He requested. Whenever we realize we should obey a particular Bible command or the Spirit conveys His guidance clearly, and we do not promptly obey, the leaven of religious compensation begins its subtle, self-deceiving work. Soon thereafter we develop a religious zeal in some area of our spiritual life other than the one in which God presently requires obedience. Ponder these illustrations.

Like Cain, religious compensators quietly refuse to offer the sacrifice God has asked of them and smilingly offer another, less demanding, sacrifice instead. Like King Saul, they refuse to utterly destroy something in their lives that displeases God and then cover their rebellion by offering Him more worship or service. As He did with the apostle Peter, Jesus asks them to wait till He comes to their aid, but they rush off instead to cast forth their gospel nets to save souls... for *God's* glory! But how can they glorify God while they are disobeying Him? Unconsciously, these people are offering up unrequested displays of spiritual fervor to appease God for His loss of their obedience. They are also attempting to ease their guilty consciences, for in their hearts they know they have disobeyed the voice of the Lord. And why is this? Because the Spirit of truth won't let them forget it. He knows well, and seeks to convince us, that nothing sufficiently repays the Lord for our failure to comply with His requests. Obedience alone satisfies the heart of God.

The Spirit's declaration through the prophet Samuel stands before us as a timeless monument of truth, "Behold, to obey is better than sacrifice" (1 Sam. 15:22). We must, therefore, always obey the Lord's words and His calls, not our personal religious preferences. We cannot be Christ's disciples on our own terms. Heaven's orders must be carried out if we hope to please the Head of the church. There are no substitutes for obedience.

~

In His infinite wisdom, God has everything wrapped up in the package of obedience. This should come as good news and a relief. We don't have to think up a 1,001 things to do to please God; we have only to keep the Word and obey the Spirit. Thus, our previously numerous spiritual responsibilities are reduced to one: follow orders. Without exception, this was the watchword of God's greatest servants. Their sterling characters are revealed in the simplest statements of Scripture.

For instance, of Noah, Moses and Joshua, and others of their mold, it is written simply that they did all that the Lord commanded. What greater testimonies could there be? To say that God spoke and His servants obeyed says everything. It proves that they possessed the heart attitudes that most delight Him who looketh upon the heart. It also reveals that one of God's most basic redemptive objectives—by grace, by faith, by covenant, by instruction, by chastening and by kindness, to convert incorrigible rebels into consistent obeyers of God—had been achieved. Obedience is the miracle of redemption in its most practical manifestation.

The way of obedience is a particularly timely topic for us in this late hour. In the coming days, two great divine objectives loom large on the saints' prophetic horizon. First, Christ will fully restore His true church in accordance with His high priestly prayer (John 17), His prophetic parables (Matt. 25:1–13), and the revelations of the epistles (Eph. 4:11–16; 5:25–27). Through mighty outpourings of the Holy Spirit, intensive teaching, extensive testing and suffering, He will raise up a company of disciples worldwide that possess the grace, truth, compassion and power of the first-century church—and even more, for the glory of the latter house shall be greater than the former. Second, at His appointed time Jesus will appear in the heavens to catch away His overcoming people. This much-anticipated event, known widely as the Rapture (1 Thess. 4:13–18), will terminate God's work in this church age; and the third person of the Trinity will return to heaven, whence He came (2 Thess. 2:6–7). The Tribulation drama will then unfold, as foretold by the prophets. What do these things have to do with obedience?

When Jesus appears, He will accept only one ticket for translation to heaven: obedience. He taught that only those who steadfastly keep God's Word in their present trials will be kept from the world's final time of testing: *"Because thou hast kept the word* of my patience, I also will keep thee from the hour of temptation, which shall come upon all the world, to try them that dwell upon the earth"* (Rev. 3:10, emphasis added). Only obedient Christians will be ready, watching and worthy when the Bridegroom appears. Consequently, they alone will be taken up unto Him. Disobedient, or foolish, Christians will be left to endure at least part of the Tribulation period. (See Matthew 25:10–12.) It is a sobering and motivating thought.

Therefore, friend, it is time to heed Mary's inspired advice with renewed earnestness: "Whatever he saith unto you, do it" (John 2:5). As you so "do," your deeds of obedience will send this message to God, loud and clear—you believe God, you have made Jesus your Lord, you fear Him and you love Him. Heaven will not fail to note your spiritually profound communiqué. And you will be abundantly rewarded in due season.

You may begin your journey of obedience today, by entering into the way of intercession.

Chapter Six

The Way of
Intercession

"And I sought for a man among them, that should make up the hedge, and stand in the gap before me for the land, that I should not destroy it; but I found none."

—Ezekiel 22:30

Prayer is more than a means for us to fellowship with God and for Him to strengthen us and meet our needs. It is also a way by which we may bring God and His blessings into other lives.

Intercession is the great hidden work of Christians everywhere. All of God's true works, His inspired initiatives, begin with intercession. The saints stand in the gap and pray to the Lord of the harvest according to heaven's will, the Spirit stirs and broods, and a work of God is called into existence: "Separate me Barnabas and Saul for the work unto which I have called them" (Acts 13:2). And many are eternally blessed by that work.

The works of God and the blessing of souls begin with ... interceding forerunners.

INTERCEDING FORERUNNERS

"After these things the Lord appointed other seventy also, and sent them two by two before his face into every city and place, where he himself would come. Therefore said he unto them...pray ye..."

—Luke 10:1–2

When Jesus sent seventy missionaries "before his face into every city and place, where he himself would come" (Luke 10:1), the first order He gave them was to "pray" (10:2). After this important initial command came other lesser orders, such as, "Go...carry...enter...remain...eat...heal... [go your ways] and say..." (Luke 10:3–5; 7–10). By ordering the seventy to pray before He assigned their other duties, Jesus gave intercession undisputed top priority. Their hidden works as intercessors were primary; their more noticeable works as missionaries were secondary. Surprising as Jesus' orders may seem to us, this was not an isolated decision.

He had given the same orders previously when sending forth His apostles on their first mission. (See Matthew 9:36–10:15, and note that this entire passage describes one occasion.) At that time He told the twelve first to "pray" (9:38), then ordered them to discharge other duties—"go... preach...heal...freely give" (10:6–8). Thus, He called them to the private ministry of intercession before He called them to the public works of apostles. This reveals that in Christ's mind intercession is the most important ministry and should be attended to before all others. Though this may seem unusual to us today, it shouldn't. Christ's orders are the biblical norm for the church, not the exception, for they are typical of the way He conducted His personal ministry.

Throughout His three-year ministry, Jesus put intercession ahead of His other spiritual labors. While we remember most vividly His public works, the gospels reveal that Jesus also gave himself regularly to the hidden ministry of prayer. Luke observes that He often turned aside from the crowds to pray: "He Himself would *often* slip away to the wilderness and pray" (Luke 5:16, NAS, emphasis added); Weymouth's New Testament in Modern Speech states He did so "constantly"; The Modern Language Bible (New Berkeley Version) reads "habitually."

The purpose of Jesus' prayer habit was twofold. First, He prayed to sustain His spiritual strength. Second, He interceded for the benefit of others. The gospel writers give us many portraits of Christ the intercessor.

Matthew writes that when Jesus' apostles were sorely tried by their all-night passage across the raging Galilee, Jesus was not with them. But He was not inactive. He was spending the night in prayer, no doubt beseeching His Father to sustain His troubled students. (See Matthew 14:23.) Then, when He finished interceding, He "went unto them, walking on the sea" (14:25).

Luke records that before Peter's fiery trial in the high priest's courtyard, Jesus interceded for him, praying that his faith would not utterly fail, even if it temporarily lapsed in the heat of the crisis, and that afterward he would emerge strong and ready to minister to his brethren: "And the Lord said, Simon, Simon, behold, Satan hath desired to have you, that he may sift you as wheat; *but I have prayed for thee*, that thy faith fail not. And when thou art converted, strengthen thy brethren" (Luke 22:31–32, emphasis added). John further discloses that on the eve of the crucifixion, when Jesus should have been preoccupied with His approaching ordeal, He took time instead to pray for His apostles and all who would thereafter believe on Him because of their testimony. (See John 17.) These descriptions of Jesus at prayer do not end with John's gospel.

The writer to the Hebrews takes up where the gospel

writers leave off, revealing that the Ascension did not end Jesus' ministry of intercession. To the contrary, it increased it. In heaven today, an ever-increasing stream of intercession flows from His heart. As our High Priest, enthroned at the Father's right hand, Jesus "ever liveth to make intercession" (Heb. 7:25) for believers everywhere.

Together these New Testament references teach us that Jesus is a perpetual intercessor. This explains why He instructed the seventy first to intercede wherever He sent them. He was only asking them to do what He would have done.

INTERCEDING FORERUNNERS

Note that Jesus sent the seventy into the very localities in which He would later visit and minister, "into every city and place, where he himself would come" (Luke 10:1). The seventy, therefore, were *interceding forerunners.* That is, they were praying ones sent ahead of Jesus, or spiritual harbingers. A harbinger is one sent ahead of a royal party to announce and prepare for the visit of a king—to herald His imminent arrival and make the necessary arrangements for his stay.

Therefore, as harbingers, the seventy were sent ahead to announce and prepare for the visits of Jesus, Israel's King, to the cities and villages of Israel. The preparations they laid were both natural and spiritual. Naturally, they secured lodging and food for Jesus and His sizeable entourage, which consisted of His twelve apostles, the women who supported His ministry (Luke 8:1–3), and other disciples who accompanied Him from city to city (Acts 1:21–22). They also located suitable places for His meetings. Spiritually, they prepared the people's hearts to receive Jesus, His message and His ministry. This was a twofold work. First, they preached Christ's words and ministered His works. By teaching His parables, telling of His compassionate miracles, and praying for the healing and deliverance of many, they gave the locals a foretaste of the Lord's ministry. Second, in obedience to Christ's initial command, "Pray ye," they gave themselves to intercession daily for the townspeople. Though hidden from public view, this was by far their most essential preparatory work. Why was intercession their primary duty?

JESUS' WAY—WE PRAY, THE SPIRIT LEADS, WE EXECUTE HIS PLANS

As stated previously, Jesus' method of life and ministry was *intercession first*. It still is. In His way, prayer leads and all our organization follows the revelation of God's initiatives. We pray, the Spirit of God moves to lead us, then we organize and execute His plans.

This is heaven's modus operandi—the way God goes about His work. Apart from prayer, He will do nothing. With prayer, He may do anything. Prayer completely surrounds everything God does. Prayer leads, preceding every true work of God. Prayer accompanies, sustaining every work with wisdom, grace and strength to carry on. Prayer follows, establishing, enlarging and protecting what God has done. It is greater than logic, overruling the wisdom of experts, opinion polls and precedents. Prayer is supernatural, surpassing human limitations. Prayer is creative, producing things previously not in existence. And not only does it create and assist God's work, prayer itself *is* God's work. Amazing things happen while Christians are praying.

Prayer is a direct spiritual attack upon the demonic spirits that hold nations, cities and individuals in the darkness of unbelief and the bonds of sin. Whenever we pray "always with all prayer and supplication in the Spirit. . . for all saints" (Eph. 6:18), God works wonders in the invisible spiritual realm. Satan's agents, demons, are paralyzed and their works are hindered. And as we persist, praying without ceasing, we prevail over these spirits and their malicious plans are defeated. As a result souls are released, enlightened, convicted, strengthened and encouraged—all while we pray. As we are in the act of interceding, therefore, God's work is being accomplished. These immediate effects are due to the work of the Holy Spirit.

The hidden labor of intercession brings the Spirit of God actively into the situations for which we pray. When He begins to move, dramatic changes occur, "not by [human] might, nor by [human] power, but by [the power of] my Spirit, saith the Lord of hosts" (Zech. 4:6). In *Disciples Indeed* Oswald Chambers wrote, "What happens when a saint prays is that the Paraclete's almighty power is brought to bear on the one for whom he is praying." Now the work of the Spirit of God is unmatched. With perfect wisdom He plans, with perfect timing He moves, with divine power He creates, with unfailing ability He accomplishes. He is unstoppable. After believing prayer, impossible things surrender to the Spirit of possibility. Doors open before us, hearts become receptive, enemies are subdued, chosen ministers come together, missions are conceived, and utterance, power, and direction are given.

Then, after the Spirit moves in answer to prayer, we respond by following His lead. Hence, we implement God's agenda, not ours. We carry out His orders, His plans, His missions, not ours. Saul and Barnabas walked in this way of intercession first. As they worshiped, fasted and [it is implied] prayed to the Lord along with the other leaders of the church in Antioch, the Spirit spoke, revealing God's plan: "Separate me Barnabas and Saul for the work unto which I have called them" (Acts 13:2). After this inspiration, they organized, making the necessary preparations and plans for their departure under God's watchful eye, and offered further prayer (13:3). Then they went forth to obey God's plan: "So they, being sent forth by the Holy |Spirit|, departed..." (13:4). Because they were led of God, theirs was a work of the Spirit, not of the flesh. Jesus understood perfectly how the Spirit works and moves and leads.

This was the reason He sent interceding forerunners to the cities of Israel. Their primary duty was to *be there and pray*, that the supernatural power of the Spirit would be activated. They did their duty—and the results were tremendous! Because of their many prayers in private, the Spirit empowered Jesus to do many works in public when He arrived. His words of truth and works of power flowed freely, like a mighty river of life...and many believed and entered God's kingdom.

This way—the way of prayer first, the way of interceding forerunners—was Christ's way of ministry.

THE LAODICEAN WAY— WE REASON, WE PLAN, THEN WE PRAY

How many Christians, churches and ministries practice Christ's way in this Laodicean Age? Many are working ardently in His name who, sadly, have forgotten His spiritual and simple method of ministry. Why? Because we have developed our own way of working the works of God.

While in preaching and praise modern Christianity exalts the way of faith, in practice far too many individuals, churches and ministries rely more on human reasoning than on the wisdom of the Spirit of God. Hence, we have departed from Jesus' way and hewn out for ourselves a new way. Our way is *reason first*. Our religious reasonings lead us, not the voice of the will of God. We reason, we plan, then we pray. We take polls, survey statistics, estimate trends and predict outcomes. Then, based upon these factors, we lay our plans. After our plans are laid, we attempt the impossible, namely, to pray down divine power and blessing upon human plans. Thus we put organization before inspiration. We organize first, then look up for heaven's blessing upon our projects and programs. In doing so, we lose simplicity and peace and gain complexity and needless pressure—and frustration, for God refuses to walk in our ways.

We also misunderstand the very purpose of prayer. We see prayer as secondary, not primary, a means of securing God's support for what we have decided to do for Him, not as the way in which He reveals what He would have us do. So we err from the way of the Lord.

The consequences of this error are devastating, for if our works come forth from ourselves, they are doomed to ultimate failure. No matter how popular or seemingly effective they may be for a season, or how eager and sincere we are, at the judgment, self-led works will be nothing but wood, hay and stubble. In a moment, they will be consumed and gone forever. Gamaliel's warning to the Sanhedrin serves also to warn us: "If this counsel or this work be of men, it will come to Inothing|..." (Acts 5:38). And that is precisely what will come of the Laodicean way...nothing! If we walk in it, we will produce nothing; nothing that is born of God, nothing that is done by His Spirit, nothing that pleases God, nothing that glorifies Him, nothing that will last forever. Jesus Himself testified that apart from "abiding" in Him—living very close to Him and following His ways—Christians would achieve, in the end, nothing. "Apart from Me [and My ways], ye can do *nothing"* (John 15:5, NAS, emphasis added). Let every heart take heed, for the Lord has spoken.

ONLY INTERCESSION BRINGS FORTH NEW LIFE

The natural birth process teaches us of its spiritual counterpart. In many aspects, spiritual rebirth is similar to physical birth. As babies are born into this world, so Christ is born into souls.

Naturally, a baby cannot be born without travail. Before every new life is birthed, its mother must labor. For hours her muscles contract, her body suffers pain, and her mind is distressed, while her whole being prays to be delivered of her young. Universally, this is the genesis of human kind. We see then that every mother pays a price for her baby's physical life. Only labor brings forth new life.

The same is true in the spiritual realm. There, too, births cannot occur without labor. Intercession is the vital travail of spiritual life. Lasting conversions cannot occur apart from the persistent prayers of the righteous. As spiritual mothers, intercessors pay a price for souls to be brought into life. Whenever they labor in prayer, the spiritual birth process begins. The Father sends His plow of trouble to disrupt the sinner's complacency and self-sufficiency. The Spirit then draws near to convict him of sin. Then He sends the Word of salvation and gives the measure of faith. Eternal life gestates in the heart for a season. Suddenly, deliverance comes. Works of repentance and faith manifest—and the sinner's soul exits the womb of darkness and emerges into a new world of light.

Thus a child is born unto the heavenly Father. But when intercessors neglect their duties, these miracles cannot occur. Why? Because where there is no labor, there is no life. Only intercession brings forth new births. Isaiah's writings confirm this: "as soon as Zion travailed, she brought forth her children" (Isa. 66:8). Zion refers symbolically to God's righteous remnant in any given generation. In this verse, Isaiah teaches that as soon as the Lord's remnant travails in steadfast, sacrificial intercession, it will bring forth children unto God. This is exactly what happened in the upper room on Pentecost Day.

The upper room was the birthing room of the church.

The 120 who gathered there after the Ascension comprised God's Zion—the remnant of Christ's original disciples. (See Acts 1:12–15, 21.) In obedience to Jesus' explicit command, they waited for the promise of the Father, and while they waited, they travailed in prayer. For ten successive days they gave themselves to unified intercession. Luke records their steadfast, spiritual labor: "These all continued with one accord in prayer and supplication" (Acts 1:14). This is not an incidental reference, a mere footnote in the story. It is a key fact, revealing that intercession was an integral part of the birth of the church. For as soon as Christian Zion travailed, she "brought forth her children" unto God. As soon as the remnant's prayer-labors were complete, the body of Christ emerged into the world.

In that miraculous moment, the Holy Spirit fell in power, Peter preached Christ, and suddenly three thousand souls believed, repented and were born anew, babes in Christ. (See Acts 2:37–41.) Thus the church, by prayer, was born.

The travail of the 120 describes perfectly the work Jesus called the seventy to fulfill when He sent them before His face to the villages of Israel. Their intercessions, like those of the 120, brought forth new life in many souls. This is the calling of God's interceding forerunners everywhere.

WE ARE INTERCEDING FORERUNNERS

Like the twelve apostles, the seventy, and the 120, Christians have been sent ahead of our Lord as His harbingers. It is our solemn duty to announce and prepare for the King's upcoming visits to the cities, regions and nations in which we live. We announce His coming by our upright manner of living, our faithful testimony, our faithful sowing of God's Word and our uncompromising loyalty to His standards. In these ways our lives and our works give others a foretaste of the life and ministry of our King. But our most important means of preparing the way for Jesus' visitation is hidden; it is systematic, faith-filled, Spirit-inspired, persisting intercession.

This is the labor that repels the forces of darkness. This is the labor by which the life of God is born into the souls of men. This is the labor that hastens the maturing of the saints. (See Galatians 4:19.) It is the labor that causes fallen Christians to repent and turn again to the Lord. This is the labor that spawns Spirit-led, God-glorifying missions and ministries. And this is this labor—the work of interceding forerunners—to which each of us is called. But one question remains to be answered: Will we fulfill our calling?

Will you, friend, accept your responsibility to be an interceding forerunner in "every city and place" in which Jesus providentially places you? Will you gladly assume the hidden, humble work of a spiritual harbinger, that, by your daily intercessions known only to God, the Lord may do mighty works in many lives in the day He visits your city? If so, you will have to walk by faith, not by sight. You have to persist in childlike belief in God's promises, confident that "the effectual, fervent prayer of a righteous man availeth much" (James 5:16b), even when lengthy delays severely test your faith. Travail sometimes lasts long, but it always brings forth a "new thing" (Isa. 43:19). Similarly, intercessors must sometimes pray for long periods of time, even years, before seeing the full fruits of their travail. Will you persevere in prayer? God is searching for those who will.

Today the Lord of the harvest needs believer-priests who will stand in the gap—believingly, patiently, immovably—for souls to be saved, Christians to be revived and divine works to be initiated. He needs ministers, churches and ministries who will walk in Jesus' way of life and ministry. Simply put, He needs spiritual harbingers. Today, by grace, through faith, and with a set mind, begin the work of an interceding forerunner.

THE KING IS COMING

And remember this: Wherever a harbinger is, a king soon follows. Kings always follow their forerunners, visiting only those places in which adequate preparations have been made—never those that are unprepared. So it is with the King of kings. Jesus always follows His harbingers. He visits only those people and places that have been prepared by steadfast spiritual travail. Never does He visit unprepared places. And, most importantly, He never fails to visit a prepared place. Never. Our King is utterly faithful: "But God is faithful..."

(1 Cor. 10:13). "Faithful is he that calleth you, who also will do it" (1 Thess. 5:24). He faithfully follows the trail of His intercessors. Wherever interceding forerunners are, Jesus soon follows.

So, amid life's infinite uncertainties, here is something that is certain: If you make it your business to intercede daily for the city and area in which you live, the King will make it His business to visit there one day. Yea, saith the Spirit, "Our God shall come . . ." (Ps. 50:3).

To be fully prepared for His visitation, learn now to walk in the way of self-examination.

Chapter Seven

The Way of
Self-Examination

"Examine yourselves, whether you are in the faith..."
—2 CORINTHIANS 13:5

To walk closely with Jesus, we must examine ourselves constantly. Determined self-examination destroys the damaging
habits of judging others and "busybody-ness"; we become so
busy judging our faults we have no time to consider the faults
of others. It's good to pray, "Search me, O God, and know
my heart; try me, and know my thoughts..." (Psalm 139:23),
but such prayers are futile, and hypocritical, if we do not also
judge ourselves. This duty demands large amounts of brutal
frankness, humility and patience, but it is only as we fulfill it
that we walk in the Spirit.

It is one thing to be born of the Spirit, another to be baptized
with the Spirit, and yet another to walk in the Spirit. There
is a natural progression here. Only those who are born of the
Spirit and baptized with the Spirit can walk in the Spirit. But,
sadly, not all who possess the Spirit walk in the Spirit. The
reason? They do not examine themselves regularly.

*The only way to walk in the Spirit is to walk in the way
of self-examination...*

SELF-EXAMINATION

"But let a man examine himself…"

—1 Corinthians 11:28

The teachings of Jesus set the standard for walking in the Spirit. Simply put, He taught that *evil thoughts defile*. "For out of the heart proceed evil thoughts…these are the things which defile a man…" (Matt. 15:19–20). That is, merely having wrong thoughts in our hearts renders us unfit for fellowship with God. In Scripture, the term heart is often used synonymously with mind. So here Jesus really speaks of our minds. If we let sinful thoughts or motives rest in our minds, our union with God is broken. We cut ourselves off from abiding in the Vine. We stop walking in the Spirit. We cease to "walk in the light, as he is in the light" (1 John 1:7) and turn aside to spiritual darkness. Jesus' standard, then, is clear: To walk with God, not only our actions but our thoughts must be right. That's a high standard. Very high.

To meet Christ's standard, the apostle Paul urges us to walk in the way of self-examination: "But let a man examine himself…" (1 Cor. 11:28). And to facilitate this self-monitoring process, he recommends that we learn to captivate every thought that enters our conscious minds: "…bringing into captivity every thought to the obedience of Christ" (2 Cor. 10:5).

61

To take every thought captive to the obedience of Christ we must do three things.

First, we must screen our thoughts, arresting or holding any the Spirit deems questionable.

Second, we must then test them, to see if they agree with God's Word. (See 1 John 4:1.)

Third, we must "cast down" (quickly reject, drop, quench) every thought that does not meet that test. Especially dangerous are "imaginations," which are daydreams and suppositions (ideas we do not know to be facts); "high things," which are proud thoughts of rebellion, vanity or unbelief; and also "every thought" of despising others for their faults, real or imagined.

By thus bringing our thoughts into subjection to the written Word, we make our minds obedient to the Living Word. As we continue this day by day, our minds become renewed and our lifestyles spiritual. This trying of the spirit of our thoughts is vital. There is no other way to walk in the light as Jesus is in the light. If we refuse to watch over our minds, we forfeit the fellowship of our heavenly—and holy—Father. Self-examination begins with the heart.

God looks always upon the heart, and so should we. Our hearts are both the seat of our affections and the home of our thinking. They are the secret chambers of our souls known and read only by God and ourselves. Wisdom bids us to guard our hearts diligently: "Keep thy heart with all diligence..." (Prov. 4:23). Why is this sustained heart-watch so important? Because everything we do originates there. Whatever is in our heart presently determines our present reaction to the spontaneous events of life: "...for out of it are the issues of life" (4:23).

Right thoughts keep us in the flow of the Spirit and inclined to react to life's difficulties from a spiritual viewpoint. Wrong thoughts quench the flow of the Spirit, leaving us separated from Jesus, our Vine, and confused in the darkness of sin. If difficulties arise, then we are likely to react in an unspiritual manner because our heart is at that moment unspiritual. So we fail and grieve the Lord and cause needless difficulties for ourselves and others. For these reasons, we must always monitor our hearts. Self-examination is designed to eliminate disobedience from a Christian's heart, and hence from his life.

Disobedience is spiritually what sickness is physically—an abnormality in God's plan for mankind. He never intended for either of them to be a part of the human experience. Jesus came to deliver man from sin and its curse and reestablish his union with God. (See 1 John 3:8b.) The angel who appeared to Joseph described the purpose of Jesus' life in these words: "...he shall save his people from their sins" (Matt. 1:21). So we see that God wants Christians saved not only from wrath but from its cause; not only from hellfire in the hereafter but from sin's control in the here and now. Although this victory over sin is God's will for all Christians, it is experienced only by those who desire it and cooperate with Him by practicing self-examination. To assist them with their inner vigil, God has sent the Holy Spirit into the world.

Jesus called the Holy Spirit the *Parakletos*, which means "one called alongside to help." Once we have received of the Holy Spirit's fullness, thereafter He lives in our bodies: "Know ye not that your body is the temple of the Holy |Spirit| who is in you..." (1 Cor. 6:19). From within us He helps us daily to monitor our spiritual condition. If we fail to maintain our union with Christ, the Holy Spirit immediately alerts us that we are disconnected from the Vine.

The moment we turn aside from the light ever so slightly, He wants us to know it. Why? Lest we enter the deceptive and dangerous realm of spiritual darkness. He knows well what Jesus testified—that anyone who walks there will soon "stumble," or fall into more open and destructive sins: "If a man walk in the night [darkness], he *stumbleth*, because there is no light in him" (John 11:10, emphasis added). To help us recognize our departure from the light, the Spirit gives us signs of spiritual darkness.

Jesus promised that signs would follow true Christians. Regarding obedient, faith-filled believers He declared, "These signs shall follow those who believe..." (Mark 16:17), and He went on to describe the miracles that appeared after the Holy Spirit came at Pentecost (16:17–18). These supernatural signs of the Spirit's presence and power authorized the early Christians as Jesus' representatives and confirmed their message in the public eye (16:19–20).

But these spectacular signs are not the only ones the

Spirit has given. There are others that attend disobedient Christians—the signs, or spiritual indicators, of spiritual darkness. Just as surely as signs of divine power follow Christians of extraordinary faith, the signs of darkness follow those who regard sin in their hearts. But they are internal, not external; private, not public; quiet, not obvious. Whenever we turn aside from abiding in Jesus and His Word, the Holy Spirit within us manifests one of His warning indicators.

Invariably, the signs of spiritual darkness come whenever we have failed to bring our thoughts into captivity to Christ or have otherwise disobeyed the Lord. When our heart vigil breaks down, the Spirit intervenes to alert us of our failure and prompt us to correct ourselves. This is His ministry of redirection. He simply reminds us of what we have ignored—thoughts or emotions we recognized as wrong yet allowed to slip into our hearts unchecked; words or deeds we knew were wrong but failed to confess as sin; words or acts that we knew gave offense yet for which we refused to ask forgiveness. It is then up to us to deal with the matter the Spirit reveals. If we do so, we escape from spiritual darkness and do not stumble. So where our self-examination fails, the Spirit's examination prevails...if we respond to the signs of broken fellowship with God.

Given below are samples of these signs.

Loss of Peace
"Let the peace of God *rule* in your hearts..." (Col. 3:15, emphasis added). This text exhorts us to let God's peace "rule," or act as judge, in our hearts. We see, then, that God's peace is the judge of our hearts. The Amplified Bible states that peace should "act as umpire continually in your hearts—deciding and settling with finality all questions that arise in your minds..." So God's peace is also our umpire. These two examples are synonymous because both judges and umpires are authorities employed to render clear, final decisions—the judge in the court of law and the umpire on the field of play. Judges rule defendants innocent or guilty, and baseball umpires rule players safe or out. So also the peace of God rules in our hearts.

The peace of God that passes all understanding should be our constant companion. If we walk in the light, our hearts abide free from agitation and filled with deep peace. Whether our surroundings are heavenly or hectic, placid or panicky, our personal inner sanctums abide at rest. The loss of this wondrous soul-rest is the surest indicator that we have erred. Whenever tranquillity exits and anxiety enters, the Spirit is rendering a decision in our soul. Judge Peace rules we are "guilty" of disobedience, and the Umpire shouts we are "out" of the Spirit.

A Dead Bible

Dwight L. Moody wrote in the flyleaf of someone's Bible, "This book will keep you out of sin, and sin will keep you out of this book." He meant simply that meditation in the Word inspires us to rise above sin and indulgence in sin inclines us to neglect the Word. Moody's proverb implies a link between inspiring Bible reading and obedience.

As long as we obey the Word, the Bible is a living thing. Every time we touch it, we have an encounter with God. It is a fountain flowing with living water, from which we refresh our spirits. It is an oven filled with freshly baked bread with which we feed our souls. It is a telephone line over which we hear direct messages from God via the Spirit. It is a temple of words, in which, awestruck, we behold the beauty of the Lord. Never does the Logos fail to bless obedient ones. Always the Bible offers, and delivers, an exhilarating touch from the living God. Hence, we are drawn steadily to it.

But if sin or self-will enters, a marked change occurs immediately. We seek drink, but our Bible fountain is dry. We seek bread, but the oven is empty. We listen for God's voice, but our line of communication is broken. We search chapter and verse for a glimpse of Jesus but are unable to see Him clearly. So we fall away from the Word...and sink and falter in the midst of life's adversities. What is wrong? Our Bible is dead. And so are we—dead in sin, selfishness and worldliness. Our disobedience has separated us from "the life" (John 14:6) and is hindering Him from inspiring us through His Word.

Fear of Evil

In the beginning, Adam knew no fear. In Eden, he had daily fellowship with God and walked with Him in unruffled confidence. But the instant he sinned, he feared and hid himself from his Creator. (See Genesis 3:7–10.) It is the same with Christians today: It is impossible to practice sin and enjoy spiritual assurance simultaneously.

Salvation brings with it the deepest confidence: "In the fear of the Lord is strong confidence . . ." (Prov. 14:26). Every Christian who trusts and obeys abides in his own divinely protected Eden—the perfect will of God—where the fear that torments cannot dwell. If it tries to enter, he easily repels it by the blood, the Word and his testimony. But disobedience spoils the believer's utopia. It drives us from Eden and from all its security, and relocates us in God's permissive will where we are exposed to evils and calamities that are not in God's plan. (See Genesis 34.)

Sensing our departure from "the shadow of the Almighty" (Ps. 91:1), as Adam did, we fear. And to our dismay, when we resist this fear, it does not flee. "Jesus I know, and Paul I know," it sneers, "but who are you?" A cloud of uncertainty then envelops us, and the dread of divine chastisement takes root in our hearts. Until we repent, this fearful looking for of judgment grows stronger by the hour. But the instant we put away our disobedience, all our anxieties evaporate and Sonshine again warms us with the security of God. So we resume life in Eden: "Whoso hearkeneth unto me...shall be quiet from fear of evil" (Prov. 1:33). And there, again, no fear can have at us.

Powerless Prayer

Because God is holy, He does not respect our prayers if we do not respect His holiness. A holy heart is one kept free from all known sin. Have the heavens been as brass to you lately? Do you pray for the things you desire and dutifully "believe that ye receive them" (Mark 11:24) when you pray, yet still suffer a nagging lack of confidence? And have your requests gone conspicuously unanswered? The presence of but one wrong attitude lodged in your heart—pride, envy, strife, malice, unforgiveness, rebellion, unbelief—is enough to render your prayers powerless: "If I regard iniquity in my heart, the Lord will not hear me" (Ps. 66:18). Only diligent self-examiners pray with confidence and see results.

Weakness

"The Lord is the strength of my life" (Ps. 27:1). If the Lord is our strength, sin is our weakness. If not immediately confessed and forsaken, sin causes an otherwise unexplainable weakening of our entire being. We have enough food, sleep and leisure time, and our health is excellent, yet we feel continually drained. "For this cause many are weak..." (1 Cor. 11:30). As a branch cut off from its vine is instantly weakened, so the Christian cut off from Jesus senses an immediate drop in vitality. For apart from Him, all we have is the strength of our old man, who is dead; and the strength of a dead man is weak. If we are plagued with weakness and sin is the culprit, no natural remedy (a cool drink, a hot meal, rest and relaxation, etc.) will restore our energy. Only confession and repentance reunite us with our power source and cause life from the Vine to again surge into, and strengthen, our branches.

Sickness

God sometimes uses the pressure of physical sickness to convince sinning Christians to return to the way of obedience: "For this cause many are...sickly among you" (1 Cor. 11:30). Typically, our physical follows our spiritual; our bodies prosper as our souls prosper: "Beloved, I wish above all things that thou mayest prosper and be in health, *even as thy soul prospereth*" (3 John 2, emphasis added). Physical health, therefore, is the norm for the believer whose faith is healthy. When sickness visits, our first concern should be to examine our hearts for a sin-cause.

If we have sinned, James gives the divine directive for both forgiveness and healing:

> Is any sick among you? Let him call for the elders of the church; and let them pray over him, anointing him with oil in the name of the Lord; and the prayer of faith shall save the sick, and the Lord shall raise him up; and if he have committed sins, they shall be forgiven him. Confess your faults [sins] one to another, and pray one for another, that ye may be healed.
>
> —JAMES 5:14–16

These inspired instructions reveal that if sin causes affliction to come, repentance alone makes it go. Without the humility of a truthful confession and a contrite, believing prayer, our bodies will remain as our souls—sick.

A Double Mind

A double-minded Christian is one who cannot make decisions with finality. Every decision he makes he reconsiders, every step he takes he reverses.

When a man of trust yields to thoughts of doubt, or through fear seeks to evade any vital issue God sets before him, he becomes a double-minded man—and unstable. "A double-minded man is unstable..." (James 1:8). Certainty flees and a plague of hesitancy infects his mind. As this sickness grows, more symptoms manifest: hesitation, uncertainty, timidity. Eventually every decision is doubted and every move questioned, until the double-minded man is "unstable in all his ways." The Amplified Bible states, "[For being as he is] a man of two minds—hesitating, dubious, irresolute—[he is] unstable and unreliable and uncertain about everything (he thinks, feels, decides)." (See James 1:8.)

When this spiritual sickness reaches the point that we labor over the tiniest decisions of daily life—whether to turn left or right at the intersection—it's time to ask ourselves, "How long halt ye between two opinions?" (1 Ki. 18:21) and to seek help, which comes via the Spirit the minute we humbly retrace our thoughts in search of the first decision we failed to make. That's where we allowed the Back-and-Forth Syndrome to begin, and that's where we must terminate it.

A Running Mind

Closely related to a double mind is a running mind. A running mind is one obsessed with thinking ahead...and consequently tormented by anxiety. It is far from the attitude of faith.

When faith is strong, we do not demand to know the future. Trust holds our soul in inspired rest. Our Father who is providing for us today will provide for us tomorrow. We don't know what tomorrow holds, but we know and trust the One who holds yesterday, today and eternity in His hands. But unchecked disobedience erodes this faith.

If we let sin rest in our minds, creeping anxiety enters and begins crawling its way to the forefront of our thoughts. Within a matter of moments, our minds are off and running. We feel driven to plan tomorrow before we have even lived today. In this state of mind, major mental storms easily erupt;

we work ourselves into a panic over problems that are months, even years, away. So we make haste in our hearts. Not only is this condition a sign of unconfessed sin, it is sin.

Isaiah forbids believers to harbor a hasty spirit: "...he that believeth shall not make haste" (Isa. 28:16). Jesus commands us to allow no anxious thoughts: "Take... no [anxious] thought for the morrow..." (Matt. 6:34, KJV). And the apostle Paul teaches us to worry about nothing: "Be [anxious] for *nothing*..." (Phil. 4:6, emphasis added)—and to pray about everything: "...but *in everything* by prayer and supplication with thanksgiving, let your requests be made known unto God" (emphasis added).

Everywhere Scripture reveals there is only one thing to do with worry: Refuse it! Christians who obediently refuse to worry reap the blessing of the peace of God that passes all understanding. Those who worry reap the curse of the running mind. And a curse it is—never do they rest, never are they free from pressure, never do they leave tomorrow in the hands of their compassionate and all-powerful Father.

A Confused Mind

Confusion is the inability to distinguish between things and is highly dangerous in the natural as well as in the spiritual. A state of confusion always creates a state of emergency.

For example, when confusion breaks out in a control tower, air traffic controllers, sensing danger, move quickly to seek its cause and eliminate it. They know well that if confusion rules, even for a short time, a collision will likely occur. So it is with us.

A Christian's mind is his control tower. Whenever confusion enters, a state of spiritual emergency exists. If we ignore the confusion, we are heading straight for a damaging spiritual collision. There is just a step between us and something evil: "...there is confusion and *every evil work*" (James 3:16, emphasis added). Like seasoned air traffic controllers, wise Christians heed the sign of confusion. They immediately examine themselves to find its cause. Confusion arises from one of several sources.

A confused mind may result from harboring envy or a spirit of strife, internal or verbal; for "where envying and strife are, there is confusion . . ." (James 3:16). It may be a sign of fear, for while the Spirit of God produces a sound mind, the spirit of fear produces just the opposite—an unsound, or confused, mind: "God hath not given us a spirit of fear, but [to the contrary, the Holy Spirit] of power, and of love, and of a sound mind" (2 Tim. 1:7). Confusion may arise from harboring pride in our hearts or from resisting God's will, for when either are present God resists us: ". . . God resisteth *the proud* . . ." (James 4:6, emphasis added).

A Confounded Mind

A confounded mind differs from a confused one in that rather than swirl around chaotically our thoughts simply grind to a halt. We experience temporary mental paralysis; momentarily we are unable to think at all. Our mind freezes, or goes blank, and we suffer an embarrassing stupor of silence. No matter how difficult our trials, it is never the Lord's will that we be confounded: ". . . ye shall not be . . . confounded world without end" (Isa. 45:17). Like other spiritual indicators, this sign of the Spirit betrays specific root causes.

A confounded mind is sometimes caused by being ashamed. David prayed often that his enemies would be confounded with shame: "Let them be *ashamed and confounded* together who seek after my soul to destroy it . . ." (Ps. 40:14, emphasis added). Isaiah promised that God will do so: "Behold, all they that were incensed against thee shall be *ashamed and confounded* . . ." (Isa. 41:11, emphasis added).

The fear of man also causes confounding. When commissioning him, God warned Jeremiah that if he feared the people's faces, He would confound him in their very presence: "Arise, and speak . . . be not dismayed at their faces, lest I confound thee before them" (Jer. 1:17).

Sudden fear, or terror, also may confound our minds. So great was the patriarchs' shock at the sight of Joseph—whom they had long assumed dead—that they could neither think, speak, nor move: "And his [Joseph's] brethren *could not answer him;* for they were *terrified* at his presence" (Gen. 45:3, emphasis added).

Carnal Cravings

Carnal cravings are bodily lusts. The apostle John warns us not to live for these or other worldly desires: "Love not the world, neither the things that are in the world...For all that is in the world, the lust of the flesh, and the lust of the eyes, and the pride of life, is not of the Father, but is of the world" (1 John 2:15–16). What many fail to realize is that the *only* way to do this is to walk very closely with Jesus daily. Paul writes, "Walk in the Spirit, and ye shall not fulfill the lust of the flesh" (Gal. 5:16). Only the Spirit has sufficient power to control our carnal cravings.

If we abide close to Jesus, the Spirit holds us above the reach of lower temptations. The power of God insulates us from the power of sin. So strong is the life of the Vine within us that the lust of the flesh cannot move us. All that we have in Jesus so satisfies us that we have no desire for all that is in the world, for in His presence is fullness of joy. But if we turn aside from our heavenly Satisfier, all this soon changes.

Our Christ-life weakens and our fleshly nature revives... and takes charge. All that we have in Jesus then seems dull and all that is in the world looks attractive. No longer satisfied in God, our soul instinctively seeks satisfaction elsewhere. We feel again the surgings of carnal desires and appetites long ago mortified. The enemy then begins moving us and manipulating us, through our desires for food, comfort and sex. And soon we find ourselves, again, yet carnal.

Lack of Brotherly Love

Jesus taught that those who truly love Him seek and obey His words: "If a man love me, he will keep my words..." (John 14:23). And the apostle John adds that those who love Jesus love His followers: "Everyone that loveth him that begot loveth him also that is begotten of him. By this we know that we love the children of God, when we love God, and keep his commandments" (1 John 5:1–2). So both loves—love for Christ and love for Christians—are shed abroad in our hearts by the Holy Spirit who is given us. It is impossible for us to love Jesus without also loving His followers.

But if we turn from the Lord to iniquity, our Christian

compassion wanes. "And because iniquity shall abound, the love of many shall |grow| cold" (Matt. 24:12). The caring spirit of Abel departs from us, the callousness of Cain enters, and we abandon our responsibility to love and help our fellow believers, reasoning in our hearts, "Am I my brother's keeper?" (Gen. 4:9). If there is no recovery, this indifference soon degenerates into enmity, and we find ourselves biting and devouring those whom Christ has called us to love. This lack of brotherly love is a sign we have lost touch with Him who first loved us and who commanded us to "love one another" (John 13:34–35). After unbelief set in, the formerly faithful servant of Christ's parable began to "smite his fellow servants" (Matt. 24:49). His is an example we should not follow.

Bodily Pain

The Book of Proverbs teaches, "The merciful man doeth good to his own soul, but he that is cruel troubleth his own flesh" (Prov. 11:17). This means that our attitudes toward others affect our souls and bodies. A merciful outlook brings God's blessing upon our minds and health, but an unmerciful heart brings stress and consequently pain, particularly upon our bodies: "He that is cruel troubleth his own flesh." In short, God is saying *cruelty inflicts pain on the cruel.* Why? It is God's judgment.

In Luke 6:36–38, Jesus commands all Christians, "Be ye...merciful," and then spells out four ways we may exercise the mercy God has placed within our hearts:

- By not judging others
- By not condemning others
- By forgiving offenders
- By giving and sharing with others

If we who are saved by mercy refuse to have mercy, we offend the Lord of mercy. And if we persist in our hardness of heart, He gives us a sign of His displeasure. Surprisingly, that sign is torment.

Yet we really should not be surprised, because Jesus warned us of this. In Matthew 18:21–35, He taught that Christians must forgive and reconcile with every offender who asks forgiveness. (In other scriptures He revealed that we must also internally forgive [forsaking anger and vengeance] offenders who do not ask forgiveness; see Mark 11:25–26.) He then revealed that unforgiving Christians stir God's wrath so greatly that He gives them over to "tormentors" (Matt. 18:34), who inflict on them the cruelty they wish upon their offenders. To torment is "to rack with pain, to inflict mental or physical agony." When considered with Proverbs 11:17, we may conclude that when we have aches and pains in our fingers, legs, joints and backs, without detectable physical causes, it may be because some form of unmercifulness—unforgiveness, vengeance, hatred, condemnation or stinginess—is resting in our hearts.

Hyperactivity

Jesus has provided spiritual rest for us now in this time: "There remaineth, therefore, a rest to the people of God" (Heb. 4:9). That rest is ours as long as we abide in faith and obedience: "For we who have believed do enter into rest..." (4:3). Really, Jesus is our rest. In Him, we rest; apart from Him, we cannot rest.

When we disobey the Lord, therefore, our spirits are troubled. And no matter how we try, we are unable to rest. This spiritual restlessness shows itself in physical restlessness. We become impulsive, hopping from one new project to another while our earlier works remain unfinished. Waiting, or inactivity of any kind, torments us. Driven to perpetual motion, we feel we must fill every moment with activity. Even our leisure time provides no rest; insomnia fills our nights with tossings and disturbing dreams. (See Isaiah 50:11.) These sorrows of hyperactivity betray our troubled hearts.

∼

These signs of spiritual darkness are corrective messages from Love. They are the gentle-but-firm voice of the Bridegroom telling His wayward bride that she has turned aside and wooing her to return to Him: "Come unto me... and I will give you rest [spiritual restoration]" (Matt. 11:28). They are a personal "word of knowledge" (1 Cor. 12:8), the Spirit's supernatural revelation of our true state. Whenever they arise, we should immediately examine our relationship to God. Somewhere our connection to the Vine is severed. Somewhere we are not walking in the Spirit. Somewhere we have entered the dangerous realm of spiritual darkness, and we are walking in the way of Achan.

When Achan sinned and did not repent, immediately God gave a sign: At Ai, Israel could not stand before her enemies and thirty-six of her soldiers fell slain (Josh. 7). If Achan had voluntarily confessed to Joshua, he may have received mercy; because he didn't, he was judged. We must learn from Achan's folly. Whenever the signs of spiritual darkness appear in our lives, we have an accursed thing—a wrong thought, motive, emotion, word or act—buried in our hearts. With the Spirit's help, a few moments of quiet, truthful digging before God will unearth our wedge of gold or Babylonish garment. We should then come to the light and make confession to our Joshua, Jesus: "I have sinned against the Lord...I saw...I coveted...and [I] took them..." (Josh. 7:20–21). He will always show us the path to full spiritual recovery. God's purpose in ordering self-examination is for correction, not penalty.

He seeks not to punish but to purge us, that we may remain in living touch with Him at all times. But for this to occur we must be correctable; that is, willing to see where we are wrong and eager to do whatever God requires to make it right. Whether we confess sin, quench wrong thoughts, plant new thoughts, put off wrong attitudes, put on the mind of Christ, ask forgiveness, give forgiveness, make restitution, we must do it quickly.

When the signs of spiritual darkness tell us, "Thou art the man...," we must not resist confession, as King Saul. When Samuel confronted Saul about his failure to kill all the Amalekites, Saul denied his true spiritual condition, insisting, "*I have performed* the commandment of the Lord . . ." (1 Sam. 15:13, see also 20, emphasis added). Instead, let us walk in the way of David. When Nathan confronted him with his errors, David quickly yielded and confessed his sins: "*I have sinned* against the Lord . . ." (2 Sam. 12:13, emphasis added).

A quick, humble confession of sin always brings us an

immediate return to favor, fellowship and fruitfulness in God. For He promises, "If we confess our sins, he is faithful and just to forgive us our sins, and to cleanse us from all unrighteousness" (1 John 1:9). It will also spare us chastisement, because if we won't judge ourselves, God will.

The failure to walk in the way of self-examination inevitably brings us into the way of divine correction.

Chapter Eight

The Way of Divine Correction

"Simon, I have somewhat to say unto thee…"

—LUKE 7:40

The One we follow said plainly He rebukes and chastens those He loves. His intention to correct us, then, is fixed. But what of our willingness to receive His correction?

One simple, quiet word of correction is sufficient to redirect a wise soul into the way of life, while a hundred lashes fail to change a fool. Which example—which way—will we follow? If Jesus' rebukes and chastisements prove that He loves us, our response to His correction proves that we love Him.

To learn to recognize and respond to His correction, we must consider His way in correction…

HIS WAY
IN CORRECTION

"Nevertheless, I have somewhat against thee, because
thou hast left thy first love."

—REVELATION 2:4

In Revelation 2–3, we see Jesus correcting His people. With
consummate love and uncompromising holiness, He
speaks to the individual needs and problems of the seven
churches of Asia. Two of these congregations needed no correction, because they had fully trusted and obeyed Him. But
five received His loving rebukes so that they might be
brought into perfect oneness with Him and full fruition unto
His Father. The manner in which Jesus dealt with these
churches is most revealing. As the Father "made known His
ways unto Moses" (Ps. 103:7), so the Son makes known to us
His way in correction.

When the Divine Corrector chastens individual Christians, local churches or ministries, He always follows the
fourfold pattern seen in these messages to the seven churches
of Asia. That pattern is: *commendation, criticism, warning,
exhortation.* He commends everything worthy of merit, criticizes whatever is unacceptable, warns us of the consequences
of disobedience and encourages us by giving incentives for
change. Let us consider these unchanging components of
divine correction and see where they appear in Jesus' message
to the church at Ephesus (Rev. 2:1–7).

COMMENDATION

Whenever possible, Jesus always begins on a positive note. If there is anything in our lives pleasing in His sight—faithfulness, diligence, wisdom, mercy, sacrifice—He commends us for it: "Well done, thou good and faithful servant..." (Matt. 25:21). Such praises reveal the things we need to continue practicing. Generally, anything that pleases Jesus needs no improvement; it merely needs to be maintained. Hence, if we are wise, we will hold fast to the things He commends: "...hold that fast which thou hast..." (Rev. 3:11). Jesus commended the Ephesians on several points.

The Christians at Ephesus were hardworking and patient: "I know thy works, and thy labor, and thy patience..." (Rev. 2:2). Being sincere, they disliked religious hypocrites: "... and how thou canst not bear them who are evil..." (2:2). Being wise, they tested teachers' claims and doctrines; more than one false minister was exposed by their examinations: "...and thou hast tried them who say they are apostles, and are not, and hast found them liars" (2:2). Being loyal, they endured sufferings and refused to faint over the course of painfully long trials: "And hast borne, and hast patience, and for my name's sake hast labored, and hast not fainted" (2:3). And being zealous, they hated sin, as did their Lord, and rejected teachings that subtly led their brethren into sin: "But this thou hast, that thou hatest the deeds of the Nicolaitans, which I also hate" (2:6). The Lord wanted the Ephesians to diligently maintain these practices, because they were His will. This praise was His way of saying, "Carry on."

CRITICISM

Despite His preference for positivism, Jesus finds it necessary at times to be negative. To perfect us, He must point out our imperfections—all of them. Hence, Jesus criticizes everything that fails to meet the standards He gives us in His Word. Always plain and precise, His fault-findings reveal the things we need to change. Their arrival creates an important turning point in our lives, a spiritual *Kadesh-barnea*, for our entire future in God rests solely on our response. If we receive Jesus' criticisms, we grow and bear more fruit; if we reject them, we give place to Satan and quickly backslide; if we ignore them, we stagnate and slowly wither on the Vine. Amid the Ephesians' many pluses, Jesus pinpointed one minus.

Their lone fault was a lapse of personal devotion. They had lost their first love: "I have somewhat against thee, because thou hast left thy first love" (Rev. 2:4). They had stopped seeking the Lord with the desire and regularity they exhibited when they were first saved. They were still dutiful, but no longer passionate; externally they were still upright, but internally they were cooling fast. Though this part of Jesus' report was negative, if heeded it would have produced positive changes—changes which in turn would have brought blessings to the Ephesians and glory to God. Ultimately, then, His criticism was a very positive thing.

WARNING

The last thing Jesus wants to do is issue warnings, but sometimes our stubbornness forces Him to do the last thing. When necessary, the Lord of Grace can issue some very stern warnings. Simply put, His warnings describe the undesirable consequences of rejecting His correction. Why does He warn us? Because His mercy endures forever. He bears long with us, patiently pursuing every avenue by which He may bring us to full union with Himself and, consequently, to the full power and blessing of His Spirit. If His commendations and criticisms fail to inspire repentance, He resorts to warnings. Always He prefers to inspire change by stirring our love for Him. But if need be, He will use fear. (See Luke 12:4–5.) He speaks to us through Jude's inspired writings: "And others save with fear, pulling them out of the fire..." (Jude 23). Jesus is the master motivator. One way or another, by wooing or warning, praising or threatening, He will get our attention. He certainly alarmed the church at Ephesus.

His warning to the Ephesians was most unsettling: "Repent...or else I will come unto thee quickly, and will remove thy lampstand out of its place, except thou repent" (Rev. 2:5). Their lampstand represented their Christian witness—their ability to share the light of the knowledge of God with others. By saying He would remove this, Jesus was threatening to take away their ministry if they did not quickly return to their former love for Him. That jolted them. For if their witness were lost, their rewards would be also. Their past works (2:2–3) and accrued rewards were great. The thought of losing them all now was unbearable. Yet they couldn't ignore His warning, for they knew all too well that His were no idle words. They knew from Scripture the bitter ends of Israel's castaways: Samson, Eli and his sons, King Saul and so on. This was a dreadful prospect, so dreadful that we may think Jesus would never dare flash it before His people. But He did, and it got their attention.

EXHORTATION

Despite the electricity of His warnings, the Lord's promises are still His best weapons against the apathy of His people. When all else fails to move us, He exhorts us with His promises. While His threats arrest our attention, it is His promises that really stir us to action. With them, He mollifies the wounds His criticisms have inflicted and douses the fears His threats have kindled. With them, He revives our broken spirits and restores our faith. With them, He sets hope before us and rekindles our sense of destiny. His promises guarantee exactly what blessings He will give us…if we will just obey His correction. These pledges, like nothing else, inspire us to rise up and obey. They were present in His exhortation to the Ephesians.

Jesus' exhortation to the Ephesians was twofold. First, He reminded them of their initial passion for Him and urged them to recover it: "Remember, therefore, from where thou art fallen, and repent, and do the first works…" (Rev. 2:5). Second, He gave them strong incentive to do so, promising to give them the right to live forever in New Jerusalem and eat of the tree of life: "To him that overcometh will I give to eat of the tree of life, which is in the midst of the paradise of God" (2:7). Jesus here implied the opposite of His previous warning—that their Christian witness would continue, and grow, if only they would correct their lone fault.

THE PURPOSE OF HIS CORRECTION

The Lord's purpose in correcting us is simple: He wants the best for us. His best is that we continue growing in Him until we become full of fruit—and rewards—in this life and the next.

Strangely, many believers are not seeking the Lord's best. Why? They covet the world's best and will go all lengths to have it. Consequently, far too many of us today accept Christian lifestyles that are less than God's best—the average, the traditional, the popular. Rather than leave us in this state until the Judgment, Jesus wants to deal with us now while we can still change. Whenever He sees us settling down into comfortable Laodicean compromise, He draws near to disturb us with His correction...to redirect us into the way of fruitfulness.

In John 15, Jesus revealed four degrees of Christian fruitfulness. The first is no fruit: "Every branch in me that beareth not fruit he taketh away..." (John 15:2). The second is fruit: "...and every branch that beareth fruit, he purgeth . . ." (15:2). The third is more fruit: "...that it may bring forth more fruit" (15:2). And the fourth is much fruit: "...that ye bear much fruit" (15:8). In correcting us, Jesus identifies the things that hinder our fruitfulness so that as we eliminate them, we eventually come to bear much fruit, and that will bring us rich rewards in Christ. It will also bring glory to God: "In this is my Father glorified, that ye bear much fruit..." (John 15:8). And that is the purpose for which we were created. But in our uncorrected state, we cannot glorify God.

Before being divinely chastened, the average Christian is a garden—"ye are God's |cultivated field|" (1 Cor. 3:9)—but one badly in need of cultivation. He is a puzzling mixture, a combination of right thinking and wrong thinking, spiritual habits and carnal ways, good attitudes and bad moods, upright deeds and questionable acts, spiritual inspirations and human impulses, godly goals and selfish ambitions.

When divine correction lays hold upon us, it divides the true from the false within our souls. For the things that are of God to grow and prosper, the things that are not of God must be removed—the weeds of stubbornness, the rocks of hardheartedness and the thorns of worldly entanglements. If not, the seed of the Word will never bring forth fruit, or, if it does, it will not be fully developed. Jesus described His disappointment at underdeveloped fruit: "And that which fell among thorns are they who...bring no fruit to perfection" (Luke 8:14). At best, such fruit will bring us limited rewards—and no glory for God. Imperfect fruit is not the kind He seeks.

81

THE FRUIT HE SEEKS

Too often we mistake Christian fruitfulness for frenzied pros-
elytizing. Novice Christians are hastened into ministry in an
effort to bring others into a relationship with Jesus that they
do not yet fully enjoy or understand themselves. This, the
fruit we seek first, is folly. The fruit the Lord seeks first corrects
this error.

That fruit grows, not in the harvest field of the world, but
in the garden of our souls, as we seek, believe, obey, and abide
closely to Jesus. It is inward, not outward; it is the evidence of
developing spiritual reality, not the results of zealous religious
activity. Scripture calls it the fruit of the Spirit: "But the fruit of
the Spirit is love, joy, peace, long-suffering, gentleness, good-
ness, faith, meekness, |self-control| ..." (Gal. 5:22–23). These
spiritual crops are nothing less than various aspects of Jesus'
nature manifested in us regularly by the power of the Spirit.
The fruit of the Spirit, then, is *consistent Christlikeness*—the
personality traits of the Son of God revisited in our lives daily.
It is this spiritual produce that makes us truly fruitful, cultivated
fields in God's sight. Then, out of such lives, He seeks a second
kind of fruit.

That yield is outward, not inward—a crop of saving works,
not of gracious personality. It is the fruit of Spirit-led Christian
service. This is human ministry through which Jesus continues
to work the works of God—saving, healing, delivering, training
and maturing predestined souls. Every Christian is familiar with
these activities. They are intercession, evangelism, Bible teaching, counseling and charity. In the beginning of the Christian
era, the Lord worked these works only through believers in
whom the fruit of the Spirit was consistently manifested; He
sent forth only those who were being "conformed to the image
of his Son" (Rom. 8:29). If the fruit He seeks first was not present, He did not grant the fruit of Christian service.

Always, the Savior could be seen in those who served Him:
"Now when they saw the boldness of Peter and John...they
marveled; and they took knowledge of them, that they had been
with Jesus" (Acts 4:13). The fruit of their souls and the fruit of
their works were inseparable. He seeks the same order of fruitfulness today, and His correction is sent to bring it forth.

CORRECTION—A CONFIRMATION, NOT A CURSE

When chastened by the Lord, some Christians fear He has rejected them. They immediately assume they are too un-Christlike for the Master's use. Some become convinced they are under the wrath of God. But these are devils' lies. Jesus' rod is not a curse; it is a confirmation.

Far from a sign of woe, divine correction proves that the root and substance of the matter are in us. God corrects us only because there is something very valuable in us—"Christ in you, the hope of glory" (Col. 1:27). The stroke of the Shepherd's rod confirms these comforting facts: Our hearts are good soil, the seed of the Word is within us, the water of the Spirit is present, and our lives are indeed fields under divine cultivation. Moreover, we are already fruitful in a measure. Jesus said His Father purges only Christians who have borne fruit: "…and every branch that beareth fruit, he purgeth…" (John 15:2). Those who bear no fruit are cast away, not purged. The Husbandman leaves them alone, wasting neither time nor effort to speak to them further. But let us not be presumptuous. The confirmation of our fruitfulness is not its completion. For that, there is something else we must do.

Despite the presence and potential of fruit in our lives, there's something else within us, something very unfruitful with which we must deal. It is our old nature. When Christ corrects us, we must *respond* by putting off the old man and putting on the new. (See Colossians 3:5–9.) This is not done in a day. The purging of our old thoughts and ways and reactions occurs daily, one decision at a time, over a season of correction. Only when it is finished does our potential fruitfulness become actual fruitfulness.

THE WAYS HE CORRECTS US

The Lord corrects us in a number of ways. He may lead us by the Spirit to Scripture portions that describe our errors; or, through our pastor's weekly sermon, over the radio, in a television message, or simply in our private Bible reading, we meet a word in season that demands we change. He may correct us through circumstances; He works all things together so that we are no longer able to indulge our disobedience.

83

He may correct us through our observations; we see His hand chastening others for the same faults we possess, and, taking their lesson to heart, we change our ways. He may correct us by dreams; many have turned back from sin and folly due to recurring visions of the night.

Or He may correct us during prayer or worship; while in His presence, we are convicted by the Spirit of truth of an error we have overlooked or neglected: "...I do remember my faults this day" (Gen. 41:9). These are the ways He prefers to correct us. If, however, we fail to respond to them, He has another method.

That method is correction through people. Our heavenly Mentor sends our fellow disciples to counsel us. This is the way He corrected the saints at Ephesus. Note His greeting: "Unto the angel of the church of Ephesus write . . ." (Rev. 2:1). The Greek word here translated angel *(aggelos)* means simply "messenger" and has a twofold application. First, it refers to the church's pastor who, as the Lord's chief spokesman to the Ephesians, delivered His messages to them regularly. Second, it apparently applied to couriers the churches of Asia sent to the Isle of Patmos to visit the apostle John during his exile. Jesus' corrective message came to the Ephesian pastor by their hand. So we see that the Head of the church corrected the members of His body through human messengers.

This should come as no surprise to students of Scripture. In biblical history, the Lord often corrected His erring servants through people. David is a prime example. God prompted Joab to rebuke David when he wept excessively over Absalom's death (2 Sam. 19:5–7); and again when David proposed numbering the people (24:3). He sent Nathan to indict David when he covered his crime against Uriah (12:1 12). And He sent Abigail to turn David from senselessly avenging himself against Nabal: "And David said to Abigail, Blessed be the Lord God of Israel, who sent thee this day to meet me. And blessed be thy advice.. .I have hearkened to thy voice..." (1 Sam. 25:32–33, 35). The same divine trend visited other saints. The Lord corrected the apostle Peter through Paul's brave rebuke in Antioch (Gal. 2:11–14). By His prophets, He repeatedly reproved Israel and her kings for worshiping idols: "And the Lord God of their fathers sent to them by his messengers . . ." (2 Chron. 36:15).

He even corrected Naaman, the proud Syrian commander, through his assistants (2 Kings 5:13). So we see our heavenly Corrector using human mouthpieces in ancient times.

Now consider this: He hasn't changed—"Jesus Christ, the same yesterday, and today, and forever" (Hebrews 13:8)—nor have His methods of correction. He still commends freely, criticizes frankly, warns firmly and exhorts faithfully—and often through men. Obviously, our challenge is this: Are we willing to hear *His* voice when our inspired counselors speak? Or will we, through pride, turn away?

SATAN'S WAYS

Satan's ways stand in sharp contrast to Christ's ways of correction. Satan is the anti-corrector—the inspirer of all opposition to godly correction. Whenever Jesus moves to correct an erring soul, Satan makes a countermove, usually through his servants, to resist Christ's agents and their corrective messages. He tries to defeat the Corrector's counsel in several ways.

First is his way of no criticism at all. Satan promotes the false notions that Jesus never criticizes anyone at anytime for anything and that all criticism is negative and mean-spirited. Through ignorance of Scripture many Christians buy this lie, not realizing that Jesus practiced constructive criticism freely in the days of His flesh and, as stated previously, in His corrective counsel to the churches of Asia. To corroborate his lie, the enemy points to Jesus' "judge not" teaching, claiming it is a blanket forbiddance of criticism, which it is not. (See Matthew 7:1–5.)

Instead the passage merely forbids that novices and hypocritical Christians attempt to correct their brethren's errors while ignoring worse errors in themselves (7:1–4). Jesus then orders us to practice vigorous, sustained self-judgment (7:5a). He ends the passage by calling on self-judged ones (mature disciples) to practice accurate and Spirit-led constructive criticism freely (7:5b)—that erring Christians may be redirected into the way of life.

Nowhere in Scripture does God advocate a policy of no criticism. Such a course only appeases our pride and encourages us to deny reality. Saints that stop speaking the truth in love and begin following an "I'm okay, you're okay" policy, eventually slip off into the abyss of carnality together. And the anti-corrector smiles.

Second, Satan inspires Christians to reject correction. He prompts us to object to the person(s) God uses to correct us. Subtly we begin thinking they are not perfect, they have this fault and that, and how dare they speak to us! But what of it? Do their shortcomings, real or imagined, make ours any less wrong? If Nathan had a discernable fault, would that have made David's sin any less sinful? Certainly not. This is the same technique used so successfully in today's courts; the defense attacks the prosecution's witnesses hoping to divert the jury's attention from the defendant's guilt! Or Satan inspires us to reason our way out of conviction. Sure, we're wrong, but look at this excuse and that temptation and our basic human frailty: We just couldn't help ourselves. So we justify our disobedience to God... and deny the voice of the Corrector. And the anti-corrector laughs.

Third, the enemy hits us with his twin sledgehammers of condemnation and despair. Unlike his other methods, this device plays not upon our pride but upon our sincerity. If when corrected we become so depressed over our errors that we forget the uplifting facts of forgiveness (1 John 1:9) and the Lord's purpose in correction, we will lie down and quit walking with Jesus. To this end, the enemy inspires thoughts of false conviction. These introspections only put us down and never lift us up; they criticize but fail to give hope; they focus on our weaknesses yet ignore God's promises to redeem our failures, refill us with grace, restore our fruitfulness, and yet glorify Himself in us. If we heed such thoughts or the people that bring them, we immediately fall. Prostrate under a juniper tree of despair, we cry out with Elijah, "It is enough" and die to the vision God has set before us. And the anti-corrector rejoices.

~

When visiting the home of Simon the Pharisee, Jesus surprised His host with a word of correction: "...Simon, I have somewhat to say unto thee..." (Luke 7:40). And surprisingly, Simon, though a Pharisee, had the wisdom to receive the Master's counsel: "...And he saith, Master, say on" (7:40). The

One who had somewhat to say to Simon has many things to say to this Laodicean generation; to our churches, our ministries, and to you and me personally. Jesus prophesied that many Laodiceans would deceive themselves by thinking they need no correction: "Because thou sayest, I...have need of nothing..." (Rev. 3:17). Don't be among them.

Learn now to recognize the voice of the Corrector and determine to receive His corrections, no matter how imperfect the messenger, how stinging the criticism, or how humbling the cost of obedience. The Book of Proverbs declares that "reproofs of instruction are the way of life" (Prov. 6:23). But that is only when reproofs are *received*. Reproofs rejected are the way of death. So despise not the chastening of the Lord, nor be weary of His correction. Christ's rebukes are the surest signs of His love: "As many as I love, I rebuke and chasten..." (Rev. 3:19). You have considered His pattern of correction: commendation, criticism, warning, exhortation. You know He seeks only the best for you. You understand the fruit He seeks. You recognize the ways He brings correction into your life. And you realize that the enemy hopes you will be fool enough to reject divine reproof. Don't be his fool.

Be God's wise child instead. Remember that God's goads keep you moving forward in the Spirit, ever stronger, ever closer to Jesus, ever freer from the power of self-deception—and ever safer from divine judgment. For that is all that remains when divine correction is rejected. When we stubbornly reject Jesus' corrections, His constructive purgings cease and His destructive punishments begin. No longer corrective and temporary, His chastisements become permanent... and lethal. It is indeed a fearful thing to fall into the hands of the living God. Divine correction, if received, will keep us from them. So be glad when the Lord corrects you, and let Him have His way: "...be zealous, therefore, and repent" (Rev. 3:19).

By walking in His way in correction, you become eligible for the way of divine guidance.

Chapter Nine

The Way of
Divine Guidance

"...I being in the way, the Lord led me..."
—GENESIS 24:27

It is gloriously possible to be led by God every day of our lives. Moreover, the Lord requires it. Self-led living is unacceptable living—and too wearisome.

Jesus calls us to rest from the weariness of self-led living by taking on His yoke: "Come unto me, all ye that labor and are heavy laden, and I will give you rest. Take my yoke upon you. ..my yoke is easy, and my burden is light" (Matt. 11:28–30). A yoke joins two as one for work. It is a strict yet liberating confinement. It is strict in that no allowance is made for deviation; yokes don't bend. It is liberating in that we now have another to help us pull our load; and He is mighty. Outside of Christ's yoke, all the heavy decisions are ours. Inside His yoke, the burden of forethought is shifted largely to God. As a result, life becomes easy. The Spirit leads and we simply follow; we go when He goes, turn when He turns, and stop when He stops. So we live in the restful yoke of Jesus.

If we are to abide in Jesus' yoke and one day say with Abraham's servant, "I being in the way, the Lord led me," we must learn the ways of Spirit-led living...

SPIRIT-LED LIVING

> "Immediately we endeavored to go into Macedonia, assuredly gathering that the Lord had called us to preach the gospel unto them."
>
> —ACTS 16:10

I t is imperative that we learn to be led by the Spirit of God, for only Spirit-led Christians truly live as God's children: "For as many as are led by the Spirit of God, they are the sons of God" (Rom. 8:14). If we are not allowing God to direct our paths, our paths are not His—and we are not on the paths of glory. The apostle Paul's experiences during his second missionary journey illustrate for us the ways of Spirit-led living.

After passing through the region of Galatia, Paul's ministry team prayerfully considered their next thrust. (See Acts 16:6–10.) Where did God want them to go? Their first choice was the large and promising field of Asia Minor. But as soon as this was proposed, the Spirit of God immediately checked them. For some unknown reason they "were forbidden by the Holy |Spirit| to preach the word in Asia" (16:6). Obediently, therefore, they dropped that initiative. Bithynia seemed the next most favorable field of service. So off they went toward that region: "...they |attempted| to go into Bithynia..." (16:7). Surprisingly, however, they were again checked: "...but the Spirit |allowed| them not" (16:7). Bithynia, too, was "out."

After receiving this second heavenly no, Paul wisely

decided to wait on the Lord until He revealed His will. So, "passing by Mysia, [they] came down to Troas" (Acts 16:8), on the Aegean coast, where they began seeking the Lord. Sometime afterwards—possibly the same evening—God made His plan known to Paul in a night vision: "And a vision appeared to Paul in the night: there stood a man of Macedonia, |beseeching| him, and saying, Come over into Macedonia, and help us" (16:9). Then Paul understood why he had twice been checked. God wanted him to go to Macedonia, not Asia Minor or Bithynia; apparently that was where the need was greatest at the time. So Paul promptly obeyed the vision, boarding a ship bound for Macedonia: "And after he had seen the vision, immediately we endeavored to go into Macedonia, assuredly gathering that the Lord had called us to preach the gospel unto them" (16:10).

Paul's obedience to divine guidance soon brought divine blessing. (See Acts 16:11–40.) God led him straight to the city of Philippi (16:11–12) and to a very godly woman, Lydia (16:13–14). The Lord opened her heart to the gospel and she became the first European convert noted in Scripture. A church was then formed in her home, which became Paul's base of ministry in the city. (See Acts 16:15, 40.) Sometime later Paul pulled down a satanic stronghold over Philippi—previously held in place through a very profitable fortune-telling operation—by expelling a demon from a young female medium (16:16–18). After a violent, but brief, period of persecution (16:19–26), more locals were converted to the faith (16:27–34), and soon the Philippian Christians became Paul's most faithful supporters, giving to his ministry wherever he went. (See Philippians 4:14–19.) In many ways God's will was done in Macedonia and His name glorified: occultism was exposed, Satan was dethroned, many were saved, a strong church was established, and Paul's ministry gained support… all because Paul walked in the ways of Spirit-led living.

In Paul's experiences we see four essential steps in being led by the Spirit of God. They are:

1. Obeying the checks
2. Waiting in the dark

3. Receiving revelation

4. Prompt obedience

Let's examine each of these steps closely.

OBEYING THE CHECKS

By not going to Asia or Bithynia as planned, Paul obeyed the Spirit's check. Exactly what is a spiritual check?

A spiritual check is an impression made upon our hearts by the Holy Spirit that we should go no further in the way we are presently going. He is saying, "Stop. This is not my will for you." He is telling us that our thoughts are not His, our plan is not His, that our present course is in some way wrong. By wrong we do not mean evil, but *something other than God's will, God's way and God's time.* What we propose is either not God's plan at all, or it is His plan but we are not going about it His way, or His time is not yet. Contrary to what some believe, being led of the Spirit is a strict spiritual discipline. God never settles for second best. If we don't do His will in His way and in His time, He will not bless our works. So we must learn to always heed His checks. If we disregard God's checks, God withholds His initiatives.

God showed Paul that he was to go to Macedonia *after* Paul obeyed His checks. We must also understand that when God checks, He does not reveal why He is checking us. He just shows us to stop and then waits for our obedience. If we demand explanations, we will disobey His checks every time—and remain without a revelation of His plan. There are several reasons why we disobey God's checks.

One reason is self-will: "But I really want this, Lord. It's my heart's desire. Please let me have it." Carnal reasoning is another: "Why shouldn't I, Lord? This is a perfectly good thing to do!" Then there is religious pride. We refuse to obey the check because that would be admitting a mistake. We can't do that because we are spiritual, and spiritual people never misread God's will—or so we think. But the Bible reveals that even deeply spiritual servants of God at times temporarily misunderstand God's will. The apostle Paul was checked twice in the passage we are considering, and he was probably the most spiritual person in the church! Joseph, that amazingly insight-

91

ful interpreter of dreams, misread God's purpose for his two sons until the Holy Spirit, through Jacob, checked him. (See Genesis 48:1–20.) While at Jesse's home, the mighty prophet Samuel erred when he assumed that Eliab, David's good-looking older brother, was the Lord's anointed. (See 1 Samuel 16:6–7.) These exceptionally spiritual servants of God learned not to take offense when God checked them. They simply submitted and obeyed, humbly and quietly altering their courses to please Him. If they accepted the Holy Spirit's correction easily, shouldn't we? It is also helpful to remember that a check is not always permanent.

Though Paul was ordered not to go to Asia Minor at this time, he was later sent there in the will of God. (See Acts 19.) In that divinely appointed day of service God used him mightily. The entire region of Asia Minor was evangelized through his ministry; a powerful satanic stronghold of idolatry was broken; multitudes were saved, healed and delivered; and many strong churches were formed. So we see that when the Holy Spirit previously checked Paul, He wasn't telling him that he would never visit Asia, just that He didn't want him to do so at that time.

WAITING IN THE DARK

Obedience to the Spirit's checks plunges us into the darkness. Not the darkness of sin, but the darkness that occasionally comes in the center of God's will. By "darkness" we mean *not knowing God's exact plan or the next step He would have us take.* Isaiah wrote of this darkness when he described servants of God who are both God-fearing and obedient, yet who find themselves in the dark: "Who is among you that feareth the Lord, that obeyeth the voice of his servant, that walketh in darkness, and hath no light?" (Isa. 50:10). Paul found himself in this darkness at Troas (Acts 16:8). For an undisclosed amount of time (several hours, days, possibly longer) he waited there until God gave him positive direction. He wasn't the only servant of God who was plunged into darkness.

Others experienced similar seasons, some quite lengthy. Abraham waited twenty-four years before knowing positively who would bear his son of promise. The light came when God revealed that his aged wife, Sarah, was indeed the chosen mother and that her son was to be named Isaac. (See Genesis 17:19.) Later Abraham endured three long, heavy days of darkness after God ordered him to offer up Isaac on the mount, unsure of how God would yet deliver Isaac and keep His promise to make him fruitful (22:1–10). The light didn't appear until Abraham noticed a ram caught in the thicket by his horns (22:13). Elijah experienced many months of spiritual darkness by the brook Cherith before God gave the light for him to proceed to Zarephath (1 Kings 17:2–9). And in Zarephath he endured many more months of not knowing his next step; then God sent the light by calling him forth to challenge Ahab and initiate the long-awaited reformation (17:10–18:1). We should follow these examples.

When God leads us into the darkness, we should wait patiently until He reveals the next step in His plan. Isaiah advises, "Let him [who is in darkness] trust in the name of the Lord, and stay upon his God" (Isa. 50:10). This will require us to:

- BELIEVE ... God's promise to send the light.
- ABIDE ... in close fellowship with the Lord daily.
- WORK STEADILY ... at our God-given duties, however difficult or mundane.
- OVERCOME ... the various offenses and subtle compromises the enemy sends to stumble us spiritually or prompt us to settle for less than God's best.
- REFUSE ... temptation, especially the desire to rush ahead of God.

Isaiah then warns us not to try to cut short our stay in the darkness by initiating fires of good works on our own. He reveals that such attempts to produce our own light only cause restlessness and end in futility: "Behold, all ye that kindle a fire, that compass yourselves about with sparks: walk in the light of your fire, and in the sparks that ye have kindled. [But] This shall ye have of mine hand; ye shall lie down in sorrow [insomnia]" (50:11).

Our seasons of darkness may be brief or lengthy. But whether they last days, months or years, we must maintain our obedience to the Spirit's checks. Impatience is one of the strongest tendencies in fallen human nature. Most Christians wait out the darkness for a while, but if no light is given in what they consider to be a reasonable time they turn back and disobey a check previously given.

When God fails to open a door within their time frame, they simply choose one He closed earlier, open it, and walk through. This rebellious presumption leads only to confusion—and humiliation—when God, as He invariably does, demands that we reverse our course. Always, we are much better off if we obey His checks. Remember, when you don't know what to do in a given matter, do nothing until God shows you what to do. No matter how long your hopes are deferred, occupy in the dark until Jesus sends the light. He hasn't forgotten you, and He isn't wasting your time.

To us, time spent in the darkness seems wasted, but it is actually time well spent. For while we faithfully abide, God works wonders in our soul. He develops His patience in us, that our characters may become mature and complete, lacking nothing. We learn to walk in the fear of the Lord as we witness and consider the adverse consequences of others who rebel against the darkness. So we enter into Jesus' yoke and learn true submission to God's guidance. As the Israelites followed the cloud in the wilderness, so we follow the Spirit's leading, going as far as He goes, stopping when He stops and staying till He moves. This conforms us to the image of Jesus, who was always led by the Spirit in the days of His flesh and never acted independently of His Father's will.

Receiving Revelation

Ever the rewarder of those who diligently seek Him, God rewards those who faithfully obey His checks and endure the darkness. To such His reward is light: "Unto the upright there ariseth light in the darkness" (Ps. 112:4). In this context, "light" means a revelation of His guidance. One day, in the midst of our uncertainty, the Lord suddenly unveils His plan, and our darkness is no more.

For Paul, the light was given in a dream that directed him to go to Macedonia. (See Acts 16:9.) He realized then why God had checked him from going to Asia and Bithynia. The need in Macedonia was greater, even urgent; it was a field white unto harvest. The Lord had shut all the other doors to direct Paul to this door. For us, the light always reveals one of three things: God's will, God's way or God's time.

God's will

God showed Philip, the evangelist, His will. When God suddenly ordered Philip to leave the revival in Samaria and go south on the Gaza highway (Acts 8:26–40), Philip obeyed (8:26–27). But while en route he walked in total darkness, knowing nothing of God's plan. Internally, his heart must have wondered: where was the need? to whom would he minister? what would God have him do and say? One ray of light shone forth the moment Philip spied the Ethiopian eunuch's caravan in the distance.

More rays filtered in when the Holy Spirit spoke to Philip's heart, "Go near, and join thyself to this chariot" (8:29). Still more light came when he noticed that the eunuch, sitting in his chariot, was reading the holy Scriptures. Full light burst in when Philip saw that the eunuch was at that very moment reading a prophecy of Christ's crucifixion (Isa. 53) and then humbly requested Philip's interpretation, even inviting him to sit in his chariot! Then Philip knew the will of the Lord—he was sent to preach Christ to the Ethiopian eunuch. And so he did: "Then Philip opened his mouth, and began at the same scripture, and preached unto him Jesus" (8:35).

God's way

God showed Joshua His way. After Israel's first, and unsuccessful, attack on the city of Ai (see Joshua 7), Joshua had no doubt as to the will of God. God wanted Israel to conquer Ai. But darkness filled another area of his mind: *How* was God's will to be done? What method, or strategy, was he to use in the battle? Joshua's darkness was mercifully brief, for the Lord soon gave him a specific strategy: "Lay thee an ambush for the city behind it" (8:2). Joshua knew then that the Lord would give victory if Israel attacked Ai by ambush—and in no other way. So he immediately ordered that an ambush be set: "And he commanded them, saying, Behold, ye shall lie in wait against the city, even behind the city..." (8:4).

God's time

The Lord showed Elijah His time. During the notorious

reign of Ahab and Jezebel, Elijah knew God's will for Israel. (See 1 Kings 16-18.) God wanted to destroy the worship of Baal and restore obedience to His law. He further knew how God wanted this end achieved. He was to first call for a drought and then later challenge the prophets of Baal to a public showdown on Mount Carmel, that God might expose Baal as false and powerless and bring judgment upon Baal's prophets. But Elijah was still in the dark on one point. He did not yet know *when* the showdown was to occur. So, as a good soldier, he occupied, awaiting further orders. Daily he attended his humble duties, alone by the brook Cherith and in the company of a widow and her son at Zarephath (1 Kings 17:2–24). Then one day in the third year, the light came. God informed his patient prophet that it was time for the great contest: "Go, show thyself unto Ahab…" (1Kings 18:1; see 18:19). So Elijah went forth—in God's time—to do His will: "And Elijah went to show himself unto Ahab…" (1 Kings 18:2).

~

The light may come to us in one of many ways. In the early morning, the Spirit may bring to mind a verse of Scripture that shows us God's will. As we pray, He may impress upon our hearts that we should wait upon God and not act in a matter. As we read our Bibles, He may quicken a passage that gives us a clear pattern to follow in our present circumstances. The Lord may give us a vivid dream, as he did Paul in Troas. His unseen hand may arrange circumstances that loudly suggest what He would have us do.

On Mount Moriah, the appearance of the ram in the thicket just after the angel told Abraham *not* to sacrifice Isaac was a divine hint; the timing told Abraham that the ram was God's substitute and he *should* offer it in Isaac's stead. (See Genesis 22:10–14.) The light may come with dramatic flair; the Lord may send a prophet to deliver a special message to us in the midst of our brethren. (See Acts 21:10–11.) Or it may come quietly. God may guide us through the private counsel of a pastor or Christian mentor. Whatever means He chooses, one thing is sure: If we obey God's checks and wait faithfully in the dark, He will send us light, and light always brings with it new responsibilities.

PROMPT OBEDIENCE

When God gives us light, He expects us to act on it. Wise souls seize every divine initiative promptly. When Paul received the vision in Troas, he obeyed it immediately: "And after he had seen the vision, *immediately* we endeavored to go into Macedonia" (Acts 16:10, emphasis added). But prompt obedience to the light requires faith, because when God gives us light He reveals only the next step we are to take, not the consequences of that step or His entire plan. We must obey, believing that the Lord has a clear plan before Him (Rom. 8:28) and will see us through whatever "fallout" results from our obedience. Mature disciples remember this adage: God is responsible for the consequences of our obedience to Him. Hence, they obey and leave everything else to God. The immature forget this and procrastinate.

Procrastination—putting off indefinitely what we should do immediately—is the age-old enemy of prompt obedience. It is also a sign of a deeper, unresolved problem. Whenever we procrastinate, some sinful attitude is lodged within our hearts. It may be fear of man: we fear that our obedience will offend certain persons, causing them to turn away from us or retaliate, so we draw back from obedience. It may be laziness: the light calls us to a duty that requires a sustained, diligent effort, and, unwilling to exert ourselves, we do not respond. It may be carnal reasoning: the vision God asks us to believe and work toward seems impossible, so in unbelief we hold back, convinced that it will surely fail. It may be selfishness: we don't obey promptly because what God asks requires us to give up a personal desire. It may be pride: the thing God wants us to do is very humbling, and we're simply unwilling to do it, so we quietly set the issue aside. These are the spiritual hurdles we must leap over if we are to become prompt obeyers of God.

Wise Christians learn to quickly vault over them and obey the light. Why? Because they realize the light is God's will—and His will is utterly dependable. Peter's obedience illustrates this.

Peter received light when Jesus commanded, "Launch out into the deep, and let down your nets for a draught [a haul of fish]" (Luke 5:4). He knew then the what, how, and when of

God's will: he was to seek a large catch; he was to use his present crew, boats, and nets; and he was to do so *now*. But the hurdle of carnal reason almost caused Peter to balk. He had fished all night without catching even one fish, so the prospects of catching a haul only hours later in the same body of water were laughably slim. Impulsively, he began to resist: "Master, we have toiled all the night, and have taken nothing..." (5:5). But then the Spirit seemed to constrain Peter. He knew he had the light—Jesus had spoken—so why not obey?

Wisely, Peter responded. Leaping over the hurdle, he decided to promptly cast his nets: "...nevertheless, *at thy word* I will let down the net" (5:5, emphasis added). He was soon shocked by God's response: "And when they had this done, they enclosed a great multitude of fish...When Simon Peter saw it...he was astonished..." (5:6–9). God's blessing was exceedingly, abundantly above anything he had imagined. Immediately, Peter discovered two truths fully known only by those who promptly obey God:

1. Ultimately, God's wisdom always proves wiser than ours.

2. Whenever God leads, God blesses...abundantly.

～

As we see in Peter's miracle catch, truly wonderful benefits await those who practice Spirit-led living. They grow ever closer to the Lord—and He becomes more real to them—as they learn to recognize and trust His personal guidance. They have extraordinarily deep peace, for "all her [wisdom's] paths are peace" (Prov. 3:17). They will be secure amid the universal insecurity of these last days, for "in the fear of the Lord is strong confidence" (14:26). They will become fruitful Christian workers, for only those who submit to the leading of the Spirit are fit for the Master's use, and they will be used extensively, for there is a severe shortage of Spirit-led ministers. They will rejoice abundantly, as God's perfect plans are accomplished perfectly through their labors time and again. And they will bring great glory to God, for He is always glorified when we do not our will but His—in His way and in His time.

In short, Spirit-led living brings Spirit-blessed results, and nothing else will. God won't bless our leadings, but He will never fail to bless His own.

As He blesses us in the Spirit-led lifestyle, increasingly we will find the Spirit leading us into the way of charity.

Chapter Ten

The Way of
Charity

"…Give ye them to eat…"

—MARK 6:37

The exact opposite of covetousness, charity is the spirit of generosity. The God who gave all to redeem us seeks those who will give freely to others for Christ's sake. The more freely and fully we give, the more we are like Him who gave all to save us.

But there is a problem: We have long lived in a world inspired by the spirit of greed. To get, to take, to have is in our blood—not to give.

If we are now to walk in the way of charity, we must study, and embrace, the principle of giving…

THE PRINCIPLE OF GIVING

"Give, and it shall be given unto you . . ."

—LUKE 6:38

In Luke 6:38, Jesus states His principle of giving: "Give, and it shall be given unto you; good measure, pressed down, and shaken together, and running over, shall men give into your bosom. For with the same measure that ye |measure| it shall be measured to you again." The application of this truth to our lives is limitless. God is our ever-present, faithful Reciprocator. Whenever we give to others for His sake, He gives to us again.

In this verse, Jesus reveals four key points concerning God's recompense. The Lord gives to us:

1. After we have given to others

2. The same substance we have given

3. In the same measure we have given

4. Through people

Let's examine these points in more detail.

He gives—after we have given to others

"[You] Give, and [then] it shall be given unto you..." (Luke 6:38). *The order of action* in this verse is most important.

Jesus says we must act first, then God will act. God will indeed give to us, but only after we have given to others. We often forget this vital order.

As creatures of sight and reason—and a touch of greed—we naturally hold back, wanting God to move first. We want Him to give to us so we will have something extra to give to others. As Gideon looked to his fleeces for encouragement, so we look for God to motivate our charity by giving us fresh blessings. But the Lord wants to reshape our thinking. He wants us to trust Him beyond sight and reason, to give now, by faith, when we have no idea when or how He will recompense us. Whatever our present resources and wherever the present opportunity exists, the word of Jesus is "Give..." Whether we are in abundance, normalcy or need, He insists that we start the process of charity.

The apostle Paul adds, "As we have, therefore, opportunity, let us do good unto all men, especially unto them who are of the household of faith" (Gal. 6:10). If we respond to Jesus' Word, He will respond to us. After we give, He will give. But always, we must give first. The widow of Zarephath demonstrates this for us.

It seemed brazen for Elijah to ask the starving widow of Zarephath to give him her last bit of food, nevertheless he asked her to give first: "And Elijah said unto her...make me of it a little cake *first*, and bring it unto me, and, afterwards, make for thee and for thy son" (1 Kings 17:13, emphasis added). Why? Because he knew well the order in which God works. Despite the widow's personal needs, God's principle of giving called for her to act first. Whatever she had, little or much, she should give it. Her giving would then release God's hands to reward her according to His Word. So Elijah promised, "For thus saith the Lord...The barrel of meal shall not |be used up|, neither shall the cruse of oil fail, until the day that the Lord sendeth rain upon the earth" (17:14). What was he saying? Exactly what Christ taught: *Give and it shall be given unto you!* Trusting God to do as He said, the widow promptly did what Elijah said: "And she went and did according to the saying of Elijah" (17:15). After she gave, God gave, providing her, her son, and Elijah with food for many days (17:15–16).

He gives—the same substance we have given

"Give, and *it* [what you have given] *shall be given unto you...*" (Luke 6:38; emphasis added). After we give, Jesus repays us *in kind*—He returns the same kinds of things we have given. He repays us in the coin we have paid.

If we give money, He gives us money. If we give clothing, He gives clothing. If we give forgiveness, He sends forgiveness. If we give time, He gives time. If we give strength, He returns strength. So the great Reciprocator recompenses us with the same substance we have given.

He gives—in the same measure we have given

"Give, and...good measure, pressed down, and shaken together, and running over, shall men give into your bosom. For with the *same measure* that ye measure *it shall be measured to you* again" (Luke 6:38, emphasis added). Jesus' words here depict an oriental marketplace, where containers in various sizes were used for bartering or buying dry goods. He says the same container we use to measure our gifts to the church or the needy will be used by God to measure His gifts to us. If we measure our gift with a cup, God measures blessing to us with that cup. If we fill a hand basket with our charity, He fills that hand basket with blessing. If we give a bushel basket, the heavenly Merchant uses the same to return His blessing to us, filling it, shaking it so it settles, pressing it down to compact its contents and then throwing in extra on top—"running over." But always, the amount we give determines the amount we receive. Christ gives to us in the same measure we have given. The same principle is seen in sowing and reaping.

A farmer expects a crop in proportion with the amount of seed he has sown. If he sows half an acre with seed, he knows he will not receive a twenty-acre harvest! Similarly, the number of charity-seeds we sow determines the amount of divine-harvests we reap. Paul taught: "He who soweth sparingly shall reap also sparingly; and he who soweth bountifully shall reap also bountifully" (2 Cor. 9:6).

He gives—through people

"Give, and...*men* [shall] give into your bosom..." (Luke 6:38, emphasis added). Jesus reveals that divine gifts are delivered by human hands. When God repays us for our giving,

His favor and grace flow to us through people and usually people and sources other than those to whom we have given. We see this in the Book of Ruth.

Ruth poured out love, loyalty, labor and support on her needy mother-in-law, Naomi, and later these very things were poured back upon her by Boaz. The reason—and real Giver of these blessings—was God. He led Ruth to Boaz, gave her favor in his eyes, prompted Naomi to suggest the proposal, inclined the nearer kinsman to waive his right to marry Ruth, and enabled Ruth to conceive and birth Obed. Behind each of these human decisions, acts and events stood the heavenly Reciprocator, repaying his giving daughter through her generous kinsman. Note that while Ruth's giving was directed to Naomi, God repaid her through another source, Boaz. When blessings come to us, do we see human generosity only? Or do we perceive the work of our heavenly Reciprocator?

We sometimes fail to recognize the Lord's repayments because they are not accompanied by shining angels, heavenly choruses and divine trumpet blasts. Instead His gifts come quietly, through ordinary folks in ordinary settings in ordinary times. But, nonetheless, God is behind them. If we believe Jesus' revelation, we will begin looking for, and seeing, His hand behind our human benefactors: "...unto them that look for him shall he appear..." (Heb. 9:28).

Let's consider some other truths that relate to Jesus' principle of giving.

He gives—sooner or later

The Lord always recompenses those who give, but not always when we expect. Sometimes our "good measure" returns to us immediately.

The apostles experienced this when Jesus fed the multitude. (See Mark 6:35–44.) It is common knowledge that when Jesus realized the multitude's need, He said to His apostles, "Give ye them to eat" (6:37). It is not generally realized, however, that He was asking them to give up *their* food to feed their brethren. The five loaves and two fishes (6:38) were the apostles' personal provisions. When they delivered them over to

Jesus, they sacrificed their supper to sustain their brethren. For this the Lord recompensed them in short order. After the five thousand finished dining, Jesus returned the apostles' loaves and fishes—now greatly multiplied, broken into bite-sized pieces and conveniently arranged in twelve hand baskets, one for each apostle (6:43). It was a sweet payback befitting the sweetness of their charity. And it came quickly, without any delay. They gave and received in one day. At other times, to test our faith and patience, the Lord defers our return.

When through Elisha God ordered the Shunammite to leave her home and sojourn wherever she could, she gave Him obedience. (See 2 Kings 8:1–6.) Though it cost her everything—house, possessions, lands, income—nevertheless she gave. And for seven years she continued giving to God, walking faithfully with Him while destitute. But during this set time, God gave her no rewards—no house, no land, no income, no nothing. To the contrary, he deliberately *withheld* His rewards to test her faith and loyalty to Him. Would she still serve Him even if His recompense appeared to fail? And serve she did...and God did not fail her.

When His appointed time elapsed, He requited her exceedingly, abundantly above all her hopes. Using King Jehoram as His mouthpiece, the Lord decreed, "Restore all that was hers, and all the fruits of the field since the day that she left the land, even until now" (8:6). Thus good measure, pressed down, shaken together and running over, it was given unto her. While her repayment was deferred, it was not denied. The bread she cast away in obedience returned, not in one day but after many days: "Cast thy bread upon the waters; for thou shalt find it after many day" (Eccl. 11:1).

FINANCIAL GIVING— UNDERSTOOD AND MISUNDERSTOOD IN OUR TIMES

In the area of finances, our generation has both understood and misunderstood Jesus' principle of giving. Consequently, some have obeyed it and others have abused it. Daniel wrote that the wise shall understand, and so they have.

Wise Christians realize that Jesus' life cannot be divorced from His teaching, so His principle of giving cannot be twisted to fit any other lifestyle than that which He lived.

105

And the ruling spirit of Jesus' life was generosity, not covetousness. His passion was to do His Father's will, not to acquire assets. Truth, not materialism, ruled His heart. With these facts in mind, we see that the essence of Jesus' principle of giving is not *give to get;* that contradicts the spirit of His life. It is rather *give to have to give again;* this is consistent with the unworldly Teacher who had not where to lay His head and who said, "It is more blessed to give than to receive" (Acts 20:35). Jesus knew that the more we give, the more God enables us to give.

The Spirit states in 2 Corinthians 9:8: "And God is able to make all grace abound toward you, that ye, always having all sufficiency in all things, may abound to every good work." First, we give, generously, if possible: "...he who soweth bountifully..." (9:6). Then God makes His grace (in the form of financial help) abound toward us to recompense us: "And God is able to make all grace abound toward you..." (9:8). One way or another, He commands His blessing on our personal economy—through unexpected gifts, salary increases, lower prices on necessities, no extra expenses for a season, friends giving or lending what we normally buy, and so on. Due to this divine favor, our personal needs are amply supplied: "...that ye, always having all sufficiency in all things..." And, to our delight, we are resupplied with extra resources in order to give again: "...[that ye] may abound to every good work." So obedience to the principle of giving establishes us in a miraculous cycle of charity—not a circle of greed. God is blessed by our generous giving; we are blessed when He recompenses us; and others are blessed as we subsequently share our new surplus. Then the whole cycle begins again, grace upon grace, blessing upon blessing, joy upon joy. But Daniel also prophesied that the wicked would not understand. And so they have misunderstood this principle.

In this Laodicean era, many false teachers have subtly twisted the principle of giving for their own financial profit. Precisely what the Spirit foretold through Peter has occurred. (See 2 Peter 2:1–3.) With feigned words, these false teachers have spread destructive heresies and made merchandise of God's naive sheep. As a result, the way of truth has been evil spoken of by many worldlings, who are sharp enough to know greed when they hear it. Even they sense innately that Jesus wasn't trying to stir covetousness when He promised His fol-lowers, "Give, and it shall be given unto you..." And Bible-wise Christians should certainly know that while God promises to meet the needs of faithful givers—"my God shall supply all your need" (Phil. 4:15–19)—He nowhere promises to make Christians financially wealthy.

The idolization of worldly wealth—the love of, obsession with and quest for money—has sidetracked innumerable saints in this Laodicean generation and ruined their spiritual potential. But now, at long last, the "supposing that gain is godliness" madness has run its course. Even the most die-hard prosperity worshipers are now realizing that Jesus was right all along: A man's life does *not* consist in the abundance of the things he possesses. (See Luke 12:15.) And they are beginning to see His purpose in teaching us the principle of giving...to deliver us from the same lethal anxieties that cause thousands of hearts to fail daily.

He hoped to lay an unshakable foundation of confi-dence in our hearts so that we will give *knowing* God sees and recompenses us every time. Thus we possess, not vast riches but something infinitely better: irrevocable confi-dence in the living God. We know we will never lack any material necessities in this life. That's divine security. That's a rock nothing in this world—recession, depression, bank failures, stock market collapses—can move. This assurance is the precious gold Jesus counsels us to buy and the wealth He urges us to desire: "I counsel thee to buy of me gold tried in the fire that thou mayest be rich . . ." (Rev. 3:18; see 1 Timothy 6:6–8,17–19). The more we practice His princi-ple of giving, the more we become truly "rich"—in confi-dence in our ever-wealthy heavenly Father.

But the principle of giving is not only about finances. Money is just one of many ways we may give.

OTHER WAYS WE MAY GIVE AND BE GIVEN UNTO

Time

When we give of our time to help others, God causes others to give of their time to help us. So the time we have sacrificed is returned to us.

Walking in His Ways

Strength
When we give our last ounce of physical strength to do God's will, God gives us a wondrous refilling of physical strength. So the strength we have given is given us again. Knowing this, Paul gladly expended His strength to help believers: "And I will very gladly spend and be spent for you..." (2 Cor. 12:15).

Thought
When we patiently and prayerfully study the Scriptures, we are giving our thoughts to God's Word. For this, God gives us inspired thoughts, or revelation, from His Word. Accordingly, the Holy Spirit urges us to give ourselves "wholly" to Bible study: "Meditate upon these things; *give thyself wholly* to them..." (1 Tim. 4:15, emphasis added)—then He may give us abundant understanding: "...that thy profiting may appear to all." So the mental effort we have given is repaid us.

Truth
Whenever we share biblical truths with other believers, God gives us new truths and new opportunities to share them. And, as always, His recompense is in proportion to our giving. The more we give, the more God enlarges our capacity to receive spiritual truth and the more knowledge we have to give away: "For unto every one that hath shall be given, and he shall have abundance [to use, to give]..." (Matt. 25:29).

First fruits of each day
The Lord promises to give bountifully to those who give their first fruits to Him. (See Proverbs 3:9–10.) The early morning hours are the first fruits of every new day. If we give this prime time to God He will give us precious blessings in return. Every morning we give to fellowship with the King: "Seek ye first the kingdom of God..." (Matt. 6:33)—that day the King returns our gift by helping us with all our worldly needs and problems that arise: "... and all these things shall be added unto you." So the day we give to God is given to us again.

Thanksgiving and worship
"In every thing give thanks; for this is the will of God in Christ Jesus concerning you" (1 Thess. 5:18; See Heb. 13:15). When we give the Lord thanksgiving and worship *in every*

circumstance, even those most displeasing, He gives us grace to bear our circumstances. So the sacrifice of praise we have given returns as an infilling of grace from the Lord.

Forgiveness

Jesus taught repeatedly that our heavenly Father forgives us "if" and "as" we forgive others: "And forgive us our debts, *as* we forgive our debtors...For *if* ye forgive men their trespasses, your heavenly Father will also forgive you [your trespasses]" (Matt. 6:12,14, emphasis added). "Forgive, and ye shall be forgiven" (Luke 6:37). When we forsake all grudges against our offenders, the Lord drops His charges against us. So the forgiveness we give others is given us by God.

Patience

When we patiently bear with those who try us, God returns the favor in kind. He moves someone to be patient with us in an area of our lives in which we presently struggle. So the patience we give is given us again.

Hospitality

The Lord loves hospitality and asks us to lavish it on one another: "Beloved, thou doest faithfully whatever thou doest to the brethren...whom, if thou bring forward on their journey after a godly sort, thou shalt do well" (3 John 5–6). Whenever we care for our guests generously, God arranges for others to warmly receive us and see to our needs. So the hospitality we give is given us again.

Compassionate assistance

"Blessed is he that considereth the poor; the Lord will deliver him in time of trouble" (Ps. 41:1). When we go out of our way to help those who are in need, God notes our compassion. And when we encounter a time of trouble, He raises up those who go out of their way to help us. Thus, the compassion we give is given us again.

Faithfulness and loyalty

When we are faithful in service and loyal in attitude to our superiors, God will cause our subordinates to follow our leadership. So the faithfulness and loyalty we have given are given us again.

Exhortation and counsel

When we give counsel and exhortation to the troubled ones God sets before us, He arranges for us to have the same when we are cast down—a Jonathan to strengthen our hand in God or a godly Abigail to turn away our anger. Thus, the uplifting words we have given are given us again.

GIVE . . . AND FREELY RECEIVE

Faith in the principle of giving changes our attitude toward receiving help. The free Christian not only gives freely, he also receives freely: " . . . freely ye have received . . . " (Matt. 10:8).

We freely receive from others because we know our Lord will faithfully recompense them. Whatever they do for us for His sake they do *unto Him*—"Inasmuch as ye have done it unto one of the least of these my brethren, ye have done it unto me" (Matt. 25:40)—and He will pay them back (Prov. 19:17). Human pride insists on doing everything for itself. It asks no help, accepts no help and despises those who do so. Christians who refuse to receive help sin against those who offer it, for they hinder them from being blessed by the Lord for giving. But those who believe the principle of giving will humble themselves and freely receive from others without either guilt or obligation: "So David received of her [Abigail's] hand that which she had brought him . . . " (1 Sam. 25:35). Why? Because they know the Lord will give to their donors. Because they have given, it must be given unto them.

GIVE . . . THE WAY THE SPIRIT LEADS

The Spirit should lead us in our giving, and the Spirit leads according to the present need.

When God brings needy people before us, we should consider the need they have at the moment and give accordingly, not according to the way we naturally prefer to give. Sometimes money is given to evade giving time, counsel, instruction or assistance; the nobles of Tekoah apparently supported Nehemiah's administration, but they wouldn't lend a hand to work on the wall. (See Nehemiah 3:5.)

At other times we give words of good cheer when God wants us to give of our supplies or write out a check; James wrote of Christians who gave starving brethren benedictions

110

instead of bread! (See James 2:15–16.) If the need before you is financial, give of your money. If it's non-financial, give in the way needed. If it's both, give in both ways; the good Samaritan gave time, assistance, materials, forethought *and* money to the wounded Jew he found in the way, because he needed help in all these ways. (See Luke 10:30–37.)

As you follow his example, you will be giving the way the Spirit leads. That will make you a true child of your Father who is in heaven.

RECEIVE . . . IN THE WAY YOU NEED

If we give to others the way the Spirit leads, God sometimes repays us in exceptional ways. As stated previously, Christ said our Father repays us *in kind*—with the same kind of substance we have given. But sometimes He works in other ways. He recompenses, not according to what we have given, but according to our present needs.

For instance, you give monies to a ministry or a financially needy saint, yet God doesn't recompense your finances. Instead, He delivers you from an oppressor who has long troubled you. Why? Because that's the help you need most at the time. Monetarily, you "have all and abound" and need no gift, but personally you are at your wits' end with your oppressor. So God gives relief there. Or you give time and counsel to a friend who is greatly distressed, yet God doesn't send you a counselor. Rather, He blesses you with extra income in the very month you are hit hard with extra expenses. The reason? That's where your need is. Or, as seen in the Shunammite's experience, He sometimes repays us according to our hearts' desires.

Second Kings 4 reveals that a prominent woman from Shunem built quarters for Elisha to rest in as he passed by her city regularly. So she gave to his ministry according to his need. For this, God gave unto her—but not in the way she may have expected. Instead of giving her an additional room or home, the Reciprocator gave her something far more valuable . . . a son. How thoughtful and personal the Lord was in His repayment! A wealthy woman, the Shunammite had no need of more possessions, but she lacked and longed for a son. That was her heart's desire. So that was what God gave her. What grace! What a God! What a Giver!

BECOME A GIVER...LIKE THE FATHER AND THE SON

If we faithfully practice the principle of giving, it will transform us. We will cease craving to get and begin delighting to give. We will pray for and receive opportunities to give and give freely whenever occasion serves. In so doing, we will become givers, like our heavenly Father, who "so loved the world, that he gave his only begotten Son..." (John 3:16). And we will be conformed to the image of His Son, who said, "The Son of man came not to be ministered unto, but to minister and to give..." (Matt. 20:28). So let this saying sink down into your ears until it permeates your entire being: *"Give, and it shall be given unto you..."*

And as we practice giving freely to people, it is only natural that we consider the most important form of giving—giving to God in the way of worship.

Chapter Eleven

The Way of
Worship

"Give unto the Lord...worship the Lord in the beauty of holiness."

—Psalm 29:1–2

Worship is the ecstasy of the spiritual life—for God and for His people—and God's worshipers are His lovers. Passionless Christians do not worship; or, if at all, they worship only in public church services. But passionate believers worship the Lord often. They know well that when the Bridegroom appears, He will take unto Himself lovers, not distant acquaintances. So they draw near and worship Him, day and night.

Personal worship is the gateway to a full and intimate knowledge of God. That God has hung this gate is our invitation. That we enter it is our wisdom—and our eternal gain. Let us therefore enter in and worship and know the Lord.

To that end, we should consider the importance
of personal worship...

THE IMPORTANCE
OF PERSONAL WORSHIP

"But the hour cometh, and now is, when the true worshippers shall worship the Father in spirit and in truth; for the Father seeketh such to worship him."

—JOHN 4:23

To worship God is to express adoration and affection for Him. By his worship, the worshiper makes known his supreme love for the One he worships. There are many different ways we may worship the Lord.

We may worship in deeds: Mary of Bethany worshiped Jesus by pouring out her most precious ointment, spikenard, on His head and feet. We may worship in words: in his psalms David penned words that expressed his love for the Lord. We may worship in thought: Hannah spoke to the Lord in her heart. We may worship audibly: Moses, Deborah and Barak sang songs of thanksgiving to the Lord for their victories. Or we may worship inaudibly: the Israelites' burnt offerings were silent but meaningful expressions of their adoration for Jehovah. We may worship in stillness: David sat still before the Lord, and then gave thanks for being established as king over all Israel. Or we may worship actively: Miriam and David each danced before the Lord for joy. We may bow to worship: Moses fell on his face, Jesus' kneeled down and Paul bowed his knee to the Father of our Lord Jesus Christ. Or we may worship standing: the priests stood when ministering at the altar, and Jesus stood by Lazarus' tomb while offering thanks for his resurrection. We may worship with hands raised: the people of Judah lifted up their hands to worship Jehovah during Ezra's revival. Or we may worship without raising our hands: many clasp their hands as if to pray while worshiping. We practice these various ways of worship in two general settings—public and private.

Public worship occurs whenever churches or other Christian groups convene openly for praise and worship. This most widely recognized worship is congregational worship. Private worship occurs whenever individual believers get alone with God and exalt Him. It is this secret place of worship that we are examining in this chapter. We call these times of private devotion *personal worship*.

WHAT IS PERSONAL WORSHIP?

Personal worship is a time of intimacy with God. A spiritual act of love, it occurs in complete privacy, behind closed doors. Jesus taught us, "Enter into thy closet, and when thou hast *shut thy door*" (Matt. 6:6, KJV, emphasis added), then express your love for God. And, like natural love, the more we express it, the more it grows.

As our love for God grows, we develop our own individual ways of expressing it. Our potential love-acts are many: We may thank the Lord for answers to prayer, blessings or other favors He has shown us, reciting them gratefully in His hearing.

We may extol His attributes: "Lord, your faithfulness is so dependable! Your goodness is so wonderful! Your mercies are new every day! Your judgments are perfectly just!"

We may repeatedly and affectionately speak His name, "Father." Jesus said, "When ye pray, say, Our Father..." (Luke 11:2).

Or we may utter the name above all names, "Jesus," slowly and lovingly. We may gently whisper a thank offering—"Thank You, Lord"—many times. Apparently, the writer to the Hebrews worshiped in this way: "Let us offer the sacrifice of praise to God continually, that is, the fruit of our lips giving thanks to his name" (Heb. 13:15).

We may offer the incense of praise, singing quietly with understanding: "Come before his presence with singing" (Ps. 100:2).

116

Or we may sing in the Spirit, letting the *Parakletos* utter through us His adoration for the Father and the Son. We may sit still in silent adoration while the eyes of our understanding envision Him who sits upon the throne. And the list of possible acts of worship goes on. Some, however, we fail to recognize as expressions of worship.

For instance, every time we obey the Bible, we are worshiping God. Every time we yield to the leading of the Spirit, we are worshiping God. Every time we give for Jesus' sake—to churches, ministries or the poor—we are worshiping God. Every time we deny ourselves and willingly bear the crosses the Lord lays upon us, we are worshiping God.

But whatever our acts of worship, our intention is the same. We are demonstrating before the Lord our personal delight in Him. To the carnal mind, this seems unimportant. But not to God. To Him, personal worship is very important. His heart yearns for it: "...for the Father seeketh such to worship him" (John 4:23).

WORSHIP—ITS PURPOSE

The purpose of personal worship is simply *to bless the heart of God.* So occupied are we with seeking needs and blessings for ourselves and others that we often overlook the fact that God needs and seeks satisfaction from us. The most important, yet least considered, aspect of ministry is ministry unto the Lord.

Recognizing this, Solomon offered "a thousand burnt offerings" (1 Kings 3:4) in love to God. David set his heart to bless the Lord with his psalms of praise. The elders of the church at Antioch gathered privately and "ministered to the Lord" (Acts 13:2). So committed to worship were Paul and Silas that, even when they were stripped of their rights, humiliated, beaten and bound with stocks and chains in Philippi, they dutifully offered God a sacrifice of praise, praying and singing praises "unto God" (Acts 16:25). God is seeking Christians today who, like these, will set themselves to bless His heart regularly: "My heart is fixed, O God, my heart is fixed; I will sing and give praise [for your pleasure]" (Ps. 57:7).

WORSHIP—ITS RESULTS

God delights to bless those who delight to bless Him. "God

is love" (1 John 4:16). As such, Love loves to be loved and freely loves His worshipers. When we set aside our desires and concentrate on blessing God, He always sends us reflective blessings. Like rays of light reflecting off a heavenly mirror, our worship ascends to God's throne, satiates His heart with joy, and descends again to bless us. It is the principle of giving applied to worship. Psalm 29 reveals this.

Like the ringing of joyous church bells, Psalm 29 opens by calling us to remember and give ourselves to the purpose of worship: "Give unto the Lord, O ye mighty, give unto the Lord glory and strength. Give unto the Lord the glory due unto his name; worship the Lord..." (Psalm 29:1–2). And it closes promising that God will give strength and peace to those who give Him worship: "The Lord will give strength unto his people [worshipers]; the Lord will bless his people [worshipers] with peace" (29:11). What is the Spirit saying to the churches? That if we will give God worship, He will give us the dual benefits of strength and peace. And that's not all. Worship opens up a fountain of blessings from which worshipers and others may drink in many other benefits.

Personal worship deepens our spiritual lives: continual intimacy with Jesus gives us a clearer understanding of the Bible, a sharper ear for the Spirit's voice and an increased awareness of God's presence. It expedites prayer: when blessed by our worship, God answers our petitions with exceptional speed and accuracy. It prompts divine intervention: Paul and Silas's worship stirred the Lord to immediately and powerfully deliver them from their Philippian torture chamber. (See Acts 16:26.) It delights our souls: knowing that our worship is pleasing to God fills us with the fullness of human joy. And it makes us more fruitful: consistent worship keeps us abiding closely in the Vine and produces a powerful outflow of the Spirit's fruits, and works. So the worshiper, being blessed, becomes a blessing to others.

WORSHIP—A REDEMPTIVE PRIVILEGE

Under Moses' law, the privilege of worshiping the Lord as priests was reserved for the sons of Aaron. They alone could enter the tabernacle to minister to the Lord. They alone could draw near His awesome presence. They alone offered incense at the golden altar. They alone offered the continual burnt offering, morning and evening, upon the brazen altar. Others were not so privileged. They did not have heaven's permission to draw near. A parallel to this exists today in the tabernacle of the church.

Christians are God's New Testament priests. Peter taught, "Ye are…a royal priesthood…" (1 Pet. 2:9). Personal worship is a redemptive privilege reserved exclusively for them. Only believer-priests may enter into God's presence by the "new and living way" Jesus consecrated. Only they may worship Him acceptably "in spirit and in truth" (John 4:23). Only they may offer the fragrant incense of prayer, song, and adoration unto the Father. Only they may offer the continual burnt offering— "the sacrifice of praise to God continually, that is, the fruit of our lips giving thanks to His name" (Heb. 13:15)—that so pleases the Most High. To others, the door to the presence is shut. Denied this privilege, they are to be pitied.

Poor unredeemed, they cannot worship whom they do not know nor can they comprehend the wonder of God! Jesus said to one, "Ye worship ye know not what" (John 4:22). Poor unredeemed, dead souls, they observe dead rituals at Athenian altars, giving worship ignorantly "to the unknown God" (Acts 17:23)! Such worship God cannot accept. It is the offering of Cain revisited, and He rejects it just as He did Cain's. Those who reject the Lamb and despise His humble way of personal repentance and faith cannot draw near God. He reserves that privilege for the redeemed, who are washed in the blood of the Lamb and born of and baptized with His Spirit. For us, then, one question remains.

Are we using, or wasting, our privilege of personal worship?

WORSHIP—PREDOMINATE IN HEAVEN

The fourth and fifth chapters of the Book of Revelation reveal that in heaven worship predominates. They describe for us what will occur there immediately after the true church is translated. By the Spirit, John identifies those who are worshiped—the Father and the Son. He also reveals who will worship them—Christians and cherubim. These will release a mighty river of worship.

The four living creatures, angelic beings who guard the throne of God, will begin the flow of praise by crying, "Holy, holy, holy, Lord God Almighty, who was, and is, and is to come" (Rev. 4:8). The twenty-four enthroned, crowned elders (overcoming Christians—the translated church) will then enter in. They will fall down before the throne of God the Father and "worship him that liveth forever and ever, and cast their crowns before the throne, saying, Thou art worthy, O Lord, to receive glory and honor and power; for thou hast created all things, and for thy pleasure they are and were created" (4:10–11). Then they will fall down before the Lamb and sing "a new song, saying, Thou art worthy...for thou wast slain, and hast redeemed us to God by thy blood...and hast made us unto our God |a kingdom of priests|..." (5:8–10). After this, an innumerable host of angels will enter in, "saying with a loud voice, Worthy is the Lamb that was slain to receive power..." (5:11–12). So we see that every creature in heaven—human and angelic—will unite in a great and glorious chorus of worship. The Spirit's message is clear: heaven will be, and now is, a place of worship, worship and more worship.

Citing this vision of heaven by John, and those of the prophets Isaiah and Ezekiel, A.W. Tozer wrote, "Every glimpse of heaven shows them worshiping." This evokes an important question. Since heaven is filled with worship, what will Christians do there if they don't personally worship God now? If suddenly caught up to God's throne, non-worshipers would be totally out of touch with their surroundings. The angels would have to walk them through a six-month orientation program before they could enter the flow of worship. True worshipers need no such introduction.

For them, heaven will be the climax of their earthly devotions. While in this world, they have praised and worshiped the Lord by faith—without seeing Him. He has imparted His peace to them countless times, and refilled and refreshed them with His Spirit, but always as the invisible God. Never have they looked upon His face. This great privilege of beholding the beauty of the Lord, so long withheld, will at last be given them when Jesus appears to escort them to paradise. When granted, this added visual aspect will be overwhelmingly joyous, or *rapturous*. Hence, Jesus' appearing is known as the *Rapture*.

WORSHIP—PREPARATION FOR TRANSLATION

Since at the Rapture translated saints will go immediately into an atmosphere filled with worship, how can non-worshipers be confident that they will be caught up? Eternally saved, yes; but selected for translation, no. Jesus' teachings shed light on this.

Whenever He spoke of His appearing (the Rapture), Jesus used three key terms to describe those who will be caught up—*worthy, watching, ready*. Note their use in these three sample scriptures:

> Watch ye, therefore, and pray always, that ye may be accounted *worthy* to escape all these things that shall come to pass [events of the Tribulation period], and to stand before the Son of Man [in heaven].
> —LUKE 21:36, EMPHASIS ADDED

> *Watch* ye, therefore; for ye know not when the master of the house cometh...And what I say unto you I say unto all, Watch.
> —MARK 13:35–37, EMPHASIS ADDED

> And while they went to buy, the bridegroom came, and they that were *ready* went in with him to the marriage...
> —MATTHEW 25:10, EMPHASIS ADDED

How can the heavenly Father, who eagerly seeks worshipers, account non-worshipers "worthy" to escape the Tribulation period? How will believers be sober-minded and alert to the times—"watching" for the thief in the night—if they do not worship? How will we overcome our present trials and be "ready"—approved unto God and exempted from further trials—when Jesus appears, if we do not worship the Lord now in our prisons, pits, and fires?

Jesus hints as much in His parable of the ten virgins. (See Matthew 25:1–13.) There He likens professing Christians living at the time of His appearing to ten virgins, five who are wise (prepared), and five who are foolish (unprepared). He then prophesies that of this vast company only half, the wise, will be "ready" to meet Him. These He will catch away to heaven, where they will attend the marriage supper of the Lamb: "And while they went to buy, the bridegroom came, and they that were ready went in with him to the marriage..." (25:10). The others will be left behind. Realizing their plight, they will beg Him to change His mind and take them anyway: "Lord, Lord, open to us" (25:11). But He will deny their request. And in His denial He will identify the chief reason they were not taken: They did not know Him closely. "Verily, I say unto you, *I know you not*" (25:12, emphasis added).

Paraphrasing, He said, "I do not know you intimately. We are not closely acquainted. You have not built a close, personal relationship with me." Since worship is an integral part of knowing God, not knowing Him implies a lack of worship. Apparently, the foolish virgins worshiped corporately, but not privately; in meetings, but not in their homes. They attended worship services but neglected their privilege of personal worship. Summing up, then, Jesus' parable implies:

- Christians who do not worship are "foolish."

- Christians who do not worship do not know the Lord closely.

- Christians who do not worship will be left behind at the Rapture.

These non-worshiping Christians are among those to whom Hebrews 2:3 was written: "How shall we escape, if we neglect so great salvation?..."—or, paraphrasing to put in the context of worship, "How shall we escape the Tribulation, if we neglect personal worship?"

～

Friend, we have here abundant proof that personal worship is important to God and should be important to us. Very important. But is it important to you—important enough to cause you to begin personally worshiping the Lord? Don't make the mistake of merely nodding in agreement with these truths. Let them move you. Today enter into the way of personal worship—"Oh, come, let us sing unto the Lord...let us come before his presence with thanksgiving, and make a joyful noise unto him with psalms...Oh, come, let us worship..." (Ps. 95:1–6)—and never depart from it.

In the way of worship you will find the inspiration to walk steadily in the way of duty.

Chapter Twelve

The Way of
Duty

"And he appointed…the Levites to their offices, to praise and minister before the priests, as the duty of every day required."

—2 Chronicles 8:14

The Bible makes much of faithfulness. The faithful God seeks faithfulness in His children. Inseparably linked to the ideal of faithfulness is that of duty. Though the word *duty* rarely appears in the Bible, it's thought is present in every chapter. Noah did his duty as ark-builder. Moses did his duty as lawgiver. Jeremiah did his duty as God's spokesman to Judah. Nehemiah did his duty as rebuilder of Jerusalem. John the Baptist did his duty as Christ's forerunner. And Christ did His duty as sacrificial Lamb. Time and print would fail me to tell of others who did their duty for heaven's sake. But what of us?

Will we walk in the footsteps of the dutiful? For this we must have a strong incentive.

That comes when we realize duty leads us to our blessings…

Duty Leads Us
to Our Blessings

"...their duty is also to minister unto them..."
—Romans 15:27

D uty is a task one is obligated to fulfill because of one's relationship, position or occupation. Since antiquity, wise souls in the church and the world have held duty in the highest esteem.

The famous British Admiral, Horatio Nelson, signaled his fleet before the Battle of Trafalgar, "England expects every man will do his duty." And at battle's end, mortally wounded but grateful for an amazing victory, Nelson's last words were, "Thank God I have done my duty." Later in the same century Robert E. Lee, the famous Southern general, said, "Duty is the sublimest word in the English language." But our generation is far removed from those of Nelson and Lee. In this Laodicean era, the ideal of doing one's duty has fallen into disfavor. To the worldling, it's neither glamorous nor high-paying enough to be interesting. And to the Christian, it seems too practical to be spiritual. How can something as dull as duty be inspirational?

Yet to God, duty is an immensely important topic. Heaven still looks for those who do their duty. We should regard duty highly, too, for although it is not exciting, it is rewarding. Very rewarding. The Bible reveals repeatedly that duty leads us to our blessings. As we faithfully perform our unexciting obligations we meet exciting blessings sent by the hand of God. Isaiah said, "Thou meetest him who rejoiceth and worketh righteousness [does his duty], those who remember thee in thy ways..." (Isa. 64:5). By faithfully executing our duties we show God we are becoming stable, mature Christians. And by rewarding us with blessings, God shows us that He notices our dutifulness and appreciates it.

And He appreciates it most when times are the worst, when we are besieged by difficulties. It is no great challenge to perform our duties when times are good. No extra effort is needed when everything we do quickly succeeds, prospers, and multiplies. When continuous prosperity is giving us regular doses of motivation, it's easy to fulfill our basic responsibilities. But when adversity strikes hard and nothing works as planned, and God neither explains things nor quickly makes a way of escape, our natural zeal quickly evaporates.

We discover then just how difficult it is to keep our hand to the plow when the winds of trial blow hard against us. New and strange burdens—sorrow, grief, anguish, hopelessness— like huge stones lay heavy upon our hearts as we trudge along the valley of Baca. Every step then becomes a challenge and every accomplishment, significant. Even the most ordinary deeds demand an exceptional effort of will. Persevering in duty amid such difficulties is like climbing Mount Everest: It demands the spirit and qualities of heroism. For this reason, when the Lord evaluates our dutifulness, He takes into account the difficulty of our circumstances. And He reserves His best rewards for the heroes and heroines of duty.

The lives of Joseph, Ruth and Paul illustrate this. Joseph pursued his duties during a long season of gross injustice, Ruth pursued hers amid the twin sorrows of bereavement and poverty, and Paul attended to his while enduring unrelenting religious persecution. And in each case, duty guided them straight to the discovery of rich blessings.

Joseph

While yet a boy, Joseph learned to love duty. (See Genesis 37.) Quite the opposite of his mischievous and unreliable elder brothers, young Joseph attended his duties faithfully. In fact, he was doing his duty—seeking his brothers' whereabouts as charged by his father—at the time his brothers sold him into Egyptian slavery (37:13–14). But Joseph refused to let their hatred spoil his love.

In Egypt, he continued pursuing his passion for duty. (See Genesis 39.) As a slave, he served Potiphar with the same dutifulness he had rendered Jacob earlier. Consequently, Potiphar soon made him the steward of his estate. But, again, trouble came when Joseph was on duty. While Joseph was fulfilling his stewardly obligations, Potiphar's wife made advances toward him which, when he rejected them, led to her false charges and his unjust imprisonment. Joseph must have wondered where duty was leading him. Twice tragedy had struck, not while he was neglecting his duties, but while he was attending them. In prison, he could have easily rebelled against his seemingly unfaithful friend, Duty.

But not Joseph. While incarcerated he continued quietly fulfilling his responsibilities. (See Genesis 39:21–23.) In time he became keeper of the prisoners, but there was nothing new and exciting about his duties, just more of the mundane. He was neither paid nor commended for looking after his fellow prisoners' needs. And to make his lowly duties seem even lowlier, there was no apparent hope for advancement as there had been in Potiphar's house. Man would never again promote him; only God could do that now. It was with this faith that Joseph kept to his tasks daily, serving meals, dispensing supplies, settling disputes, and encouraging downcast inmates; he also performed spiritual duties, interpreting the dreams of Pharaoh's butler and baker (40:1–19). A wonder to all, Joseph was as dutiful in prison as he had been in Potiphar's service and Jacob's household. Why? Because of his faith. Joseph believed that those who do their duty please God. And he was right.

One day God revealed just how pleased He was with Joseph. (See Genesis 41.) Suddenly, mighty Pharaoh summoned lowly Joseph for an interview. Suddenly, the interview led to a position, which turned out to be the highest in Pharaoh's court. It was a miracle! In the twinkling of an eye Joseph's long trial was over, and he leaped from drudgery to ecstasy. The forgotten prisoner was now the favored prime minister of Egypt. Though miraculous, this was not accidental. It was the very place for which God predestined Joseph.

All his past life had been but a divinely arranged preparation for that post, that hour, that high calling. And it was duty that led him there. Joseph's interview with Pharaoh was a direct result of his performance of his spiritual duty—as an interpreter of dreams—while in prison. If he had failed or refused to interpret the dream of Pharaoh's butler, the butler would never have recommended him to Pharaoh. So duty led Joseph to his destiny.

Ruth

When Naomi and her daughter-in-law, Ruth, returned to Bethlehem, Naomi was elderly, bereft and destitute (Ruth 1:19–22). Too old to remarry, too exhausted for hard work and too disillusioned to be optimistic, Naomi was desperate. Seeing this, Ruth felt obligated to help her needy mother-in-law. So she volunteered to go to work gleaning the barley harvest: "And Ruth, the Moabitess, said unto Naomi, Let me now go to the field, and glean ears of |grain| ... " (2:2). Now gleaning was no easy task. It was exhausting labor and its returns were usually slim. But being youthful and strong, Ruth knew it was her duty to support Naomi. So she went forth seeking employment: "And she went, and came, and gleaned in the field after the reapers..." (2:3). What she found far exceeded what she sought.

Not only did the Lord give Ruth job and wages, His unseen hand directed her straight to the fields of Bethlehem's finest and wealthiest bachelor, Boaz: "...and she happened to come to a portion of the field belonging unto Boaz..." (Ruth 2:3). One of Naomi's near kinsmen, Boaz was a potential redeemer of her late husband's estate. And as Ruth soon learned, fulfilling that role would require Boaz to marry her and father children to receive the name and property of her late husband, Mahlon. Now by no woman's standards was Boaz ordinary. He was in every way an exceptional find. Spiritual, stable, honorable, humble, courteous, thoughtful and generous—the epitome of a godly husband—he was clearly the best husband heaven could have bestowed upon Ruth.

Paradoxically, Ruth found her dream husband while *not* seeking one. Though she must have desired a husband, Ruth chose to seek after duty rather than men. Daily she worked the fields to provide her and Naomi's needs instead of going to the usual places single women met single men in Bethlehem. Apparently, she believed Jehovah would provide her with the right husband at the right time. And hers was no passing faith. She continued gleaning and trusting "until the end of barley harvest and of wheat harvest" (Ruth 2:23), a period of six to eight weeks. It was this exceptional virtue—placing duty before heart's desire—that deeply impressed Boaz and made Ruth all the more attractive a candidate for marriage. He told her, "Blessed be thou of the Lord...inasmuch as thou followedst not young men, whether poor or rich...for all the city of my people doth know that thou art a virtuous woman" (3:10–11). And soon the two were married in the will of God (4:13).

Ruth's marriage illustrates the principle of Matthew 6:32–33. Ruth herself had pressing human needs: "...ye have need of all these things..." Yet she continued to seek her kingdom duty first, before her needs: "But seek ye *first* the kingdom of God, and his righteousness..." (emphasis added). And because she did so, God added all the things she needed—and desired—in a single, sudden reward: "...and all these things shall be *added* unto you" (emphasis added). In Boaz, God gave Ruth love, security, companionship, children, abundant provisions, and honor. And it was duty that led her to Boaz. Clearly, then, duty guided Ruth to her heart's desires.

Paul

As an extraordinary apostle subjected to extraordinary persecution Paul needed extraordinary help. During his second apostolic mission, Paul drew near to the city of Lystra. Reason would have advised Paul to turn away, had it been permitted to speak, for Lystra only meant trouble for him. His enemies had brutally stoned him there during an earlier visit. (See Acts 14:19–20.) What might they do this time?

Whether Reason thus challenged Paul is not stated, though other references reveal that thoughts of impending persecution sometimes harassed the apostle. (See Acts 18:9–10.) But if Reason spoke, Paul cast down its arguments. A man given to duty, he knew well his ministerial obligations in Lystra. The fledgling Christians there needed many things—instruction, guidance, exhortation and fellowship—if they were to be permanently established in the faith. These vital tasks were the very reasons God sent Paul on this follow-up mission (Acts 15:36) and the cause of Paul's trust that God would shield him from his enemies. So, putting his duty before his safety, he ventured into the spiritual war zone of Lystra: "Then came he [Paul] to…Lystra;…" (Acts 16:1). To Paul, who faced danger often, the day he entered Lystra probably seemed like any other—just another unexciting day of duty.

But it wasn't. That day was different, wonderfully different. That day Paul became personally acquainted with Timothy: "And, behold, a certain disciple was there, named Timothy, the son of a certain woman, who was a Jewess, and believed…" (Acts 16:1). Saved under Paul's ministry during his previous visit to Lystra, Timothy was a jewel of a Christian, a rare find, an extraordinary disciple who soon became Paul's closest friend, brightest understudy and most trusted ministerial associate. (See Philippians 2:19–22.) In the years to follow he ministered large doses of assistance, consolation and encouragement to the oft-troubled apostle.

Note the role of duty in this key union. Paul returned to Lystra, not seeking helpers for his ministry but determined to fulfill his apostolic duties, and there he found his greatest helper. Had he opted to neglect his duties for fear of mistreatment, his and Timothy's paths may have never again crossed, and Paul would have been minus one extraordinary helper. Thus, duty led Paul to the help he needed.

DUTY'S HOST OF HINDERERS

If we are to please the Lord, we must do our duty: "It is required in stewards that a man be found faithful [dutiful]" (1 Cor. 4:2). And to do that we must overcome duty's host of hinderers—the army of spiritual obstructions that infiltrate our circumstances to prevent us from doing our duty. While their full number is potentially infinite, here are a few hinderers that all Christians face:

Unbelief

Unbelief is duty's greatest foe. Doubting that the Lord is

130

a rewarder of them that diligently seek Him results in immediate slackness and eventual abandonment of our duties. We must believe the prophecy of Azariah—"Your work shall be rewarded" (2 Chron. 15:7)—and keep our hands to the plow.

Persecution

Satan stirs his servants to accuse, plot and work against dutiful Christians for one purpose: to weaken their hands and stop their works. Therefore, amid their onslaughts we must pray with Nehemiah, "Now therefore, O God, strengthen my hands" (Neh. 6:9), and continue doing our duty.

Injustice

Injustice is a hard pill to swallow, but swallow it we must. Jesus promised us occasional collisions with unfairness. When compelled to go a second, third or fourth mile without cause, we sometimes rebel and cast off our duty to protest the injustice. But instead of "I quit," we must declare, "Not my will, but Thine be done," remembering injustice is no excuse for unfaithfulness.

Weariness

Physical weariness may hinder duty. We must maintain our spiritual attitude even when exhausted. When fatigued by righteous labors, we may begin resenting the sheer strenuousness of our duty. Then lying thoughts seep in: "I just can't do this any more; it's more than I can bear; no one can be expected to keep this up." When weary in well doing, we should simply rest to recover our strength rather than despise and forsake our duties.

Selfishness

Sometimes faithfulness to duty requires that we deny ourselves needs, wants or pleasures. In such seasons, the tempter may try to woo us from our duty by offering us our hearts' desires on his, not God's, terms. When selfishness shouts "Yes!" we must respond "No!"

Leisure

An occasional rest is necessary—or what's a Sabbath for? But work should always take priority over play. Vacations must not be taken at the expense of duty. If so, we may bring temptation or trouble upon ourselves. If David had been doing his duty (leading Israel's armies in battle; see 2 Samuel 11:1), he probably would never have laid eyes upon Bathsheba and brought upon himself all the woe that followed.

Undutiful people

We alone fully understand the duties with which God has charged us. And we alone are responsible to discharge them. Other people—including Christians—who do not understand our duties, or perhaps do not have a strong sense of duty themselves, occasionally ask us to do things that would require us to neglect our work. Understanding their misunderstanding of our duties, we must graciously decline their offers and continue pursuing our Father's business.

How easy it would have been for Joseph, Ruth and Paul to *not* do their duties due to pressures such as these. But they overcame their host of hinderers. Joseph accepted cruel treatment, denied the voice of self-pity, and went on in duty. Ruth accepted hard labor, denied her natural desires and went on in duty. And Paul submitted to thorny persecutions, refused to be intimidated, and went on in duty. As these committed ones proved, Christians who discern and circumvent their host of hinderers become faithful and wise servants whom their Lord, when He comes, will find "so doing" their duties. (See Matthew 24:44–51.) And in His millennial kingdom, truly, He will make them "rulers over many things."

CHRISTIAN, DO YOUR DUTY!

If Nelson and England expected that every man would do his duty, how much more does Jesus? Will you, then, do *your* duty? Will you do it today? Remember and believe the promise, "No good thing will he withhold from them that walk uprightly" (Ps. 84:11). Then follow your duty—quietly, patiently, passionately—till it leads you to the doorstep of your blessings.

To walk steadily in the way of duty, and not faint, you must build and maintain trust in God. For that, consider now the way of faith.

Chapter Thirteen

The Way of
Faith

"But without faith it is impossible to please him
[God]..."

—Hebrews 11:6

Faith is confidence in the unfailing character and words of
God. It is a gift from God by which we are saved. Faith is
given us when we first hear the gospel; it grows as we continue hearing God's Word; and it is developed and perfected by
trials of faith and patience. Without this confidence we cannot please God or fully do His will; hence, without faith we
cannot glorify God.

Accordingly, Jesus praised people with great faith, reproved
those of little faith, and upbraided those with no faith. He
cited faith as one of three "weightier matters" of Bible doctrine and rebuked the Pharisees for not emphasizing it in
their teaching. Why? Because after we are saved by faith the
God of faith wants us to live by faith: "The just shall live by
his faith" (Hab. 2:4).

*To help us do so let us consider the ups and
downs of growing faith...*

THE UPS AND DOWNS
OF GROWING FAITH

"Thou shalt hear what they say; and afterward shall thine hands be strengthened..."

—JUDGES 7:11

Thou shalt save Israel from the hand of the Midianites" (Judges 6:14)—from the moment Gideon heard this startling promise until the day God performed it, his faith was sorely tried. In Gideon's experiences we see the ups and downs of growing faith.

When he enters the biblical story, Gideon is a deeply discouraged soul (Judges 6:1–10). Seven years of cruel Midianite oppression have taken their toll. Gideon's words make it evident that he is highly offended with God. When the angel of the Lord speaks, he responds bitterly and openly doubts God's promises: "If the Lord be with us, why then is all this befallen us? And where are all his miracles which our fathers told us of, saying, Did not the Lord bring us up from Egypt?" (6:13). To Gideon, it seemed that the God of Israel, the miracle-working God of the Exodus, was nowhere to be found.

To drive away this doubt and establish a firm foundation for faith, the angel of the Lord gave Gideon some unmistakably clear promises:

The Lord is with thee, thou mighty man of valor.

—JUDGES 6:12

Go…and thou shalt save Israel from the hand of the Midianites.

—JUDGES 6:14

Surely I will be with thee, and thou shalt smite the Midianites as one man.

—JUDGES 6:16

These three inspired utterances contained four vital revelations to Gideon. They were:

- God was about to deliver Israel from the Midianites (Judges 6:14).

- This deliverance would come through Gideon (Judges 6:14, 16).

- God was with Gideon in an unusual way and would therefore, stand by him throughout the deliverance (Judges 6:12, 16).

- Gideon would become a courageous leader (Judges 6:12).

So overwhelming was this divine news flash that Gideon asked the Lord for a confirmation: "If now I have found grace in thy sight, then show me a sign that thou talkest with me" (Judges 6:17). God then permitted the angel of the Lord to demonstrate his supernatural powers (6:17–24). When fire came forth from his rod and consumed the sacrifice Gideon had prepared, Gideon knew he had indeed heard from God. "Alas, O Lord God! For I have seen an angel of the Lord face to face" (6:22). Inspired by the wonder, his faith was at an all-time personal high.

But immediately, "the same night" (6:25), a test came. Before Gideon would do battle with the children of sin, he must contend with the sin of the children of God (6:25–32). And God ordered him to begin in his own family: "Throw down the altar of Baal that thy father hath, and cut down the |images| that are by it; and build an altar unto the Lord thy God…" (6:25–26).

As Gideon considered the consequences of obedience—the probable reaction of his father, Joash, and the men of the city—thoughts troubled his heart and his faith plummeted. He knew well that the hometown folks would not take kindly to someone destroying their idol. Baal was a very popular deity, and to dismantle his altar was to invite disaster. Also, to destroy his father's most treasured possession—his shrine to Baal—would make Gideon appear to be a disrespectful son; many Israelites would condemn him as a violator of Jehovah's commandment to honor one's parents. But despite these fears, Gideon obeyed: "Then Gideon...did as the Lord had said unto him..." (6:27). His obedience, like his faith, was hesitant, not bold: "And so it was, because he feared his father's household, and the men of the city, that he could not do it by day, that he did it by night" (6:27). But the mustard seed moved the mountain. Despite the smallness of Gideon's faith, the Lord gave him victory.

By night Gideon successfully destroyed Joash's altar to Baal and built an altar to God in its stead. And to his astonishment, instead of his actions enraging his father, they converted him. Joash saw for himself just how unreal and impotent Baal was. And when the men of the city rose up to kill Gideon, Joash defended him and delivered him from their hands, declaring Baal, not Gideon, worthy of judgment: "If he [Baal] be a god, let him plead for himself, because one hath cast down his altar" (Judges 6:31). This turn of events was exceedingly abundantly above anything Gideon had asked or imagined. Once more, his faith was stimulated and his spiritual confidence high. And this time, at least temporarily, Gideon held fast his confidence.

When the Midianites and their allies established their war camp in the valley of Jezreel (Judges 6:33), Gideon did not waver. He quickly took the initiative, calling Israel to arms: "The Spirit of the Lord came upon Gideon, and he blew a trumpet..." (6:34). He had seen one deliverance and was confident he would now see another. Immediately, the people responded to their leader's faith: "...and Abiezer was gathered after him" (6:34). Then something happened.

As Israel prepared to make camp, Gideon apparently began considering the harsh realities of war. It's one thing to be willing to go to war; it's another thing to go. Battlefields inspire fears that melt the impulsive bravado of eager volunteers.

Whatever his thoughts, clearly fear began working on Gideon's mind. His doubts are betrayed by his utterances. First, he reverted to using the "if" word: *"If* thou wilt save Israel by mine hand, as thou hast said..."* (Judges 6:36, emphasis added). Second, he requested two additional signs. The first night he asked, "Behold, I will put a fleece of wool in the floor; and if the dew be on the fleece only..." (6:37). And the next day he asked just the opposite, "Let it now be dry only upon the fleece, and upon all the ground let there be dew" (6:39). Again God responded graciously, twice causing the dew to fall exactly as Gideon requested (6:36–40). His quivering faith stayed by these signs, Gideon bravely took the next step toward the conflict by establishing Israel's war camp: "Then Jerubbaal, who is Gideon, and all the people who were with him, rose up early, and |encamped| ...so that the host of the Midianites were on the north side of them..." (7:1). Finally, Israel's soldiers—and Gideon's faith—seemed ready for battle. Then the Lord placed another hurdle before his son of faith.

On the eve of battle, God unexpectedly reduced Gideon's army from thirty-two thousand men to three hundred. (See Judges 7:2–8.) Suddenly, the entire picture changed. With thousands of Israelites behind him, Gideon had been confident Israel would prevail. But with only *three hundred* now he could see no way through to victory. Despite frantic searchings, Reason found no way of escape and reported to Gideon's heart that defeat and disaster were imminent. Only a great miracle, a powerful divine intervention, could save the Israelites. The new odds shook Gideon badly. God's message to him at this point reveals Gideon's terror. After ordering him to begin the attack (7:9), God adds, "But if thou fear to go down, go thou with Purah, thy servant, down to the host. And thou shalt hear what they say; and afterward shall thine hands be strengthened to go down unto the host" (7:10–11). The words "if thou fear" and "afterward shall thine hands be strengthened" betray two facts; first, Gideon was fearful; second, his hands were weak with anxiety. Gideon confirmed his fearfulness by promptly visiting the Midianites' camp: "Then went he down with Purah, his servant, unto the |outermost part| of the armed men who were in the host" (7:11). But what happened there quickly raised his spirits.

Upon entering the enemy's camp, Gideon overheard one of the Midianites interpreting a dream to his fellow soldier: "...into his [Gideon's] hand hath God delivered Midian, and all the host" (Judges 7:14). Stunned, Gideon realized that it was the same report God had told him earlier (6:14, 16)! With that, Gideon's weary faith revived—this time permanently. He refused to tolerate doubt any longer. It was embarrassing for Israel's leader to have less faith than the heathen. If even his enemies, the Midianites, believed God's report, so must he! Immediately, he returned to the camp, ordered the attack, and, with God's help, prevailed (7:15–25). So his turbulent trial, with its peaks of faith and valleys of fear, ended.

And that end proved everything God said from the beginning. It was a perfect example of Isaiah's later prophecy: "I am God, and there is none like me, declaring the end from the beginning..." (Isa. 46:9–10). Specifically, the Lord fulfilled the four promises He gave at the outset of Gideon's trial. They were:

- God delivered Israel from the Midianites.

- The deliverance came through Gideon.

- Throughout the crisis God was very close to Gideon. He stood by giving him timely encouragements and specific instructions.

- At last Gideon became a courageous leader, truly a "mighty man of valor."

SUMMING UP GIDEON'S FAITH

Though by trial's end Gideon walked by faith, during the trial he was a man of faith living by sight. *It is noteworthy that every change in his faith, downward in discouragement or upward in renewed confidence, was caused by the "things seen" and not by a word from God.* God never changed His plainly stated will during the test, but because Gideon occasionally lost sight of God, his faith went up and down like a jack-in-the-box. Something encouraging happened—a victory in a smaller trial, a supernatural sign or a report of his enemies conceding defeat—and he became inspired and confident. Then something discouraging occurred—he was given an unpopular task, faced with a dangerous conflict or struck by a sudden reduction of resources—and he became discouraged again. Because he failed to continue meditating on the faithfulness of God and the comforting promises God gave him, Gideon was repeatedly taken captive by fearful imaginations and tormented in Reason's dungeon. Yet through it all God stood by him.

Every time Gideon sank, the Author and Finisher of faith intervened and lifted him up. God persisted with his weak-minded, vacillating son of destiny. He simply refused to give him over to unbelief. Finally, the divine effort paid off. Out of weakness Gideon was made strong; he grew valiant while fighting; then he routed the armies of his enemies. Afterward Gideon, and all Israel, rested in their newfound confidence in God for an entire generation. "And the country was in quietness forty years in the days of Gideon" (Judges 8:28). There are clear parallels between Gideon and the apostle Peter.

Peter's Faith

Peter is the Gideon of the New Testament era. Like Gideon's faith, Peter's confidence in God wavered for a season. And, like Gideon, Peter gradually grew more confident of God. Ultimately, Peter became an outstanding leader of his brethren, just as Gideon. As Gideon had shown valor on the field of battle, so Peter manifested remarkable courage in preaching the gospel: "Now when they saw the boldness of Peter and John...they marveled..." (Acts 4:13). Through Peter's ministry, multitudes of Jews entered the rest of faith in Christ, just as their forebears had received rest from oppression through Gideon's leadership. Let's consider Peter's faith in its season of wavering.

One of Peter's most well-known trials of faith occurred when, authorized by a word from Christ, he left the safety of his boat and walked briefly on the stormy waters of Galilee. (See Matthew 14:22–33.) Of this episode Mrs. C. Nuzum, a seasoned missionary to Mexico and woman of exemplary faith, writes:

> God warns us, in the case of Peter, to never look at our circumstances and feelings. The waves were just as high

when Peter walked perfectly on the water as when he sank. While he did not look at them, they could not hinder him; but the minute he looked at them, he doubted and went down. The wind also was just as great when Peter walked perfectly, as when he sank. When he did not pay any attention to it, it could not hinder him. God here teaches us that if we are occupied with looking and feeling, instead of with Him and His Word, we will lose all He offers us. On the other hand, by steadfastly refusing to see anything but God and what He says, we shall have and keep everything that He says He has given us.

Satan is busy trying to take from us what we take from God, and so God bids us "Hold fast that thou hast" (Revelation 3:11). Jesus gave Peter power to walk on the water, but the devil took it from him by getting him to fix his attention on the wind (representing things we feel), and on the waves (representing things we see). Peter had the power, and used it; but lost it by doubting.*

This faith of which Mrs. Nuzum writes, though still forming in Peter on this occasion, is seen in its fully developed state in the centurion.

The Centurion's Faith

Christ commended only two people publicly for having "great" faith—the Syrophenician woman and the centurion. What was special about the centurion's faith?

Obviously, the centurion believed that Jesus was a healer, a doer of the impossible, for when his servant was stricken by palsy he called on Christ for healing. (See Matthew 8:5–13.) He was humble, because he felt unworthy even for Christ to enter his home (8:8). He believed that prayer was not limited by distance, because he did not ask Jesus to come touch his servant but rather to pray for him where he was (8:8). He believed that faith was chiefly an exercise of authority. A man of authority himself, he recognized Christ as the ultimate authority, the very Creator, who spoke this world into existence with His word and whose word still ruled both

---

*From *Christ the Healer* by F.F. Bosworth, p. 119; copyright © 1973 R.V. Bosworth, published by Fleming H. Revel Company, Old Tappan, New Jersey.

its spiritual and material realms. He was convinced that if *Jesus* commanded or promised something, it would have to follow: "Speak the word only, and my servant shall be healed" (8:8). After Christ proclaimed healing for the servant, there is no mention of the centurion having any doubt. Thus he was steadfast, holding firm his faith until his servant's healing manifested. And as he believed, so it was done unto him: "...his servant was healed..." (8:13). Of the centurion's faith this much we know, for these truths are stated.

And though unstated, other aspects of the centurion's faith are evident. That he held fast his confidence until his messengers confirmed his servant's healing (see Luke 7:10) implies that his heart was perfectly focused. If contradictions had arisen, he would not have sunk into unbelief; rather, he would have kept his thoughts fixed on Jesus' proven character as a compassionate healer, and on Jesus' authoritative words—"As thou hast believed, so be it done unto thee" (Matt. 8:13)—knowing that they had to come to pass. Thus doubts would have found no place in him. Jesus' description of the centurion's faith as "great" (Matt. 8:10) confirms this; if the centurion had been a doubter, such a description would have been incorrect. He would have had "little faith" (Matt. 14:31), not great faith. We know this was not the case, for Jesus never errs in His judgments.

FINDINGS OF FAITH

The experiences of Gideon, Peter, the centurion and other children of faith reveal the following about the way of faith.

In its essence, faith is trust in God's faithfulness. It is confidence in His character that He is utterly trustworthy and always reliable. Because God's character and His words are inseparable, to trust His character is to believe His words. And, conversely, to doubt His words is to question His character. Faith means I believe in God, that He is utterly faithful, and I believe His statements, that they are infallibly true, irrespective of the contradictions that arise from adverse occurrences or shifting appearances. When God seems indifferent and His promises untrue, I stay myself (lean, rest) upon the character of God. I say with confidence, "I don't understand what my heavenly Father is doing now, but I know *Him*. He has shown me

His goodness and the veracity of His Word many times before, and I choose to trust Him again. He will yet make a way of escape for me and one day explain everything that presently baffles me. Though He seems strangely slow in rendering aid, yet will I trust Him. Though injustice, affliction, even death is my portion, yet will I trust Him." Every Christian who persists in this faith, focusing and refocusing on it, invariably receives whatever God has promised in His time. These are the biblical findings of faith.

~

Friend, in you and in me, and in every other Christian, there are two different believers. There is a Gideon—a willing-but-weak believer destined for God's work but presently lacking the assurance to do it. There is also a centurion—a soul utterly confident of God and His every promise. In Gideon's trial, we see what we are; in the centurion's, we see what we may become. In the way of faith, God works to shift the balance between these two mind-sets, to decrease Gideon and increase the centurion.

He does so by sending encouraging words and signs and reports when faith is low, just as He did with Gideon—all meant to remind us of His unchanging character and promises, so we will be not faithless but believing. The quicker we identify Gideon's doubt in our hearts and eliminate it, the less we will experience his ups and downs. And the more we practice the single-minded trust of the centurion, the stronger and more stable our faith will grow. Then one day, as at the end of Gideon's trial, our faith will remain "up," permanently established in confidence in God: "But the God of all grace …make you perfect, |establish|, strengthen, settle you" (1 Pet. 5:10).

And only God knows what deliverances, blessings and joys faith will bring us and countless others—and what hope it will give to many who are oppressed. For wherever there is faith, there is hope.

Chapter Fourteen

The Way of
Hope

"It is good that a man should both hope and quietly wait for the salvation of the Lord."

—LAMENTATIONS 3:26

Against hope Abraham continued to believe in hope—and became the father of many nations. When the apostle Paul lost all hope that his ship would be saved, he kept hope alive—and escaped a watery grave. Later, under direct inspiration, Paul concluded that hope was one of the three most fundamental Christian attitudes: "And now abideth faith, hope, love, these three..." (1 Cor. 13:13). But what exactly is Christian hope? And why is it so important?

We find these answers, and more, as we explore
the necessity of hope...

THE NECESSITY OF HOPE

"Hope thou in God..."

—PSALM 42:11

Hope is the one thing a suffering Christian must have. With it he can bear the unbearable. Without it he sinks into a horrible pit of despair, and life itself becomes intolerable, a kind of walking death. What is hope, then, to the Christian?

Much more than wishful thinking, Christian hope is a very sure thing. It is a conviction, a strong belief in a better tomorrow based upon an infallible revelation from God today. Vague, vain or impulsive aspirations disappear as quickly as they appear, leaving the tribulated soul sinking in misery, but divinely inspired hope lifts us from that deadly quicksand and plants our feet firmly on the eternal Rock. David wrote, "He brought me up also out of an horrible pit, out of the miry clay, and set my feet upon a rock..." (Ps. 40:2). Truly, ours is no ordinary hope. It is unshakable. Though torrents of malicious waters beat against our weary souls, we can stand fast in the faith we hold dear. What is the source of this undefeatable hope?

While bursts of inspiration may come from many sources, the Bible remains the Christian's chief source of hope. Nothing in this fallen world—the most profound philosophies, the most

145

beautiful poetry, the most positive thinking, the most militant determination, the strongest grit—will impart the mysterious soul energy that stirs the exhausted believer to refuse to quit. Such hope is born of faith: "Now faith is the substance of things hoped for..." (Heb. 11:1). And faith is born of God's Word: "So, then, faith cometh by hearing, and hearing by the word of God" (Rom. 10:17). Christian hope, therefore, is really a type of faith in the Promiser and in His Word.

In what way does it differ from faith? Faith typically applies to things we believe we have already received, things that exist now though we cannot see them now: "Now faith is...the evidence of things not seen" (Heb. 11:1). Hope is a different application of the same faith. It is confidence concerning things we expect God to do for us in the future. Why is this so important? Because hope is the power source of tried souls.

David, whose faith and patience were often tried, testified that hope saved him from dying in many a pit of unbelief. When his strength failed, seeing good things didn't revive it, for such things were not there to see; believing to see good things re-energized him: "I had fainted, unless I had *believed to see* the goodness of the Lord in the land of the living" (Ps. 27:13, emphasis added). Truly, amazing energy is generated by hope. We can wade through rivers of fiery torments if we are convinced a foretaste of paradise awaits us on the other side. With hope we can face any enemy, fight any battle and overcome any wound. Satan's darts may pierce us, but the anticipation of approaching blessings, like a miraculous balm, will soothe and heal us. Somehow the prospect of a better tomorrow takes the sting out of a bitter today.

For this reason the Lord always grants us a word of promise or an encouraging inner vision at the onset of every new trial. To inspire hope, the lifter of our heads reveals the end of our test from its beginning. (See Isaiah 46:9–10.) Knowing that end keeps our faith from being slain by the contradictions that attack us in the interim. Though we suffer delays, spiritual wounds and death-blows, we hold fast our hope of what God will yet do for us and for others in the land of the living. This is the way God sustained Joseph.

When Joseph was seventeen years of age, God gave him

two dreams that revealed his destiny: He would one day rise to a position of great authority. (See Genesis 37:5–11.) Convinced of the heavenly vision, Joseph believed he would help many people in the day of its fulfillment, even his own family. It was this vision, given shortly before his brothers betrayed him, that gave him hope; and it was hope that gave him the inner strength to endure the cruel mistreatment he received in the ensuing years of trial.

Similarly, God gave Saul of Tarsus a sure hope at the beginning of his Christian experience. On the Damascus road the Lord showed Saul he would one day become His special messenger to the Gentiles (Acts 26:16–18), and that as Paul the apostle he would preach the gospel before kings and turn many people from darkness to light. It was this vision of future usefulness that kept Paul's hope alive during the surprisingly long period of church rejection, hidden preparation and testing that followed. And Paul was not the last of the children of hope.

Today the Lord still gives sustaining hope to tried Christians. Before our unpleasant experiences begin, He reveals their pleasant outcome: "I will visit you, and perform my good word toward you...for I know the thoughts that I think toward you, saith the Lord, thoughts of peace, and not of evil, to give you an expected end" (Jer. 29:10–11). It is this revelation of our "expected end" that saves us from the death of despair, for expectation strengthens not only our souls but also our bodies.

Jacob illustrates the physical power of hope. For twenty-two years after Joseph's supposed death, Jacob lived without hope. Bereft of Rachel and disappointed with his older sons, Jacob was convinced he would never again see his beloved and most promising son, Joseph, in this world. Though not directly stated, it is implied that his health declined during these dark years of hopelessness. Old and aging fast, Jacob's remarks reveal he was a soul preparing for death, psychologically and physically. (See Genesis 42:38; 45:28.) Then a remarkable change occurred—Joseph was reunited with his brothers in Egypt! When Jacob heard his sons' report, "Joseph is yet alive, and he is governor over all the land" (45:26), and Joseph's personal message (45:27), and beheld the caravan of unmistakably Egyptian wagons and gifts sent by Joseph, "the spirit of Jacob...revived" (45:27); and with it, his health. That Jacob regained full physical strength is implied by the fact that he lived seventeen more years in Egypt with Joseph (47:28). The reason for Jacob's miraculous reversal of health? Hope. Just the thought of seeing Joseph, not the blessed spectacle itself, brought revival.

In his fascinating and informative book *None of These Diseases*, Dr. S. I. McMillen discusses the differing effects of despair and hope on the physical health of persons in very stressful circumstances. He cites Dr. Harold Wolff's belief that a sense of despair led to the death of eight thousand Allied servicemen interned in Japanese prison camps during World War II. These discouraged prisoners simply gave up hope that they would ever be released. With hope gone, writes Dr. Wolff, even though enough food for survival was offered him, "the prisoner became apathetic, listless, neither ate nor drank, helped himself in no way, stared into space and finally died." Dr. Wolff then observes, "Hope, like faith and a purpose in life, is medicinal."

In support of Dr. Wolff's finding, Dr. McMillen describes how hope made the difference between life and death for his Japanese Christian friend, Dr. David Tsutada, who was also imprisoned by the Japanese government and subjected to even more horrible treatment than that received by the Allied prisoners of war mentioned above. He writes:

> When Japan entered World War II, the Japanese government put him [Tsutada] in prison because of his belief in the return of the Lord to reign on this earth. The government tried to starve him to death and his weight dropped to seventy pounds. He was even confined in a cold, damp hole in a prison that was utterly filthy. As he sat on the floor, he wondered if this was the way the Lord was going to take him home to heaven. If it was, he was perfectly resigned to it. He wasn't frustrated by the bars or the mud or the Lord's apparent lack of care for him. If Dr. Tsutada had not adapted himself and resigned himself, I am convinced that the stress of self-pity, added to the severe stress of starvation, would have killed him.

After Tsutada accepted his adversity, terrible though it

148

was, God gave him the hope that enabled him to endure his otherwise unendurable plight. Dr. McMillen continues:

> While he was in prison, the Lord began to reveal to him plans for a Bible school. Dr. Tsutada worked out many details for the school while he sat in the darkness and stench of the death cell. When the war was over, he was released and immediately he put his plans into operation. Today this man has one of the finest Bible training schools in Japan. All of this transpired because he didn't fret about evildoers (Psalm 37) but trusted, committed himself to, and delighted in God's Word. Dr. Tsutada created his own environment.

As Dr. McMillen concludes, it is obvious that without the hope of the Bible school Tsutada would have been overwhelmed by the combined physical and emotional stresses to which he was subjected. With hope he endured, won deliverance, and afterward brought forth much fruit unto God. As Dr. Wolff stated, hope proved a remarkable medicine indeed—a miracle drug—for this bitterly mistreated Christian.

~

The Bible itself attests to the necessity of hope. The central purpose of apocalyptic writing is to create hope—uncrushable optimism amid crushingly pessimistic times. The Book of Revelation, the most extensive end-time vision and the culmination of all the prophetic writings, exists to uphold the church with the hope of a sure end during these extremely unsure last days before the Rapture of the church. John's vision will also sustain hope in the Jewish and Gentile converts of the Tribulation period as they await their mid-Tribulation translation. And it will inspire expectation in the hidden remnant of Jewish Christians during the Great Tribulation as they await Jesus' return to earth at Armageddon to liberate them and other survivors from the Antichrist's tyranny. Now consider this: If in planning the grand finale of world history God devoted an entire book of the Bible to prophecies that assure us the chaos of the Tribulation will end in the utopia of the Millennium, to Him the creation of hope in our minds is no mere trifle. Obviously, He considers it a great necessity.

It is the same for you in this hour. In your present trials of faith, hope is not optional: it is imperative. When the clouds of gloom gather over you and threaten to seal out your last glimmer of hope, recognize the evil one's strategy and refuse to succumb to it. Before unbelief fills your soul with darkness, turn to the fountain of hope—the Bible—and by meditative reading and prayer drink deeply from the promises of its Author. And drink again. And again. And again... until the vision God has given you reappears before the eyes of your understanding. Once you recover the vision, hold it fast until all your future hopes end in joyous fulfillments.

Truly, "Where there is no vision, the people perish" (Prov. 29:18). But where hope is kept alive, we endure and live to see another day—and to walk in the way of love.

Chapter Fifteen

The Way of
Love

"A new commandment I give unto you, that ye love one another; as I have loved you, that ye also love one another. By this shall all men know that ye are my disciples, if ye have love one to another."

—JOHN 13:34–35

As stated previously, the three most fundamental Christian attitudes are faith, hope and love. "But," the inspired apostle concludes, "the greatest of these is |love|" (1 Cor. 13:13). Accordingly, Jesus' greatest commandment is that we love one another as He has loved us. One of the most practical ways we love one another is by forgiving one another. In a world—and a church—filled with people inclined to offend, Jesus would have us inclined to forgive. By practicing forgiveness we walk in the way of love.

Walking in love consistently is arguably the hardest grace to master. To forgive bitter enemies, we need divine inspiration.

We will find this as we meditate on good reasons to forgive . .

GOOD REASONS TO FORGIVE

"And when ye stand praying, forgive, if ye have |anything| against any[one] ..."

—MARK 11:25

Repeatedly the Bible teaches Christians to forgive: "And when ye stand praying, *forgive*..." (Mark 11:25–26, emphasis added). But exactly what does its Author mean by "forgive"?

Forgiveness implies a previous offense—someone has treated you unfairly or unkindly. If you have not been insulted, cheated or injured, you have no opportunity to forgive. When offenses come, anger inevitably arises within our hearts. Whether we show it or not, we are immediately indignant at our mistreatment. Forgiveness deals with this turbulent internal reaction. It is a determination not to harbor a spirit of anger. It is a firm decision to let it go, let it drop, and give it up. Whatever the provocation, even when we have every right to be angry from a human perspective, we choose to obey God's Word and "fret not thyself because of evildoers...cease from anger...forsake wrath..." (Ps. 37:1, 8). This is the essence of forgiveness.

Forgiveness benefits us immediately in several ways. It prevents the bitter seeds of resentment, hatred and vengeance from taking root in our hearts. This, in turn, prevents many foolish acts of retaliation from springing up to trouble our lives and others'. Forgiveness also leaves us free to seek God and pursue our duties without distraction. Saved from the paralyzing venom of hatred we rest and grow and prosper, even while our offenders show no remorse. And finally, forgiveness prepares us for reconciliation with our offenders.

While forgiveness sometimes leads quickly to reconciliation, at other times it does not. Why? Because for some reason reconciliation is not possible at present. Our offenders may be arrogant and scorn the thought of reconciliation. They may remain very hostile toward us and, thus, dangerous. They may be practicing sinners, and thus people whose company would corrupt us. (See 1 Corinthians 15:33.) Or they may be determined to prove their innocence—and our guilt!—and so argue constantly. In such cases normal friendship is impossible, for there is no basis of truth and mutual respect upon which to build. Yet even then we can forgive privately. This is what we are considering in this chapter. At its core, forgiveness is a decision we make before God, not a discussion we have with our offender. Joseph's life illustrates this.

When Joseph's brothers sold him into slavery, he quickly forgave them. Though the Bible does not state this, we know it because the fruits of spiritual liberty appeared in his life immediately after his betrayal. The Lord was "with Joseph" in Egypt (Gen. 39:2); He prospered all of Joseph's labors (39:2–3, 5); and He gave Joseph great favor with his master, Potiphar (39:3–4). God doesn't do such things for unforgiving souls! If Joseph had had a root of bitterness, such fruits could not have manifested. (Every tree, and its roots, are known by its fruits; see Matthew 7:18, 20.) Instead, God would have withdrawn His presence and withheld His blessing and favor. And rather than prosper in his extraordinary difficulties, Joseph would have become hard and cynical and a failure. The fact that he did not self-destruct proves he had forgiven his brothers. Now consider another key fact.

During these difficult yet fruitful years Joseph had no relationship with his wayward brethren. Not once did they seek, write or visit him. After Joseph became Egypt's ruler, they still had no relationship with him. They never thought to visit him and God never prompted him to visit them. Not until God's time—twenty-two years after their crime—did a reunion occur.

Then they willingly confessed their sins and received the brother they had rejected. Then their relationship to him was restored on a basis of truth and mutual respect. (See Genesis 42–45.) In this we see that forgiveness is not about attempting to restore relationships with unrepentant offenders; Joseph did not do this. Instead, it is primarily a matter of correcting our attitudes toward them while our relationships are still unrestored. And forgiveness isn't optional; Jesus commands it!

Now besides Jesus' command to forgive, the Bible reveals many good reasons why we should do so—reasons which we ignore at our peril and obey to our credit and blessing. Here are some of them.

That we may be forgiven

From a practical perspective, forgiveness is a matter of giving to get—we give up something to get something else we vitally need. Because we still possess an old nature we all occasionally fail, falling short of God's high standards in thought, word or deed: "For in many things we |all stumble|..." (James 3:2). Having sinned, we need to be cleansed and restored in our fellowship with our heavenly Father. (See 1 John 1:5–10.) In short, we need forgiveness.

If we want to receive forgiveness from God, we must give it to people. If we refuse to forgive our offenders, God refuses to forgive our offenses. Jesus declared this repeatedly: "But if ye do not forgive, neither will your Father, who is in heaven, forgive your trespasses" (Mark 11:26). "And forgive us...as we forgive [others]..." (Matt. 6:12). "Forgive [others], and ye shall be forgiven...For with the same measure that ye |measure| it shall be measured to you again" (Luke 6:37–38). Realizing that he must either forgive his offender or forfeit the fellowship of a holy, forgiving God, the wise believer decides to forgive.

That our prayers may be effective

In three New Testament passages, Jesus linked the topics of prayer and forgiveness. In Matthew 6:6–13, He prescribed how we should pray. Then in the next two verses He spoke of the importance of forgiveness (6:14–15). In Mark 11:22–24, He taught us the command of faith and the prayer of faith. Then in the next two verses He again spoke of forgiveness,

155

linking those comments with His previous statements on prayer with the introductory words, "And when ye stand praying, forgive..." (11:25–26). In Matthew 18:18–20, Jesus taught us the prayer-command of binding and loosing, and the prayer of agreement. Then in the following passage He taught both by precept and parable that we must forgive all offenders (Matt. 18:21–35). Again, His comments on forgiveness are linked to His previous teaching on prayer by the introductory words, *"Then came Peter* to him, and said..." (Matt. 18:21, emphasis added). Apparently, Peter asked Jesus about forgiveness just as He finished speaking on prayer.

None of these text linkups are accidental. They are divinely planned. Why? Because the subjects of prayer and forgiveness are inseparably connected. If we want our prayers answered, we must forgive. If we refuse to forgive, God refuses to answer our petitions. Even when our petitions are according to God's will and offered fervently with faith and thanksgiving, we will receive nothing if we harbor an unforgiving spirit toward any soul.

That we give no "advantage" to Satan

In 2 Corinthians 2:9–11, the apostle Paul warned the Corinthian Christians that if they refused to forgive someone, they would give Satan an "advantage" over them. That is, Satan would gain the upper hand in his ongoing spiritual battle against them. He would gain a *controlling position*—the ability to influence and, thus, manipulate them. Satan is a supernatural being. As long as we obey God, the blood of Jesus and the armor of God shield us from Satan's power, while the Word, the Spirit, prayer and our testimony provide us with spiritual power and spiritual weapons superior to those of our adversary. Thus, when he tries to deceive and mislead us, we can successfully discern and resist him and hold fast to the straight and narrow way. But if we refuse to obey God over any issue, including forgiveness, the balance of power shifts in Satan's favor. By rebelling we remove God's armor and expose our souls to Satan's arrows of deception. Thus he gains a spiritual advantage over us, afterwards influencing and manipulating us at will. (See 2 Timothy 2:26.)

In Romans 6:16, Paul sheds further light on this advantage:

"Know ye not that to whom ye yield yourselves servants to obey, *his servants ye are* whom ye obey, whether of sin unto death, or of obedience unto righteousness?" (emphasis added). When we yield to the spirit of disobedience, we give Satan, the arch disobeyer, the legal right to bind us as his slaves—and to continue holding us in spiritual captivity until we confess and forsake our disobedience. As long as we abide in this spiritual captivity, Satan has the advantage over us. In such times, he may inflict great damage on our souls and on others through us.

Having gained the advantage, our new spiritual master immediately makes the most of it. Using cords of fear, anger, pride, greed or lust, he moves us to speak and act in an un-Christlike manner. Witnessing this, family, friends and fellow Christians stumble—they become disillusioned with Christianity and disbelieve in the Son of God. If our rebellion and consequent service to Satan continue, our whole Christian witness is eventually inverted. Instead of being transformed into Christ's character-image, we are transmuted into Satan's. Instead of showing others the beauty of the Lord, we show them the ugliness of the devil. Instead of spreading light, we spread darkness. Instead of being a way of life and blessing to others, we are a way of death: "He who neglects or refuses reproof [not only himself] goes astray, but causes to err and is a path toward ruin for others" (Prov. 10:17, AMP). These are the terrible results of giving an advantage to our malicious supernatural enemy through unforgiveness. Clearly, it is an advantage none of us can afford to give.

To avoid God's wrath and preserve our health

Christ's parable of the unforgiving servant reveals that an unforgiving attitude angers God. (See Matthew 18:21–35.) In this lesson, Jesus describes a servant who received forgiveness from his lord, yet refused to forgive his fellow servant. This was both unfair and unkind. It is highly unjust for those who have received forgiveness to refuse to give it. And it's cruel to deny mercy to a broken, humble soul. As a result of this servant's unforgiveness, "his lord was |angry|" (18:34).

But the story didn't end with this comment. The lord's wrath brought swift and painful punishment. The unforgiving servant was "delivered...to the *tormentors*, till he should pay all that was due unto him" (Matthew 18:34, KJV, emphasis added). While some modern translations alter the word "tormentors" to "jailors" (NIV; PHILLIPS), others use such words as "torturers" (AMP, NAS) and "scourgers" (MODERN LANGUAGE BIBLE, BERKELEY VERSION). Because torment is clearly implied, I prefer the word used originally by the King James translators, "tormentors." The unforgiving servant was sent to a torture chamber where pain was deliberately inflicted on him to evoke a change of will. And this ministry of pain continued until his will *was* changed: " . . . till he should pay all that was due unto him" (18:34).

Surprisingly, Jesus says this is a perfect example of the treatment God gives unforgiving Christians. They, too, are placed in a spiritual torture chamber: "So likewise shall my heavenly Father do also unto you, if ye, from your hearts, forgive not every one his brother his trespasses" (Matt. 18:35). In their self-appointed dungeon of horrors, unforgiving Christians suffer much. Mentally, they are bound and beaten by recurring memories that produce fresh anger and pain every time they strike. Refusing to forgive, they find themselves unable to forget; we cannot escape from thoughts of those whom we hate. Emotionally, they use a vast amount of soul-energy harboring grudges and constantly plotting and talking against their offenders. Consequently, they live life half-alive. Never cheery, they are always dull and half-hearted. Physically, their bodies suffer psychologically induced aches, pains and illnesses, so they abide weak and unhealthy. Socially, they lose friends on every side. It's not fun keeping company with a bitter soul. So, abandoned, the bitter become even more bitter. All of these sufferings need not be. None would be theirs if they would just forgive.

The lesson here is simple: God, who is love, loves mercy and despises hardness of heart. When Love sees unforgiveness, His wrath is stirred. His chastening then swiftly and painfully visits. The cruel in spirit reap cruelty. Therefore, to preserve our own health and well-being—mentally, emotionally, physically, socially—we should always forgive our offenders. Why should we put ourselves in torture chambers?

Here is an interesting afterthought. When centenarians are asked to reveal the keys to a long and happy life, often they cite the importance of not holding grudges. Somewhere early on they chose not to torment themselves with unforgiveness and thus add to the stresses of life. It was a wise decision, and health, happiness, and long life were their rewards.

That others may be released

Jesus taught that our forgiveness releases our offenders: "Whosoever's sins ye remit, they are remitted unto them..." (John 20:23). And in the same breath He declared that our unforgiveness prevents them from receiving mercy: "...and whosoever's sins ye retain, they are retained." Thus He places both a great privilege and a great responsibility in our hands. By holding offenses, we become responsible for keeping our offenders from the Lord. By forgiving them, we exercise the privilege of releasing them to be drawn to Jesus and repentance by the Holy Spirit. Stephen's forgiveness of Saul of Tarsus illustrates this.

When Stephen was stoned, young Saul of Tarsus stood by supporting Stephen's executioners enthusiastically. (See Acts 22:20.) But just before he passed, Stephen did something very significant. He prayed for his enemies, forgiving both his murderers and their accomplices: "And he [Stephen] kneeled down, and cried with a loud voice, Lord, lay not this sin to their charge..." (Acts 7:60). For a long season it looked as if Stephen's prayer was unanswered, because Saul of Tarsus became the church's worst enemy, leading the growing anti-Christian movement in Jerusalem and imprisoning and executing Christians by the score (8:1–3). But one day the effectiveness of Stephen's petiton suddenly manifested. En route to Damascus, where he hoped to persecute still more Christians, Saul was abruptly halted and powerfully converted by a personal appearance of the risen Christ (9:1–9). Far from being an accident, this was a direct fulfillment of John 20:23. Saul was brought to repentance because Stephen's forgiveness had released him to be drawn to Christ and convicted by the Spirit. Had Stephen not forgiven his persecutors, the kingdom of God would have suffered an immeasurable loss. Saul, the frightful persecutor, would never have become Paul, the fruitful apostle. And Stephen would have been responsible!

This provokes a very motivating thought. It is a pure joy

to be used of God to help a soul find the Savior. But on the other hand, it would be an unbearable burden if at the last we discovered that our unforgiveness had kept someone—any-one—from entering the kingdom of God. There is only one way to be sure you will never bear that burden: Forgive every offender every offense every day.

Because God permits offenses for good purposes

The Book of Job reveals that God has placed a supernatural hedge around every righteous person, and nothing may pass that barrier and touch his or her life without God's personal permission (Job 1:10–12; 2:6). If He permits an offense, He has a good purpose for doing so, for He works "all things"—not some or most but *all*—together for the good of those who love Him. (See Romans 8:28.)

In the day of his offenses Joseph saw God. Looking beyond His callous brothers, Joseph soon detected the Lord's hand behind their cruel betrayal. Eventually he became convinced that God merely used their acts to facilitate His own, so much that he declared three times that God, not they, sent him to Egypt. (See Genesis 45:5, 7–8.) While Joseph was fully aware of his brothers' murderous intentions, he focused instead on God's larger purpose, concluding, "God meant it unto good" (50:20). It is a sterling example to follow. In the day of your offense, imitate Joseph. Look to God for a revelation of His purpose.

Is the situation that offends you the Lord's chastening? Is He allowing you to reap the same kind of offense you have often sown? Then thank Him, because you are learning to fear the Lord, to respect the fact that He keeps His Word to all. Even His children must reap His rod if they sow folly. Has your offense come to test you? The only way God can test your obedience regarding forgiveness is to send offenders and offenses your way. Then thank Him, for by obeying the word of forgiveness you will become "approved unto God" (2 Tim. 2:15) and "|fit| for the Master's use" (2:21). Is your offense a cross? Has it come not because of disobedience but because of obedience, because you *have* obeyed the Lord's Word in all the general areas of Christian living, including that of forgiveness? Then thank Him, because as you forgive additional

160

offenses, these additional blessings will be yours: God will further transform you into the character-image of the ultimate forgiver, Jesus. He will finish breaking your self-will that you may be more useful to Him in His work; and you will receive more rewards in this life and the next, for every cross borne willingly wins its bearer yet another crown.

Is your offense especially humiliating? Then bless the Lord, for He is preparing you for promotion. God sends indignities to condition us to bear honor humbly: "Before honor is humility" (Prov. 18:12). And if He plans to take us especially high, He ordains great humiliations that take us very, very low. If considered, these examples help us see God in all situations, even those most offensive.

And if we believe that God, not the devil, is the mastermind behind our offenses, we can easily forgive our offenders. They are but instruments in His hand. Then all our trials will end as Joseph's. The cruel harm our offenders hoped to inflict, "as for you, ye thought evil against me..." (Gen. 50:20), will be swallowed up by the larger, eternal good God has purposed for us, "...but God meant it unto good..."

That we may bear more fruit

In his ongoing effort to quench our fruitfulness in Christ, Satan employs many strategies. One of his more subtle ones is to move his servants to offend us, hoping thereby to provoke us through pride and stubbornness to harbor unforgiveness. (See 2 Corinthians 2:9–11.) Knowing well Jesus' Word, "Forgive, if ye have anything against any," he tempts us to disobey it, and thus defy our Lord. Then he has us right where he wants us—in rebellion to Christ and unfit for His use.

All too often this strategy succeeds because even when we are obedient in other areas of our Christian walk we may find ourselves inclined to not forgive, especially when the offense is very unjust, personal or cruel. If we refuse to forgive, Satan gains an "advantage" (2 Cor. 2:11) over us. There are many adverse consequences of this, but the greatest is that we lose our fellowship with Jesus. Then, with our connection to the Vine broken, our present fruitfulness quickly withers. Truly, offenses are Satan's shears with which he seeks to lop off every fruitful branch in the church and so end their fruitbearing. Surprisingly, he seems

161

quite willing to risk the alternative: If we overcome our offenses, just the opposite occurs—our fruitfulness increases dramatically. Jesus' teaching confirms this.

The Lord declared that the Father deliberately purges fruitful Christians that they may bear more fruit: "Every branch that beareth fruit, he purgeth it, *that it may bring forth more fruit*" (John 15:2, emphasis added). When we are offended—cheated, slandered, falsely accused, forsaken, betrayed, supplanted or rejected by men—our spiritual "branch" is cut back. That is, our spiritual life is wounded and our Christian service temporarily interrupted. But the moment we forgive our offenders, our wounds begin to heal. Soon we regain full spiritual strength, and, eventually, in the very areas in which we were cut back, new fruit appears. This new fruit is higher in quality and greater in quantity than that which we bore earlier. Our character is more refined and established. Educated, strengthened, and purged by our painful ordeal, we find ourselves free from many of the faults that previously hindered us. Thus, we emerge in every way more productive. The inward fruits of Christ's Spirit are more manifest, and our outward fruits, our deeds of Christian service, are more numerous. Ultimately, then, the heavenly husbandman uses the enemy's offenses as His own purgings. Satan's shears serve God's will. Instead of decreasing our fruitfulness, they increase it. The ministry of the apostle Paul bears this out.

Who suffered more wrongs, more ill treatment at the hands of enemies, than Paul? The numerous insults, injuries and injustices he catalogs in 2 Corinthians 11:23–33 would dismay and dizzy even the most stalwart Christian soldier. Yet not one of these offenses quenched Paul's fruitfulness: "But none of these things move me..." (Acts 20:24). If Paul had held unforgiveness at any point in his ministry, his extraordinary Christian fruitfulness would have ceased. The lush spiritual blessings that his life produced—conversions, deliverances, healings, revelations, epistles, exhortations, mercies, prophecies—would have withered away. But this never happened. Why? Because, wise to the enemy's devices, Paul forgave his offenders religiously: "I forgave it, for your sakes... lest Satan should get an advantage..." (2 Cor. 2:10). His fixed habit of forgiveness ensured that, despite many offenses, his spiritual branch would continue bearing ever more fruit for the nourishment of the saints.

Because no offense is unforgivable

Except for blasphemy of the Holy Spirit, God forgives all kinds of sins and sinners. Jesus said, "All manner of sin and blasphemy shall be forgiven men..." (Matt. 12:31). And like God, like people. If our heavenly Father forgives all kinds of sins and sinners, so must we. Accordingly, whenever Jesus taught on forgiveness He used the broadest possible terms, such as "anything" and "anyone." "Forgive, if ye have *anything* against *any[one]*..." (Mark 11:25, emphasis added). Thus He stresses that to us there are no unforgivable sins.

When we allow ourselves to consider any offense unforgivable, we deceive ourselves. We erect a wall of falsehood behind which we hide our hard hearts from the conviction of the Spirit. Offenses seem unforgivable usually because they are directed at us.

To me, the thing that hits me is far worse, far more grave and serious an injury than the injustice I see you suffer. Why? Because it has hit *me*! And you are likely to feel just the opposite—that the injury you have received is much worse than the one I have suffered. Why? Because of the selfishness and pride of our old natures. It is healthy for us to remember that the trials of life are common to us all. Whatever has hurt us has hurt thousands of other Christians also. (See 1 Corinthians 10:13a.) If we are wise, we will remember this and not overly inflate the seriousness of the sins committed against us. This will help us keep things in right perspective and save us from the snare of self-deception. No longer will we use the lie, "It's unforgivable," as an excuse for an unforgiving spirit. And we will more readily forgive all our offenders.

～

Along with the foregoing reasons to forgive, consider these additional facts on forgiveness. They, too, help us leap over mountainous offenses.

Deeper than emotion

Forgiveness runs deeper than emotion. It is a matter of will, not of feeling. For this reason, we forgive by a choice of will, not

163

a surge of emotion. Regardless of how we feel toward our offenders, we *choose* to forgive them. It is a matter of law, not emotion.

In the court of the soul, the mind informs the will that Christ's Word is heaven's law. And in the matter before us, the mind argues, His Word is, "Forgive, if ye have |anything| against any..." (Mark 11:25). Furthermore, unforgiveness stirs the wrath of God and brings serious punishments upon the unforgiving. Acting as judge, the will then rules, ordering our mind and heart to forgive in compliance with the Word. These subordinate faculties then dutifully submit, uttering the words, internally or audibly, "I forgive..."

Our emotions then follow these acts of our wills. By stirring the love of God shed abroad in our hearts, the Holy Spirit manifests feelings within us that confirm our obedience. We sense a complete release from anger. Grief lifts off of us, and the joy of the Lord descends upon us in its stead. The peace of God fills our hearts. And, remembering the many mercies Jesus has shown us, we feel the compassion of Christ stirring us to release our offenders as our Forgiver has released us. By these internal emotions we know all is well. God has seen our choice of will and approved it. Forgiveness is in effect. And we are free.

Forgive immediately

Our consciousness of an offense is not incidental; that passing internal awareness is the Spirit's call to forgive. Forgiveness should then be exercised immediately. The moment we realize we've been offended is the moment we should turn to God and give up our right to anger. If we delay, we disobey—and quickly lose ground spiritually. The sooner we surrender to the Word, the surer is the safety and joy of our souls. Immediate forgivers live an abundant life, totally free from deception and bitterness. Slow forgivers waver between victory and defeat. They endure life when they should be enjoying it.

Form the habit of forgiveness

Forgiveness is an acquired habit. And like any other habit, it is formed by many starts and maintained by a steady, determined effort.

We should set our hearts to practice forgiveness at fixed times—when drawing near to God in the early morning, before taking rest every evening, and when praying. We should also resolve to practice it spontaneously—the moment offenses arise throughout the day. If ever we fail to do either of these, then we should confess our sins of unforgiveness to God, receive cleansing (1 John 1:9) and then reset our minds to forgive every offender every offense every day. As we thus restart this vital practice of love, the habit of forgiveness is formed. Each time we repeat this process, the habit is strengthened. Eventually it takes over. Forgiveness becomes second nature to us, and our way of life is forever changed for the better.

Forgiveness is forever

Forgiveness is forever. That is, it applies to all offenses, past and present. To be free indeed, we must forgive every offender we have ever known.

Some Christians are bound because they have not forgiven current offenders, such as family members, co-workers, neighbors, fellow church members and others nearby. Others hold bitterness toward those who are far removed from their daily experience, past offenders who now live, work or worship elsewhere. Still others refuse to forgive offenders who are now deceased. Apparently, they believe the adage, "Time heals all wounds," but this is false. Only business-like obedience to Jesus' command to forgive heals our wounds. Committing them into the hands of time by ignoring them only permits them to fester and grow. The truth is that distance and death change our fellowship with people, but not our *attitudes* toward them. We may be just as bitter toward a distant or deceased offender today as we were in the day they offended us. To become current on forgiveness, we must forsake anger toward all offenders, distant and near, living and deceased. Then no bitterness can bind us.

～

In light of these biblical reasons and facts, begin today forming the habit of quickly forgiving every offender by a choice of will. What reason is there not to?

The habit of forgiveness will help you greatly as you pass through the valley of trial.

Chapter Sixteen

The Way of
Testing

"Beloved, think it not strange concerning the fiery trial which is to test you . . ."

—1 Peter 4:12–13

Christian sincerity becomes Christian reality only through divine testing. Thus, to make us real, God must test us. Spiritual potential becomes actual fruitfulness only through divine testing. Hence, if we are to bear fruit, God must test us. Saving faith is distinguished from mental assent only through divine testing. So, to discover who really trusts Him, God must test us. Bible knowledge is transformed into personal knowledge of God only through divine testing. Therefore, if we are to truly know Him, God must test us. For these and other reasons, the Spirit of God exhorts us to "think it not strange" when our time comes to enter into the demanding-yet-rewarding way of testing.

To endure that way, we need a special spiritual strength that comes only from the strong meat of the Word.

*For that, let us feed upon, and thoroughly
digest, the lessons from Job . . .*

LESSONS FROM JOB

"There was a man in the land of Uz, whose name was Job…"

—JOB 1:1

The Book of Job reveals God's permissive will in His testing of the righteous. It discloses such vital information as: the kind of Christian God tests, the types of difficulties He permits to test them, why He permits these tests, the end of His testing process and His own actions before, during, and after our tests. Surprisingly, this seemingly negative book contains some very positive truths.

The first two chapters are the most revealing. They are a spiritual telescope by which we may look through the natural barriers and view the supernatural realm beyond us. These passages describe the heavenly preludes to Job's earthly trials—and those of every obedient Christian. They show that before each of Job's tests, Satan challenged God to prove that Job would continue trusting and serving Him in the midst of great and inexplicable adversity. Satan hoped, and plainly stated, that Job's trials would cause him to break relations with the Lord: "Touch all that he hath, and he will curse thee to thy face…" (Job 1:11). "Touch his bone and his flesh, and he will curse thee to thy face" (2:5). This is a revelation every zealous Christian should take to heart because it explains the reason for many of the trials we face in our own lives. Job's trials, therefore, are model tests. They are divinely designed troubles similar to those we face, carefully recorded to comfort, educate and inspire us in our day of adversity.

Before each of our trials visit us, a reenactment of the preludes to Job's tests occurs. God and Satan have a chat concerning us in heaven. Satan challenges our heavenly Father to try us, claiming that we will "curse God and die"—turn away from the Lord and self-destruct—if he is allowed to have at us. God then accepts Satan's challenge, granting permission for him to trouble us without cause. But, conversely, He hopes that we will continue to trust, cling to and serve Him despite the difficulties and pains He permits. In these respects our examinations parallel those of the great saint, Job.

But let no reader misunderstand: The kinds of ordeals Job endured in the book that bears his name are *not* those Christians face every day. They are major tests, master trials—final exams in the school of the Spirit. They are therefore distinctly more severe and lengthy than the trials we face in the early and intermediate stages of our Christian development. Not until we reach the end of our spiritual testing process does God expose us to distresses that approach in severity those that suddenly engulfed Job. Nevertheless, the same characteristics we see in his trials are also present in every test we face, regardless of its difficulty or duration, from the first to the last day of our Christian walk. Most importantly, God's actions will also be exactly the same. Everything He did for Job before, during and after his trials, He will do for you and me when He thrusts us into the furnace of testing.

Let us now examine in detail God's actions in Job's trials.

The Qualifier

Christians must qualify for the kind of testing represented in the Book of Job. God doesn't put driftwood through his refining process. It burns up too quickly in fiery trials, and, if it does survive, what value would it hold? Fired driftwood is still driftwood and still worthless, like hay and stubble. Only gold and silver—valuable and useful souls—qualify for trials like those Job faced. As the Qualifier, God reserves His hardest trials for His most promising servants.

And so we read that Job was tested severely because he was

the best man God had. On heaven's witness stand, God raised His right hand and testified of Job's character, "My servant, Job ...*there is none like him in the earth*, a perfect and an upright man..." (Job 1:8, emphasis added; see 2:3). The words "none like him in the earth" are most significant. They set Job apart from his peers worldwide. The evidence we find in the opening chapters alone corroborates God's testimony and establishes that Job indeed had a soul of the highest caliber. In its first two chapters, heaven's court record states the following:

- Job feared God (1:1).
- Job avoided sin (1:1).
- Job loved his children (1:5).
- Job rose early to commune with God (1:5).
- Job was "perfect," or spiritually mature (1:8).
- Job interceded regularly (1:5).
- Job understood fallen mankind's inclination to sin (1:5).
- Job had formed the habit of worship (1:20–21).

And the verdict is: perfect and upright, fearing God and eschewing evil, Job represents maturing Christian disciples, not novices. He typifies vessels aspiring unto honor, not vessels living dishonorably. He is the embodiment of the words, "approved unto God" (2 Tim. 2:15) and "sanctified, and |fit| for the master's use" (2:21). Case closed.

Like Job, only upright, seeking Christians qualify for strong testing. These are born again, Spirit-baptized, instructed in the Word and ways of God, and obedient; and they have already proven themselves in ordinary Christian trials. The Qualifier passes over all other kinds of Christians—the newly converted, the unspiritual and the disobedient. He is not interested in firing babies or carnal ones, and certainly not driftwood, hay or stubble.

The Protector

Because of his faithful intercessions (Job 1:5), Job's family lived gloriously untouched by adversity for many years. The troubler could not and did not penetrate the divine protection that surrounded Job, his family and his possessions. Grudgingly, Satan bore witness to this miraculous shield, likening it to a hedge: "Hast not thou made an hedge about him, and about his house, and about all that he hath on every side?" (Job 1:10). Job's hedge was an impassable angelic barrier. God charged angels to encompass and guard Job's world: "For he shall give his angels charge over thee, to keep thee in all thy ways" (Ps. 91:11). No evil could pass this barrier unless God personally permitted it. (See Job 1:12; 2:6.) Therefore, God was Job's personal Protector.

The same Protector and same spiritual hedge surround the personal world of every obedient Christian today. This is the fulfillment of God's promise to the patriarch of faith, Abraham. Early on in Abraham's spiritual life, God revealed Himself as Abraham's personal shield: "Fear not…I am thy shield…" (Gen. 15:1). And He has never forgotten this promise. To this hour, He still shields every true child of Abraham. Under orders from the Protector, angels guard our bodies, families, homes and possessions day and night. Supernaturally secure, we can rest in the supernatural peace of God in this day of unprecedented terror and universal fear, knowing that the God who shielded Abraham and Job also shields us. But some may disagree.

Considering the breech in Job's protection, some may think the Book of Job a strange source of confidence. But we must put things in right perspective. Largely, the Book of Job records a very brief period in Job's life, about one year (Job 1:6; 42:15). During the remainder of his very lengthy lifetime—possibly totaling two hundred years!—Job was not touched by Satan. Not even once! (See Job 1:1–5; 42:16–17.) That kind of security cannot be duplicated by human means; it is divine! unfailing! miraculous! Therefore, instead of inducing the fear of sudden calamity, Job's biography should inspire faith in Job's Protector.

Satan's malicious invasions into Job's world were not divine failures. God's omnipotence cannot lapse. Rather, they were calculated changes in the divine plan, necessary only for a season to test and establish Job's faith. Instead of focusing on the fact that Job's hedge was broken through and worrying that God may permit the same in our lives, we should remember the many years of Job's security. Before and after Job's personal tribulation period God's protection held off the destroyer perfectly, and God will do the same for every Christian who trusts and obeys. Should we not, then, put our trust anew in our unfailing Protector?

The Competitor

When Satan insulted Job and God and issued his challenge, "But put forth thine hand now, and touch all that he hath, and he will curse thee to thy face" (Job 1:11), surprisingly, God immediately accepted the challenge: "Behold, all that he hath is in thy power..." (1:12). Unintimidated, God showed no inclination to avoid a contest. The same God who regularly protected Job from destruction readily exposed him to severe testing. Heaven's Coach did not hesitate to send His best player onto a very demanding playing field. To gain the joy of victory, God was ready to risk defeat. Clearly, He was a bold Competitor.

He still is. God never shrinks from the enemy's challenges, nor holds us back from our tests. Once we have had ample time to become rooted in the words and ways of God and have gained vital wisdom and experience from lesser trials, a season of strong testing will unexpectedly visit our lives. As in Job's life, an evil day will dawn: "Now there was a day..." (Job 1:13; see Ephesians 6:13). In that day, the Competitor will without hesitation thrust us, His trained gladiators, into an arena of final testings. On that spiritually lethal field of play, our faith and loyalty to God will be severely tested that they may be established for all time and eternity.

Are we readying ourselves for this competition? Now is the time to build our strength and hone our skills in our preparatory trials. There will be no time to prepare when the Competitor suddenly thrusts us into arenas like Job's.

The Initiator

God, not Satan, initiated Job's trials. He is, therefore, the Initiator. Foreseeing Satan's hateful challenges and Job's faithful endurance, God sparked both of the heavenly conversations that led to Job's two fiery onslaughts: "And the Lord said unto Satan, Hast thou considered my servant, Job, that there is none like him in the earth?" (Job 1:8; 2:3). On each of these two occasions, Satan turned his attention to Job and conceived the cruel attacks only *after* the Lord had spoken well of Job. (See

1:9–11; 2:4–5.) This reveals that the Lord, not the adversary, was in control of everything that followed. It also proves that Job's adversities were not accidental but providential. Satan did not conceive them; God authored them. The Mastermind's thoughts were far ahead of the misery-maker's. Job's heavenly Trainer was wiser than his diabolical troubler and immensely larger than his colossal troubles. God was in complete control from alpha to omega. Obviously, He knew He could trust Job. If He didn't think Job could stand the flames, He would have held back the words that ignited them, for as the Bible repeatedly states, and as we repeatedly learn in life, the Initiator is faithful: "God is faithful, who will not |permit| you to be tempted above that ye are able... " (1 Cor. 10:13).

He is equally faithful in sending our trials. Satan attacks us only after the Initiator has spoken well of us in heaven. The enemy's onslaughts, then, reveal that God is pleased with our current spiritual development. We should then remember these truths from Job's trials: Our trials are not random happenings, but the plan of a Mastermind. The Initiator, not the enemy, started them and is in unrivaled control of them from beginning to end. Furthermore, He planned them for our good, not our ruin. Their very presence in our lives proves that He trusts us to stand true to Him. If He didn't, He would have held back the spark that enflamed the enemy against us. The Initiator never permits us to be tested above what we are able to bear. So His commencement of our trials proves that we are presently able to rise above them in Him.

The Limiter

If left to his own designs Satan would have killed Job—and that on the first assault! But God did not let Satan do as he pleased. In both assaults He carefully limited Satan's actions. The Lord opened a door in Job's hedge and permitted the thief to steal his dearest possessions and relationships: "All that he hath is in thy power" (Job 1:12). But then the Lord limited Satan by erecting a wall beyond which he could not pass: "Only upon himself [his body] put not forth thine hand... " (1:12). In the second assault, the Lord again limited Satan. He permitted him to afflict Job's body with sickness: "Behold, he is in thine hand" (2:6). But He then forbade him from killing his prey: " ...but save his life" (2:6). So God the Limiter contained the evil one.

God does precisely the same in our trials. Since the author of malice knows no bounds, God sets them for him. Try as he may, the enemy *cannot* advance one step beyond the Limiter's precisely set limitations: "|Thus far| shalt thou come, but no farther..." (Job 38:11). When the enemy comes at us, charging furiously and barking loudly, it is immensely comforting to know this: Though we see it not, the beast has a leash on him—held firmly by Him who sits on the throne.

The Observer

After authorizing the holy contest, God became an attentive spectator. With great interest He sat by, watching Job's reactions. When Job *accepted* his adversity as being divinely permitted for a good and wise purpose, thanking and worshiping God in the midst of his trouble instead of cursing Him (Job 1:20–21; 2:10), the Observer took note. He then promptly reported His prize overcomer's performance to his accuser: "And still he [Job] holdeth fast his integrity, although thou movedst me against him, to destroy him without cause" (2:3). Had Job known that the Lord was praising his endurance, it would surely have inspired him to carry on. Unfortunately, he did not know it.

But we may know it. The words of Job's Observer are recorded solely for our benefit. They encourage us to believe that every time we hold fast our faith and uprightness amid perplexing distress, the Observer sees our progress and reports it to our accuser, who then, of course, has to shut his mouth: "Whose mouths must be stopped..." (Titus 1:11). That's a victory so sweet that it should cause us to open our mouths and praise our God, the Observer. This is the gospel to the discouraged. Fearing their devotion has gone unnoticed, many lose heart when their trials wear long. Discouraged and weakened, they stumble. How comforting it is to know that the eyes of the Observer are present, watching us day and night, and He who sees us in secret will reward us openly...and speak well of us in heaven.

The Terminator

Had it been Job's companion, Fear would surely have told

173

him his torment would never end, for every shred of evidence affirmed that conclusion. But one day the improbable happened. Job's ordeal ended. And the One who ended it was the same who started it. At trial's end, the Initiator reversed His role and became the Terminator: "And the Lord turned [ended] the captivity of Job, when he prayed for his friends..." (Job 42:10). He had sent the trial to achieve a high purpose in Job—to further purify and humble His pure and humble servant. When at long last Job abandoned his animated self-defense and spoke words of pure surrender—"Behold, I am vile...I will lay mine hand upon my mouth...I abhor myself, and repent in dust and ashes" (40:4; 42:6)—God knew His purpose was achieved. As the Terminator, He then moved swiftly to end Job's seemingly interminable nightmare. It was as simple as that.

It's still that simple. When our pride has been thoroughly crushed, our spirits broken, and our hearts purified, when our works have demonstrated our faith and submission so clearly that even Satan cannot conceive further accusations and the Spirit has made us truly fit for the Master's use, then the Terminator will faithfully end our captivity: "God is faithful, who will...make |the| way to escape, that ye may be able to bear it" (1 Cor. 10:13). And out we will come, instruments of gold bound for glory.

The Vindicator

In his hour of crisis Job's closest friends turned against him. Because his circumstances were so incriminating, their traditional beliefs led them to conclude Job had to be a secret sinner. The righteous, they judged, do not suffer, so Job's flood of adversity was overwhelming evidence that he was not—he could not be—righteous. Therefore, they began heaping condemnation on him for refusing to confess his supposed sins. This unjustified reproach provoked a spirited self-defense by Job that led to a religious and philosophical argument of epic proportions (Job 4:1–31:40). During the lengthy debate, it looked as if Job's good name would never be restored; his very closest friends despised him, while neither man nor God spoke a good word in his behalf. Finally, after Elihu's preparatory rebuke, God broke His silence, rebuking Job for indulging in the pride and strife of self-defense. Then, as the Vindicator, He suddenly turned and humbled Job's critics. First, He shocked them by informing them that Job was more righteous than they were, driving His point home by referring four times to Job, and not them, as His "servant." "Ye have not spoken of me the thing that is right, *as my servant* Job hath..." (Job 42:7, emphasis added). Then He shook them with a test, ordering them to go to Job for prayer: "Therefore...go to my servant, Job... And my servant, Job, shall pray for you..." (42:8). Thus the accused was vindicated and his accusers humbled. At long last, the record was set straight.

As we see in Job's experience, misjudgment is an unavoidable phase of our Christian trials. Jesus Himself was falsely accused and grossly misjudged, and He taught us to consider ourselves blessed when we receive the same. (See Matthew 5:11–12.) Why do we, and who are we to, expect better treatment? When misjudgment comes for Christ's sake, our reaction is critical. If we rebel, striving by word and deed to justify ourselves in the eyes of our critics, we fall into Job's snare—the pride and strife of self-vindication—and bring upon ourselves an eventual divine rebuke. In that case, God will only turn our captivity if we repent of our uplifted attitude and return to a humble spirit, as Job did. But there is yet a better way.

That way is the attitude of acceptance. Job walked in full acceptance in the opening days of his great dual trials (Job 1:20–21; 2:10), and supernatural peace was his reward. Any of us may walk in the same overcoming attitude, if we will. Even backslidden Eli accepted the unacceptable on one occasion, uttering words of godly resignation: "It is the Lord; let him do what seemeth to him good" (1 Sam. 3:18). If we accept misjudgment as part of God's plan and do not defend ourselves before men, God will delight in us. By accepting rejection we gain a victory that eluded even Job for a season. And eventually, the Lord will come to us as He did Job. As the Vindicator, He will bring forth our righteousness as the light and our justice as the noonday. In that day, all those who were incensed against us shall be ashamed and confounded, and our name, previously maligned, will be cleared.

The Rewarder

The end of Job's sufferings was not the end of his story.

175

There was more. Much more. After turning Job's captivity, God recompensed him richly for his pain. Everything Satan had stripped from him—children, friends, flocks, herds, even time— was returned and *doubled:* "The Lord gave Job *twice* as much as he had before" (See Job 42:10, emphasis added; 42:11–17). Why did the wealthiest of all the men of the East suddenly become twice as prosperous as he was before his ordeal? Because God always honors the faith that honors Him. Job's double portion was not coincidental; it was God's reward for his faith. Because Job chose to trust God while passing through a nightmarish valley of contradiction, the Rewarder chose to restore him to the high lifestyle he had known before. Two truths are evident in the final chapter of the Book of Job. First, God rewards those who perseveringly trust Him. Second, those who endure intense testing receive immense blessing.

That's good news for every sorely tried believer, for Job's Rewarder is ours also. At the end of our fiery trials there await us a host of good things lovingly placed there by our Lord, the Rewarder. If we hold fast the word of His patience, one day He will surprise us with them. He will release us from every hindrance, recompense us for every loss and double the blessings we enjoyed in the days before our adversity. And He gives not grudgingly, but with delight: "...the living God, who giveth us richly [abundantly and freely] all things to enjoy" (1 Tim. 6:17). It is the Rewarder's good pleasure to give richly to those who endure unto the end.

～

Truly, the Book of Job is filled with weighty matters. Its revelations are the heaviest of the words of God. Yet, instead of increasing our sorrows, they relieve them. When its revelations of God as Qualifier, Protector, Competitor, Initiator, Limiter, Observer, Terminator, Vindicator and Rewarder are pondered by heavily tried souls, surprisingly, their burdens are lifted. May they comfort you today.

Disciples of Christ often need such consolation, because the way of the Lord is sometimes a very lonely and separated way.

Chapter Seventeen

The Way of
Separation

"Wherefore, come out from among them, and be ye separate, saith the Lord...and I will receive you."
—2 CORINTHIANS 6:17

Admittedly, the way of separation is an unpopular subject. Healthy souls innately want to love and be loved by everyone and recoil at the thought of walking a path apart. Social by nature, we all prefer to be united with, not divided from, other people.

But the Bible gives Christians a higher perspective on this subject. Repeatedly and unmistakably, the Scriptures make this revelation: In a fallen world, disciples of Christ must at times endure periods of separation from unspiritual ones. When faced with God's call to "be ye separate" (2 Cor. 6:17), believers must remember that the alternative—spiritual compromise—is far worse and more damaging than separation. While compromise pleases people, it offends God. In fact, it nauseates Him who would have us hot or cold but not lukewarm, and unfits us for His service.

To please God, therefore, we must at times detach ourselves from people. To understand this, let us ponder the facts of biblical separation...

BIBLICAL SEPARATION

"If a man, therefore, purge himself from these, he shall be a vessel unto honor, sanctified, and |fit| for the master's use…"

—2 TIMOTHY 2:21

The ideal of full spiritual maturity is captured in the thought of walking with God. Those who live close to God walk with Him—and those who do not walk with Him do not deeply know Him. Enoch, Noah and Abraham walked with God in ancient times, as did John the Baptist, Jesus of Nazareth and the apostles in the dawn of the Christian era. Therefore we enter into an elite company indeed when we learn to walk consistently with God. But if we aspire to that high and holy walk, there is one vital truth we must consider. To walk *with*, we must walk *apart from*.

Walking with God requires that we walk apart from people who do not walk with Him. Unity with God means separation from everyone not united with Him. Why? Because the Bible and life repeatedly teach that two cannot walk together unless they are in agreement:

Can two walk together, except they be agreed?

—AMOS 3:3

Though love wishes otherwise, truth lays down the law of biblical separation: We cannot walk faithfully with Jesus and at the same time walk closely with those who are unfaithful to

Him. This will mean abandoning close friendships with people who are not committed to the Lord, non-Christian and Christian alike. The Lord had this in mind when He urged us to "come out from among them, and be ye separate, saith the Lord" (2 Cor. 6:17). The thought of separating from unsaved sinners is understandable. We are well acquainted with the dangers of associating with the ungodly. But the idea of severing ties with certain professing Christians is not. It may even shock some. Why would the Lord require us to separate from some of our very own brothers and sisters in Christ? Because sadly but truly, many Christians refuse to walk with God.

The infallible Word declares there are two general types of Christians in the church—the committed and the uncommitted. They are like two kinds of furnishings in a large mansion—the honorable and the dishonorable: "But in a great house there are not only vessels of gold and of silver, but also of wood and of earth; and some to *honor*, and some to *dishonor.*" (2 Tim. 2:20, emphasis added.) In this passage the "great house" is the church, the current manifestation of the kingdom of God. The vessels of "gold and of silver" are spiritual Christians, who are of great value to God and are therefore reserved for honorable use. The vessels of "wood and of earth" are carnal Christians, who are worth little to God in their present state and are therefore fit only for dishonorable use.

The key thought here is that to be vessels unto honor we must be fully sanctified (made holy), or separated unto God. For that we must "depart from iniquity" (2 Tim. 2:19), that is, forsake all forms of sin, including close companionship with sinners. This is necessary because all forms of sin are highly contagious and "evil |company| corrupts good |morals|" (1 Cor. 15:33). But we must note the separation referred to in this passage (2 Tim. 2:19–21) is not from unsaved but from saved sinners, the vessels unto dishonor in God's house. To comply, then, we must avoid building close relationships with carnal Christians. If we do so willingly, separating ourselves from vessels unto dishonor, we may go on to full sanctification and usefulness: "If a man, therefore, purge himself from these [vessels unto dishonor], he shall be a vessel unto honor, sanctified, and |fit| for the master's use..." (2 Tim. 2:21).

This requirement should not surprise us, for carnal Christians are one in spirit with unbelievers. They are unbelieving believers.

Unbelieving believers are Christians who profess faith in the Lord without currently possessing it. Some are churchgoers who have never been truly born again. Others have been spiritually reborn but are currently walking in sin and unbelief rather than faith and obedience to the Lord. Something has arisen to offend them, their faith has lapsed, and they now live as if they were never saved. These unbelieving believers have nothing in common with true believers. They are infatuated with this world, not with Jesus. They think carnally, not spiritually. Their goals are worldly and temporal, not kingdom-centered and eternal. They are self-servers, not Christ-servers. They are unruly to God, not submissive. They rely on human reasoning, not the divine Word. They follow popular trends, not the leading of the Spirit. They prefer to live outside, not within, God's plan for their life. They are on the low road to ruin, not the high way to glory. Consequently, they walk with sin, not God.

Vessels of honor cannot be yoked to such Christians *and* Jesus simultaneously. To answer Jesus' call to take His yoke— "Come unto me...take my yoke upon you..." (Matt. 11:28–30)—vessels of honor cast off the yokes of unbelieving believers. So they abide free from the bondage of unequal yokes: "Be ye not unequally yoked together with unbelievers..." (2 Cor. 6:14; Gal. 5:1). This way of separation is not new. It began with the father of the way of faith, Abraham.

Abraham and Lot

Both Abraham and Lot were right with God. (See 2 Peter 2:7–8.) In their days of salvation each of them saw the Light and by faith came to Him. So they two were justified by faith. But while both were converted, both were not equally committed.

Abraham set his heart to continue walking in the Light, but Lot did not. Consequently, as Abraham went on with God, he reached a point where he could no longer remain close to Lot (Gen. 13). Why? Outwardly, because their flocks were too large to share the same pasturage (13:5–9). But inwardly, the deeper reason was their hearts were set in oppo-

181

site directions—Lot's toward the prosperity and prominence he hoped to gain in Sodom, and Abraham's toward the fruitfulness and glory he sought in God. Lot was consumed with desire for temporal success and gave no thought to God's plan for his life, while Abraham looked for eternal fulfillment in "a city which hath foundations, whose builder and maker is God" (Heb. 11:10) and cared little for the things Lot held dear. Their dominant motivators—the flesh and the Spirit—were locked in fundamental disagreement. And "can two walk together, except they be agreed?" (Amos 3:3). Hence, an unavoidable day of separation dawned, and "they separated themselves the one from the other" (Gen. 13:11).

After their parting, the two never again reunited. On one occasion years later they visited briefly (Gen. 14:13–16), and on another Abraham's intercessions prevailed to deliver Lot from death (Gen. 18–19), but they never again walked together as companions. Lot spent the rest of his days walking with Sodomites, and Abraham spent his walking with God.

DANIEL, THE THREE HEBREW BOYS, AND THEIR JEWISH PEERS

When King Nebuchadnezzar placed Daniel, Hananiah, Mishael and Azariah in his three-year-long Babylonian educational program (Dan. 1:3–6), it wasn't long before the four faced their first recorded test of faith (1:8–20). Nebuchadnezzar placed all the students in the College of Babylon on a special Babylonian diet, which included forbidden foods by the Mosaic Law, such as meats that had been offered to pagan gods or were not properly bled. Immediately Daniel "purposed in his heart that he would not defile himself with the portion of the king's meat, nor with the wine which he drank" (1:8, KJV), and bravely defied the king's orders, subsisting instead on food and drink sanctioned by God's law. And, bravely, his three friends followed suit. But no other students joined the cause of the courageous four. Even the other Jewish scholars in the program drew back from their example.

Daniel and his friends were not the only Jewish youths enrolled in the king's program. Nebuchadnezzar had selected many young men from Judah for "Babylonization." "And the king spoke unto Ashpenaz...that he should bring certain of the children of Israel, and of the king's seed, and of the princes, |youths| in whom was no blemish..." (Dan. 1:3–4). Daniel and his famous three companions were merely four "among these" (1:6). The Babylonian students adopted the king's diet readily, as we would expect, for it was their native cuisine. But the other Jewish scholars, Daniel's peers, should have followed Daniel's example. They knew God's law as well as he. They also knew the severe consequences of disobeying God; their captivity, their very presence in Babylon, was the result of God's wrath at Israel for not keeping His law. Nevertheless, they did not side with Daniel.

Soon a rift developed between the two groups of Jewish youths, and they parted ways. Daniel and company lived on vegetables and water to escape the wrath of God, while their Hebrew peers feasted on the school's diet to avoid the wrath of Nebuchadnezzar. For three years Daniel and his companions lived separated lives, severed not only from their Babylonian classmates but also from their uncommitted Jewish friends. During this season, their mealtimes were holy-yet-lonely affairs. But the four of them got together and made the best of it. They willingly paid the cost of walking with God.

HAVE YOU COUNTED THIS COST?

In His teaching, Jesus urges believers to count the costs of Christian discipleship. (See Luke 14:25–33.) His reasoning is simple. A man estimates the costs of building a house before he begins construction; if he doesn't and later finds he is unable to finish his house, he is mocked at the last as a fool. A king estimates his soldiers' chances of defeating their foes before he sends them into battle; if he doesn't, and marches boldly into disaster, history will adjudge him a foolish general. Accordingly, Jesus says we should consider the unavoidable costs of biblical discipleship now, before setting our feet to that unchanging way. If we don't, and later turn back from our holy quest, we will be the fools.

Associating costs with Christianity seems strange to many today, for this Laodicean generation has been largely deceived. We have been led to believe that there is no unpleasantness in the Christian way of life. But this is just not so. Jesus plainly taught otherwise, and we may as well discover it now. One of the costs is separation from unspiritual people. Have you counted this cost? Every seeking Christian eventually finds there are two lanes of traffic on the King's highway. Some Christians are following the Master's footsteps on that straight and narrow way, marching steadily forward with the cross before them and the world behind them; others have given up and turned back for the comparative safety of worldly ways, temporal goals and the approval of unbelievers. So we find the farther we go on, the greater the distance that separates us from those who go back.

Progress on the King's highway is, therefore, marked by milestones of separation. On looking back, you see time and again that because you chose to go on, God separated you from others—Lot types—not equally resolute. One of your closest Christian companions turned back in your college days, and your paths soon parted. Another changed spiritual direction in your early adulthood, and you gradually lost touch with him. A decade later, a dear brother lost his faith and reverted to his former ways, separating you from his company. The apostle Paul was well acquainted with these painful partings. He shares with Timothy his grief over his separation from his former assistant, Demas: "For Demas hath forsaken me, having loved this present world, and is departed" (2 Tim. 4:10). Though he realized separations were unavoidable, Paul never desired such severances. We feel the same way. We never want them; they just happen. Our forward momentum pulls us apart from those who lag back. The two most righteous souls in the pre-flood era experienced this.

While we do not know when, how or from whom they were detached, Enoch and Noah were well acquainted with the way of separation. That much we know, for it is written they "walked with God" (Gen. 5:22, 24; 6:9) in a very ungodly world. Obviously, they would not have escaped the flood if they had chummed with those who refused to believe it was coming and prepare. Their brief record speaks volumes to us in these last days, for another flood, a deluge of apocalyptic judgments, is soon to come upon our world. Are we, as Enoch and Noah, separating ourselves from those who mock the End-Time prophecies and refuse to prepare themselves spiritually and morally to escape in the Rapture? Or are we quenching the Spirit by stubbornly maintaining ungodly ties and unequal yokes in a vain attempt to save our former lives? As with Enoch and Noah, this Laodicean generation is now faced with two choices: separation or judgment.

If we refuse the way of separation, we will never know God's full blessing or walk in the power of His Spirit. And what is worse, we will seriously endanger ourselves. King Jehoshaphat almost died as a result of being yoked to his ungodly fellow Israelite, King Ahab. (See 2 Chronicles 18:31.) After his deliverance, Jehoshaphat was rebuked for his failure to separate from an idol worshiper: "Shouldest thou help the |wicked|, and love them who hate the Lord? Therefore, there is wrath upon thee from before the Lord" (2 Chron. 19:2). To avoid the wrath that rocked Jehoshaphat, we should take his rebuke to heart.

The next time you come to a fork in the road and the hand of God separates you from someone unspiritual, accept it. You must walk apart from them to keep step with Him. Only by disengaging from those who follow not can you follow on to know the Lord: "Then shall we know [Him, the Lord], if we follow on to know the Lord..." (Hosea 6:3; John 8:31–32).

And while you count and pay the costs of the way of separation, remember this: Your obedience will bring consolations—deeply satisfying blessings—your way.

THE CONSOLATIONS OF THE WAY OF SEPARATION

Special rewards and gifts

God richly repays those who suffer separation to remain united with Him. To them He grants special rewards and spiritual gifts.

"After Lot was separated from him" (Gen. 13:14), Abraham was taken aside by God and given a surprising, sweeping promise. Because Abraham's obedience to God had required him to forfeit a very prosperous way, God revealed He would ultimately reward him with great prosperity: "And the Lord said unto Abram...Lift up now thine eyes, and look...for all the land which thou seest, to thee will I give it, and to thy seed forever..." (Gen. 13:14–17). It was a very special reward for a very severe separation. To others, God

185

imparted remarkable spiritual gifts.

After Daniel and his three friends chose separation rather than defilement, God rewarded them with special spiritual gifts. All four were given superior understanding and knowledge: "As for these four |youths|, God gave them knowledge and skill in all learning and wisdom..." (Dan. 1:17). So great was God's intellectual endowment that their knowledge excelled not only their fellow students, but even the famous sages of Babylon (Dan. 1:18–20). In addition, Daniel received two special gifts. First, the ability to interpret dreams: "...and Daniel had understanding in all visions and dreams" (1:17). Second, the gift of prophecy. Daniel's prophecies rank among the Bible's grandest. These were extraordinary gifts for extraordinarily detached souls.

Other disciples will follow

Believers watch other believers very closely and often opt to simply do as they see. Hence, the sacrifice of one inspires the sacrifice of another. And then another. And another.

Christians who have endured the way of separation before us are our examples. Like spiritual pioneers, they blazed the trail we now follow. And like spiritual lighthouses, their experiences release timeless light-beams of truth that guide us in our strange and stormy trials of separation. Their examples lessen the confusion, and hence the difficulty, of our way. When faced with separations, we should remember that our examples, too, will one day be followed. This will transfigure our tests into wonderful opportunities—rare chances to be spiritual pioneers and saving lighthouses to many. If we obey, our experiences will embolden struggling disciples to forsake their timidity and follow our example. (See Philippians 1:13–14.) They in turn will inspire others. In the end, we will find our obedience has given light to many, dispelling their confusion and thereby making their way easier.

Power with God

Separation from unspiritual ties leads us into full sanctification, if we also continue seeking and obeying God and examining ourselves. And sanctified souls have exceptional prayer influence with God. Full union with God enables us to intercede effectively for everyone—including the very people we separated from for righteousness' sake. Both Abraham and Daniel prayed with the power of a separated life. Abraham's prayers delivered Lot and his two daughters from total judgment in Sodom. (See Genesis 18:22–33; 19:29.) And Daniel's fervent intercession delivered his fellow wise men and himself from Nebuchadnezzar's hasty execution order (Dan. 2:1–23).

The same exceptional prayer power is attainable for us today. If we live separated lives, our prayers will cause God to give life to many, even those we left by the wayside in our pursuit of God: "If any man see his brother sin a sin which is not unto death, he shall ask, and he shall give him life for them that sin not unto death..." (1 John 5:16).

Power with men

God gives unusual spiritual power to separated ones that they may help His people with unusually powerful words and deeds.

Before his personal departure from the land of Pharaoh, Moses attempted to deliver his oppressed brethren. Though it was bold, his premature exodus failed for want of power. Young Moses had the desire but lacked the dynamic to fulfill his destiny. Then came a strange hiatus in the vision God had given him. Without warning, God drove His chosen deliverer away from his oppressed brethren—the very ones he was called to deliver—and plunged him into forty years of heart-rending separation. But though painful, this season of divine purging was productive. As soon as it ended, its glorious fruit manifested. God sent Moses back to Egypt to deliver his brethren from bondage, this time in the power of God. Divinely inspired words and acts of power flowed from his innermost being, and every man took heed: the Hebrews believed, the Egyptians feared, the Pharaoh bowed and deliverance followed in short order. Thus Moses, the separated one, had power with men to deliver his people.

The same pattern is evident in the life of John the Baptist. Though born among the thousands of Israel, in his youth the son of Zacharias and Elisabeth was led of the Spirit into the wilderness for a special time apart. When John's separation ended, Israel's sanctification began. John, the set-apart one, returned from the wilderness with words of immense spiritual power. So great was their impact that they turned an entire nation back to God. The source of John's power? The messages he received from God. And their source? His years apart in the wilderness with God.

Unity with separated ones

Separation is not isolation. God severs bonds to forge new ones, not to leave us alone. He detaches us from one only to attach us to another. Abraham discovered this after he lost Lot to the way of gain.

Though severed from Lot, Abraham still had Sarah and many servants for fellowship, and later God gave him Isaac. When his heart was lonely for Lot's companionship, Abraham could go to these others and find sufficient consolation. More importantly, his separation from his carnal brother brought him into a new and deeper intimacy with God. He found fellowship with his new Friend far more satisfying than the fellowship he experienced with Lot. So, rather than complain about the friend he lost, Abraham no doubt gave thanks for the friends—human and divine—he had gained. Thus, his division led not to isolation but to a new and better unity. God does the same with us today.

The Lord separates us only to unite us with Himself and with other separated ones. After disconnecting us from uncommitted Christians, the Husbandman works providentially to join us to other disciples who have made similar sacrifices to preserve their spiritual lives and fruitfulness. The cutting of ties, therefore, is merely His necessary preparation for grafting us in with new, purged and more fruitful branches in the vine of Christ. (See John 15:2.)

Reconciliation

While some separations are permanent, others are only temporary. With God, all things are possible, and He can reunite separated ones just as easily as He severed them. God changes times and seasons...and hearts. And when divisive attitudes depart, miraculous reunions occur with His blessing.

For instance, who would have imagined that, after years of deathly separation, Joseph would be reunited with his brothers—those mean-spirited, lying, plotting, murderous siblings! Yet he was. Why? Because in the day they came to Egypt seeking bread, the patriarchs were changed men. Through the passing of time, the ministry of grief, and the conviction of the Spirit, God had purged their hearts of the envy that drove them to hate and persecute their gifted brother. Joseph tested them for this very purpose, to prove they were indeed then "true men" (Gen. 42:11, 19). Afterwards, he freely reconciled with them. Peter and John afford us another clear example.

Hand-picked as leading apostles, Peter and John were close companions during Christ's three-year ministry. Jesus was their common link. Because they each walked with Him, they also walked together. But Judas' betrayal created a crisis that separated them. In the garden, Peter's trust lapsed and he followed the Lord from afar, while John kept the faith and walked closely with Jesus throughout His sufferings, from the high priest's court to the council chambers to Pilate's judgment seat to the cross. Hence, the two parted ways. Not because John was proud or unconcerned about Peter, but because Peter turned back in the hour of suffering. Their separation, however, was short-lived. Only hours later Peter repented of his unbelief and returned to full faith in Christ—and full fellowship with John. In agreement again, the two apostles then resumed their walk together: "Now Peter and John went up *together* into the temple at the hour of prayer..." (Acts 3:1, emphasis added). Such reunions breed hope.

The biblical reasoning here is simple. If the Lord separated Joseph and his brothers and then reunited them, and if He detached John and Peter and then rejoined them, who knows what He may do in the hearts of your former companions if you endure faithfully to the end of your season of separation? So don't look back now. Finish your separation, that God may bring you reconciliation in His appointed time and way.

～

The Christian who isolates himself because he feels superior is disapproved of God and unprofitable to man. He edifies his ego, not his faith, and injures both his own soul and others'. Such separation is harmful, not helpful. While biblical separation may appear outwardly to be the same, it is totally different. It occurs when developing disciples, forced to choose between separation and stagnation, go bravely "outside the camp" (Heb. 13:13) of the uncommitted to draw nearer to Jesus and join ranks with others of their kind. Like Joseph, these souls eventually become both blessed of God and blessings to men: "The blessings of thy father...they shall be on the head of Joseph...him that was separate from his brethren" (Gen. 49:22–26). Therefore, beloved, if the nail-scarred hand of Him who was despised and rejected of men points you toward a path apart, fear not to walk in the way of biblical separation.

When you do so, you will soon find yourself called to the Lord's work, for the Lord of the harvest delights to use set-apart ones in His service.

Chapter Eighteen

The Way of
Service

"... and his servants shall serve him."

—REVELATION 22:3

Serving God does not cause us to know Him. To the contrary, we must know God well before we can serve Him acceptably. But once we know God, serving Him is both our delight and our destiny. There is no higher calling than to be a servant of the living God. The greatest apostle introduced himself to the church at Rome as simply, "Paul, a servant of Jesus Christ..." (Rom. 1:1). In the way of service, as in every other way, Christ is our pattern.

Christ was born to serve His Father's will. Though He was God's Son, yet He made himself His servant—and served Him from the cradle to the cross. We, too, were born to serve the Lord. Our Christian service is an expression of gratitude. By serving our Redeemer, we say thank you for paying a debt we could never pay and giving us a salvation we could never earn. It is a message that will never end, for when our service in time ceases, our service in eternity will commence. And throughout the endless days of New Jerusalem, "his servants shall serve him" (Rev. 22:3).

Has it ever struck you? You were delivered to serve the Lord...

DELIVERED TO SERVE THE LORD

"Let my people go, that they may serve me."

—EXODUS 8:1

Six of the seven times God ordered Pharaoh to release the Hebrews, He added, "that they may serve me." (See Exodus 7:16; 8:1, 20; 9, 13; 10:3.) And in the remaining reference, He clearly implied the thought of service: "...that they may hold a feast unto me in the wilderness" (Exod. 5:1). We see, then, that in God's mind deliverance and service are vitally linked. He delivered the Israelites *that they might serve Him.*

In light of this, let us consider these three closely related truths:

- We must be delivered to serve the Lord.

- God delivers us to serve Him, not ourselves.

- God always delivers faithful servers.

WE MUST BE DELIVERED TO SERVE THE LORD

God calls every Christian to be a deliverer of souls. This was the destiny of the One whom we follow. Jesus said, "The Spirit of the Lord God is upon me...to proclaim liberty to the captives" (Isa. 61:1). And as He is, so are we in this world. We have received Jesus' nature and the Holy Spirit that we may set captives free in His name and power. But before we can liberate others, we must be liberated ourselves. Captives can't liberate captives; only free men can loose their bonds. To be spiritual liberators, then, we must be "free indeed" (John 8:36). Before we can run the race of Christian service, we must lay aside everything that binds us.

Our weighty chains of sin must be broken: "For sin shall not have dominion over you..." (Rom. 6:14). Sin must not be habitually present in our thinking, speech, or behavior. If it is, our ability to serve the Lord is quenched. Why? Because we are presently Satan's servants, not the Lord's. Wherever there is sin, there is servitude to Satan: "Know ye not that to whom ye yield yourselves servants to obey, *his servants ye are whom ye obey*, whether of sin unto death, or of obedience unto right-eousness?" (Rom. 6:16, emphasis added). Only Christians who forsake all known sin truly serve Jesus. Even one point of habitual disobedience renders us unfit for the Master's use. After forty years of special preparation, Moses had one point of disobedience remaining. Only one! But God's severe disci-pline of His yet-to-be deliverer in the inn by the way proved that one was too many. Moses' lone sin had to go. (See Exodus 4:24–26.) Only after Moses yielded was he released to serve the Lord in Egypt.

We must also be delivered from all forms of spiritual immaturity. Babes in Christ cannot conquer the enemies of the Lord. As long as we harbor timidity and fear we will flee, not fight, the Lord's battles. At his first encounter with intense spiritual warfare, John Mark withdrew himself from the service of Jesus. (See Acts 13:13.) As long as we indulge ourselves with excessive pleasures and comforts and refuse to endure hardness as good soldiers of Jesus, we unfit ourselves for God's army. Not only the fearful but the self-indulgent were expelled from Gideon's army (Judges 7:4–7); deliverers they were not. As long as we demand our way, we cannot serve God's will. Selfishness only serves itself, always. As long as we are fascinated or delighted with worldly things, we are unfit for the Master's use.

When Demas' worldly interests became more important to him than doing God's will, Demas forsook Paul's ministry: "For Demas hath forsaken me, having loved this present world, and is departed..." (2 Tim. 4:10). As long as we indulge in thoughts of envy and words of strife, we are still carnal: "For ye are yet carnal; for whereas there is among you envying, and strife, and divisions, are ye not carnal?..." (1 Cor. 3:3). And carnal Christians cannot teach others to walk in the Spirit. No matter how much these kinds of Christians may wish to, they cannot serve the Lord.

Furthermore, Christ's servants must be free from oppressors and hindrances. Luke's gospel declares that we must be delivered from the control of our enemies to serve the Lord. "That he [God] would grant unto us *that we, being delivered out of the hand of our enemies, might serve him* without fear..." (Luke 1:74–75, emphasis added). To this yea, the Bible and history add a long string of amens. To serve God in Canaan, Israel had to be freed from Pharaoh's oppression. To serve as Israel's king, David had to be delivered from King Saul's lethal and relentless persecution. If Hezekiah's kingdom was to continue serving the Lord, the blasphemous Assyrian intimidator, Sennacherib, had to be stopped. Before Mordecai could serve Jehovah by writing royal decrees that benefited the Jews, God had to deliver him from his sworn enemy, Haman. If Zerubbabel was to rebuild God's temple, the "mountain" of Samaritan opposition in Jerusalem had to be flattened. (See Zechariah 4:7.) To finish his course of apostolic service, Peter had to be delivered from his oppressor, Herod. (See Acts 12.) To reestablish the Jews in their ancient homeland (1948), that they may eventually believe and serve Messiah Jesus, God had to crush their cruel oppressor, Adolph Hitler (1945).

GOD DELIVERS US TO SERVE HIM, NOT OURSELVES

After the Lord liberates us from the control of sin, immaturity, hindrances and oppressors, we must realize the purpose of our deliverance. While He delights to shower us with blessings, and does so freely, God has not delivered us merely to bless us. Nor that we may serve ourselves. Nor that He may serve us. He has liberated us to serve Him. One way we serve the Lord is by helping the people He brings into our lives: "For, brethren, ye have been called unto liberty; only use not liberty for an occasion to the flesh, but by love *serve one another*" (Gal. 5:13, emphasis added). Oswald Chambers called this service, "Ministering as occasion serves."

After Jesus healed Peter's mother-in-law, she immediately began serving him and the other guests God providentially brought into her home (Luke 4:38–39). When Jethro heard how the Lord had delivered the Israelites from Egypt, he believed in the Lord (Exod. 18:8–12); within hours he began serving Him by offering wise counsel to His overworked servant, Moses (Exod. 18:17–23). When in his fortieth year Moses heard God's call, he realized why he had been delivered from a watery grave in his infancy: He was saved to serve the Lord. Immediately he chose to live humbly with God's people and serve them rather than indulge himself in the pleasures and riches of Egypt. When Saul of Tarsus [Paul] first believed, he immediately abandoned his religious ambitions and set his sights on one goal—knowing God fully and doing everything God wanted him to do: "But what things were gain to me, those I counted loss for Christ…that I may know him, and…that I may apprehend that for which also I am apprehended of Christ Jesus" (Phil. 3:7–12).

Each of these redeemed ones shared a common purpose. They sought not what God could do for them but what they could do for God. They longed not for God to serve their worldly interests but to know and serve God's eternal interests. They prayed not for Jesus to help them build kingdoms for themselves but rather for Him to lead and use them to establish His authority in many lives. Their lofty purpose has been long forgotten in our time.

Today many see their salvation very differently. They believe that the Lord has saved and sanctified them to help them do their will in life. To them Christianity is a higher kind of self-realization in which we choose our own goals and pursue them with full supernatural aid—divine strength, ability, guidance, protection, favor and prosperity—in tow. They have forgotten or have never read that Jesus repeatedly asked disciples to *give up* their plans and ambitions to pursue His plans for their lives. (See Matthew 19:16–22; Mark 1:16–20; Luke 9:57–62.) Consequently, by pursuing their natural ambitions in life, they misuse their Christian liberty for an occasion to serve the flesh—the desires of the natural man—and ardently follow a false vision. The true gospel teaches that the Savior has not come to assist us; we are here to assist

Him. Jesus ever lived to do His Father's will, not His own: "I do nothing of myself...I do always those things that please him" (John 8:28–29). And we are called to follow His footsteps. If Jesus always served His Father's will, shouldn't we do the same? Shouldn't we cease praying, "Lord, I want this, that, and the other..." and begin praying with Paul, "Lord, what wilt thou have me to do" (Acts 9:6)?

GOD ALWAYS DELIVERS FAITHFUL SERVERS

Steadfast servers of God qualify for special divine deliverances. King David, who served God faithfully, testified, "Great deliverance giveth he to his king..." (Ps. 18:50). By habitual prayers and unswerving loyalty to God's law, Daniel served God day and night. (See Daniel 6:10.) Therefore, as Daniel entered the jaws of a great death-trap, God inspired the king of Persia to prophesy, "Thy God, whom thou servest continually, he will deliver thee" (Dan. 6:16, 20). And so it was. Daniel the faithful server was faithfully delivered by his God (Dan. 6:23). This was his entire life's story. Because Daniel served God continually, God continually delivered him. Regardless of the dangers he faced, the outcome was always the same: "Thy God, whom thou servest continually, he will deliver thee." Daniel was not the only steadfast servant who received special deliverances from on high.

Though betrayed and abandoned by his family, wrongfully convicted by an Egyptian court, and left to rot in a gloomy dungeon, Joseph continued serving the Lord: "...and he served them [the king's prisoners]...a season" (Gen. 40:4). After more than two years of this remarkable service, God delivered Joseph, raising him to a place of special honor and extraordinary influence. The apostle Paul served God continually during a long ministry filled with constant peril. (See 2 Corinthians 11:23–33; Acts 28:30–31.) As a special reward for his extraordinary perseverance, God released Paul after his day in Caesar's court, allowing him to resume his beloved missionary work. And Paul wrote: "...I was delivered out of the mouth of the lion" (2 Tim. 4:17). Before Peter's sudden arrest by King Herod (Acts 12), the apostle served the Lord continually in many ways: he led the church in its infancy (Acts 1–5), helped the Samaritans receive the Holy Spirit (8:14–25), healed the sick at Lydda (9:32–35), raised the dead at Joppa (9:36–43), evangelized the Gentiles at Cornelius' house (10:1–48), and reported faithfully to the church in Jerusalem (11:1–18). Because of this continual service, the Lord faithfully delivered Peter from Herod's executioners—and Peter immediately put his hand again to his apostolic plow.

The remarkable deliverances of these faithful servers reveals this fact: *God holds special regard for those who serve Him continually.* Because they never fail to serve Him, He never fails to save them. Thus they reap what they sow. Their seed-acts of reliable service produce a reliable harvest of divine deliverances. Faithful servers also demonstrate the principle of giving. Because they give, it is given unto them; and as they give, it is given unto them. They give God service liberally, so He gives them deliverance liberally. Wherever they go, whatever difficulties or impossibilities they meet, whoever tries to hinder or harm them, God stands by, ready to rescue His faithful servers in His own way and time.

~

Friend, the God who delivered Israel "that they may serve Me" has not changed. He has saved you for one purpose—to know Him closely and, with that knowledge, to serve Him continually. The heavenly Husbandman desires a rich harvest of service from the field of your life. To that end, remember the following: You must first be delivered. Let the Holy Spirit finish purifying your soul until it is without spot, wrinkle or blemish. Let Him finish maturing your character until it is established, strengthened and settled. You are on this earth to serve the Lord, not yourself, so always do His will first, before your pleasure or comfort. To help you do this, meditate on the Lord's promise to Daniel: "Thy God, whom thou servest continually, he will deliver thee" (Dan. 6:16). It is an inspired thought and will fill your spirit with inspiration. Finally, set your heart to abide in close fellowship with the Lord daily. And from that basis, serve Him.

In whatever you do, sacred or secular, serve God: *"And whatever ye do, do it heartily, as to the Lord, and not unto men, Knowing that…ye serve the Lord Christ"* (Col. 3:23–24, emphasis added). In drawing near to God and waiting on Him every morning, serve Him. In praying always, serve Him. In searching of the Scriptures, serve Him. In discharging your occupational duties, serve Him. In fulfilling marital and family obligations, serve Him. In supporting the weak, warning the disobedient and sharing with the poor, serve Him. In attending and supporting your local fellowship, serve Him. In giving to faithful ministries, serve Him. In ministering the gospel to the world and the Word to the church, serve Him. In praising and worshiping, serve Him. Always let your service be steadfast.

Serve the Lord diligently "in season, out of season" (2 Tim. 4:2). When you see results, and when you do not see results, labor. When you feel inspired and when you feel weak, carry on. When you are popular and when you are despised, do your work. In prosperity and in poverty, be diligent. In sickness and in health, go forward. In times of blessing and in times of trouble, accomplish your tasks. Let nothing and no one keep you from fulfilling your service to the Lord: "Be ye steadfast, unmovable, always abounding in the work of the Lord..." (1 Cor. 15:58). Be faithful—regular, reliable, dependable.

As you serve God continually, have faith. God works in your life only if you believe in Him. To receive from Him, you must believe He will help you, that "he is a rewarder of them that diligently seek him" (Heb. 11:6). So believe that "your labor is not in vain in the Lord" (1 Cor. 15:58). Believe that your service will be noticed and blessed by the Lord of the harvest, "for God is not unrighteous to forget your work and labor of love, which ye have shown toward his name..." (Heb. 6:10). Believe that one day He will reward you for every act of service you have rendered: "... your work shall be rewarded" (2 Chron. 15:7; Ruth 2:11–12). And as you have believed, so it shall be done unto you. Everyone who sows in tears shall reap in joy, and you will be no exception. In some distant fiery furnace, in some yet unforeseen den of lions, your God, whom you serve continually, will deliver *you*.

To help you serve God continually, please consider now, and begin practicing, the way of rest.

Chapter Nineteen

The Way of
Rest

"Rest in the Lord…"

—PSALM 37:7

The way of service is closely linked to the way of rest. To serve God well, we must rest well. Fruitful Christian workers invariably rest wisely, while those who neglect periods of rest produce works of inferior quality. They believe in the Lord and work for the Lord but do not rest in the Lord. Hence, stressed and weakened by fatigue, they bring no fruit to perfection. Eventually, these overzealous servants collapse. Too weary to run farther, they never finish the race set before them.

To "run, and not be weary; and…walk, and not faint" (Isaiah 40:31), we must practice the way of rest. That is, we must know when and how to find sufficient relaxation. Foolish Christians consider rest time wasted time. But wise believers understand that times of rest are times well spent—the preparation required for further work.

With this in mind, the wise thank God for "R-time"…

"R-Time"

"He maketh me to lie down in green pastures; he leadeth
me beside the still waters. He restoreth my soul..."

—PSALM 23:2–3

R-time" refers to the times in which we deliberately turn
from work to rest. In such times, concentration, exer-
tion and stress cease, and relaxation, refreshment and recreation commence. Wisely timed periods of rest are essential to
maturing Christians. Jesus Himself recognized and practiced
this vital truth.

In the days of His flesh, Jesus walked in the way of rest. In
focusing on His amazing labors, we may forget His leisure. But
in presenting the complete picture of Jesus' life, the Bible
reveals that He not only knew when to attend to His Father's
business, He also knew when to take a break. Several of the
Lord's intermissions are noted in the gospels. When traveling
through Samaria He made a rest stop at Jacob's well: "Jesus,
therefore, being wearied with his journey, sat by the well..."
(John 4:6). During a very busy period in His traveling ministry
He found it necessary to take a short nap in a boat: "And he was
in the stern of the boat, asleep on a pillow..." (Mark 4:38).
When the press of the crowds became so relentless that the
apostles couldn't find time for lunch, He called them to accom-
pany Him on an impromptu spiritual retreat: "And he said unto
them, Come |aside| into a desert place, and rest a while...and

they departed into a desert place by boat secretly" (Mark 6:31–32). So the Great Physician prescribed a brief getaway for His patients and for Himself, to avoid excessive stress. Though the idea of Jesus resting may surprise us, it shouldn't.

From the beginning, the Lord rested. After completing His work of creation, He rested the seventh day. Thus, He set an example for us—one seventh of our week should be devoted to rest. Later He ordained rest as an integral part of His people's earthly experience. In His law He provided and commanded regular periods of rest for the Israelites. They were not to do any work on the seventh-day Sabbath. They were not to work their fields and vineyards every seventh year. They were to observe various feast times annually, during which they ceased normal activities and gathered to worship God and celebrate their faith. These Sabbaths and feasts served more than religious purposes. They gave the Jews physical and psychological breaks from the weariness and monotony of their daily occupations. This provided refreshment for body and mind, as well as time for spiritual enrichment. Hence, by God's design, they ministered to the whole person.

This is the work of the Good Shepherd. (See Psalm 23.) The psalmist reveals that the divine Shepherd periodically leads His sheep beside "still waters" (23:2), or quiet settings. There He urges us to "lie down" (23:2), or physically relax. And while we are in this state, He "restoreth" our souls (23:3), or refills our inner being with strength. Thus we, the Lord's sheep, do not "want" (23:1), or lack spirit or strength for the task at hand. But sheep—the divinely chosen symbol for Christians—are notoriously stupid creatures. We should remember this. When we permit carnal reasoning or pride to move us, we can do some pretty "sheepish" things.

For example, we can refuse to rest. We may consider R-time unnecessary. We are too busy for it. We want to go all-out all the time, so we allow no breaks, no rests, no letups. Our wisdom says inactivity is ignorance. But wise sheep learn to take rest whenever the Good Shepherd provides it. Doing otherwise puts our wisdom above His; it implies we know what we need better than He does. That's pride. It's also stupidity. But our Shepherd knows how to deal with it. If in our unbridled zeal we spurn seasons of recuperation, He presses the issue by using His

rod and staff to force us to rest: "He *maketh* me lie down..."
(23:2; emphasis added). How does He do this? He simply lets us
wear ourselves out. And if self-induced exhaustion fails to get
our attention, His rod and staff visit again, this time with a heav-
ier blow. He may permit a mild sickness or injury to slow us
down. Then, in our weakness, He draws near and gently
reminds us that *He* led us to the "still waters," not the enemy.
We were presumptuous and proud to override His wisdom and
continue working. And suddenly, we see how stupid and how
impatient we were to refuse to rest.

Christian workers, who should be the first to understand
and practice R-time, are often the last to accept it, and one of
the chief reasons we do so is impatience. At the root of this is
a wrong understanding of the ministry race God sets before
us. We imagine that the Lord's work is a mad, religious sprint.
As Ahimaaz, we seek eagerly to run for God—now, always
now: "...Let me *now* run..." (2 Sam. 18:19–32, emphasis
added). Ministry is indeed a race. The writer to the Hebrews
spoke of "the race that is set before us" and the apostle Paul
alluded to a race when he testified he had finished his ministerial "course." (See 2 Timothy 4:7.) But our race is a spiritual
long distance run, not a short dash. It is a test of endurance,
not speed. We must pace ourselves if we want to finish our
course. So the Spirit wisely admonishes us to run patiently,
"Let us run *with patience* the race that is set before us" (Heb.
12:1, emphasis added). In our conception of a diligent servant
of God, we must make room for R-time. If we don't, we may
do considerable harm to ourselves. Elijah's fall suggests a connection between unbridled zeal and self-destruction.

After his great victory over the prophets of Baal on
Mount Carmel, Elijah girded up his loins and outran Ahab's
speeding chariots to Jezreel. (See 1 Kings 18:45–46.) It was an
amazing seventeen-mile sprint; only the power of the Spirit
enabled him to do it. But that very afternoon, when he was
probably still fatigued, Elijah's faith collapsed at Jezebel's surprising murder threat (19:1–2). Dismayed, the mighty prophet
suddenly turned his back on everything—his nation, his
labors, his sufferings, even the miraculous divine intervention
he had just witnessed—and fled for refuge in the desert: "And
when he saw that [Jezebel's threat], he arose, and went for his

life…" (19:3). Thus his illustrious ministry abruptly halted, far short of its intended finish line (19:16). Could it be that overexertion, brought on by unbridled zeal, helped make him vulnerable to sudden fear? Did physical fatigue cause him to let down his guard spiritually? Undoubtedly, it was one of the factors contributing to his shocking free-fall. Jesus never suffered the overexertion of haste.

One thing the Son of Man did *not* do during His earthly ministry was rush. He took one day at a time, one work at a time, one need at a time. His was a masterful, controlled pace of ministry. Even when Herod threatened to arrest and execute Him, He refused to overexert Himself to hasten His departure from Herod's territory. Many would have attempted to do three days' work in one day—and exhausted themselves. But not Jesus. With rhythmic precision He continued to work during the day and take rest each evening, traveling only a reasonable distance every day: "I cast out |demons|, and I do cures today and tomorrow, and the third day I shall |have finished|" (Luke 13:32). In Christian work, our aim should be to imitate Him: "For even hereunto were ye called…that ye should follow his steps" (1 Pet. 2:21). Jesus mastered the art of working without overworking. Our wise use of R-time will help us do this.

Periods of rest are entirely consistent with a working God and His working people. The Scriptures reveal God providing R-time for His weary servants.

THE PROVIDER OF R-TIME

The Israelites

After their traumatic Red Sea crossing and three days of hardship at Marah, the Israelites were in need of a respite. Just then they arrived at Elim, an oasis with "twelve wells of water, and threescore and ten palm trees . . ." (Exod. 15:27). And for approximately three weeks, "they encamped there by the waters."

This was providential, not accidental; it was the work of God, not chance. The divine Shepherd led His sheep beside still waters hoping to restore their souls and prepare them for their next trial, which followed shortly in the "wilderness of Sin." (See Exodus 16:1–3.)

The prophet Elisha

The Lord made special provision for His traveling prophet, Elisha, to have a place of rest. (See 2 Kings 4:8–11.) He prompted a prominent woman of Shunem to build an extra room onto her house for Elisha to use, as needed, for refreshment: "Let us make a little chamber, I pray thee, |with walls|; and let us set for him there a bed…and it shall be, when he cometh to us, that he shall turn in |there|" (4:10). Wisely, Elisha made use of this special provision often: "…and he turned into the chamber, and lay there" (4:11). Many times he prepared himself there for further travel and ministry.

The apostle Paul

After several tedious court hearings, a lengthy imprisonment and a tempestuous journey at sea—ending with a violent shipwreck and deadly snakebite—the apostle Paul was worn to the point of exhaustion. There is a limit to what even the foremost apostle can take. But just then, Paul found himself the recipient of a heavenly gift: three months of peace and quiet on the island of Malta (Acts 28:1–11). Free to fellowship, minister and witness to the Maltese, and to be entertained and honored by their leaders, Paul must have enjoyed his unscheduled furlough immensely. This was the hand of God giving his sorely tried messenger a well-deserved rest. It was a necessary retreat, which allowed Paul time to fully restore himself before his busy period of ministry in Rome (28:11–31).

A PERSONAL SPIRITUAL RETREAT

Like Paul's sabbatical on Malta, our R-times serve as personal spiritual retreats. Some Christian positivists despise the very thought of the word retreat because they associate it wrongly with surrender. But well-timed retreats are an important phase of effective spiritual warfare. To grasp this, we must understand the purpose of a retreat in military combat.

In conventional war, a retreat is not a surrender. Surrender occurs when one of the combatants capitulates, or gives up the fight, and seeks terms of peace. It is an open concession of defeat. A retreat, however, is a completely different act. While it appears to be a submissive or cowardly maneuver because one's forces are moving backward and not forward, it is actually a positive, offensive move. It is a deliberate halt of advancement, a disengagement and a pulling back—but only to regroup and continue waging war, that subsequent attacks may be made with greater strength and effectiveness. Retreats, then, are aggressive in nature, not passive. While the army that surrenders has no fight left in it, the one that retreats is still seeking victory. Many battles have been turned and wars won because wise commanders perceived the time was right for retreat. And many saints have turned impending defeats into roaring victories simply because they recognized when to pull back and restore their souls. We do well to follow their examples.

FIND REST BY VARYING YOUR WAYS

The thing that recreates us is not always bed rest and plenty of fluids. In fact, if not needed, these remedies may produce lethargy instead of energy. Rather, a little variety, a change of scenery, something different from our usual daily round, often refreshes our dull spirits and reinvigorates our weary bodies. Winston Churchill said, "A change is as good as a rest," and strongly urged others to acquire a healthy hobby that they might find that elusive blessing—recuperation. In his biographical gem, *Never Give In*, Stephen Mansfield writes of Churchill, "The legendary sharpness of his mind and endurance of his body were enhanced by his belief that a change is indeed as good as a rest, and that the best work is done by those who know when to stop working." Truly, variety is the spice of life. It is our wisdom to occasionally vary our ways to find rest.

And there are a variety of ways in which we may do this. R-time does not take the same form in every Christian's life. Because we labor in different ways, we find refreshment in different ways. For instance, the man who labors outdoors all week may enjoy spending time indoors, while the man who works at a desk may enjoy getting outdoors for a walk or participating in an appropriate recreative sport. "Bodily exercise," writes the apostle, "profiteth [a] little" (1 Tim. 4:8), so it profits us to give a little time to it. The man who travels constantly may find rest by staying in town while the man who rarely leaves his place of business may drive out and view the countryside. The home-bound housewife with young children may be blessed by a meal at the local cafeteria or restaurant, while the active business-woman may find relaxation in a quiet sandwich at home.

BE TRUTHFUL WITH YOURSELF

To practice R-time profitably, we must be truthful with our-selves. If we're not, we may willfully misread what the Lord is trying to tell us, and deceive and oppose ourselves. Depending upon our attitude toward work, we may err in one of two ways—resting when we should be working or working when we should be resting. Let Christian workaholics take heed.

Sometimes we truly need to take a break, but simply refuse to do so. We have worked so long and hard that our minds and bodies are no longer responding to our tasks as they should. If we are diligent, we may feel the urge to keep at it, to press on, to finish the job, even though the Holy Spirit, in His wisdom, is quietly urging us to come aside. He knows that with a little R-time—a fifteen-minute walk in the fresh air, a short excursion in our automobile, a picnic in the park, a few minutes off our feet, or an hour given to Bible reading and prayer—we will regain our strength and later resume our work with more proficiency. But the choice is ours. We may obey or ignore His still, small voice. If we pretend we don't hear Him, we quench the Spirit of Truth and deceive ourselves. We also disobey the Scripture, which commands us to not stifle the Spirit's voice: "Quench not the Spirit" (1 Thess. 5:19). As a result, neither our soul nor our work is up to standard. So we work against ourselves, for poor work is worse than no work, for it always has to be redone. Christians with lazy streaks should also consider this warning.

There are also occasions when we should continue work-ing despite our weariness. Sometimes others' needs are greater than ours, or more immediate, and God expects us to help them right away, weary or not. Though he preferred to min-ister in Asia or Bithynia, the apostle Paul was summoned to Macedonia with urgency: "Come over into Macedonia, and help us [now!]" (Acts 16:9). So, despite His personal desires, he responded immediately: "And after he had seen the vision, *immediately* we endeavored to go into Macedonia..." (Acts 16:10, emphasis added; see also Philippians 1:23–25). We should follow Paul's example. When conflicts arise between our desires or needs and the greater needs of others, we should set our interests aside and help them. And promptly. If we are lazy and stubborn, we may delay rendering aid. If we are lazy and crafty, we may try to use R-time to cover our selfish, rebellious spirit. How? By pretending that we hear the Good Shepherd calling us to a time of refreshment beside still waters. What we hear is the voice of indolence, not the voice of Jesus. If we deny this, we begin living a lie and lose touch with the God of truth. The way of rest must not be used as an excuse for the ways of laziness and apathy.

This is why honesty is crucial. Every truth is beautiful in its time (Eccl. 3:1–8). Used out of season, however, truth becomes ugly, harmful, even diabolical. (See Luke 4:9–12.) There is a time for rest and a time for work; truthfulness alone will help us distinguish between the two. The honest soul will never confuse profitable times of rest with unprofitable times of neglect.

~

Friend, if you have workaholic tendencies, R-time will prove a powerful tonic. If taken regularly, it will provide a surprising boost to both the spiritual and natural phases of your life. Truly, "There remaineth, therefore, a rest to the people of God . . ." (Heb. 4:9–11). Will you labor to enter the way of rest in the proper time and way? Through Jethro, the Holy Spirit said to Moses—and to you and me—"If thou shalt do this thing, and God command thee so, then thou shalt be able to endure..." (Exod. 18:23). Take His words to heart today and begin practicing R-time wisely. This will help you avoid excessive toil and its troublesome consequences. More importantly, it will conform you to the image of Jesus, because you will pace your living and ministering as He did— one day at a time, one task at a time, steady as you go.

Soon you will realize that the way of rest often requires the submission of your will to the will of God.

Chapter Twenty

The Way of
Submission

"...Father, if thou be willing, remove this cup from me; nevertheless, not my will, but thine be done."

—LUKE 22:42

Nevertheless, not my will, but thine be done." With these words Jesus submitted His will to His Father's will. We are called to live in the spirit of His surrender.

Generally, there are two means by which we walk in the way of submission. First, we submit by yielding to God in our daily living. We do this by willingly obeying our God-ordained authorities "as to the Lord" (Colossians 3:23); children to parents, wives to their husbands, employees to employers, younger Christians to elders in the faith, and all believers to pastors, and to government authorities, etc. As we subject ourselves to these people for Christ's sake we grow spiritually, even as Jesus, who "increased in wisdom...and in favor with God and man" (Luke 2:51–52) during His years of subjection to Joseph and Mary. Second, we demonstrate Christian submission by obeying Christ's call to sell out. Though these calls occur very rarely, sellouts are larger and more revealing tests of our submission to the Father's will. They are defining moments, major decisions we make at the crossroads of our lives.

The following describes the costs and results of selling out...

SELLING OUT

"...sell what thou hast, and give to the poor..."
—MATTHEW 19:21

There are crucial times in our lives when the Lord calls upon us to make costly sacrifices for His kingdom's sake. Our generation's prevailing belief—that Jesus promotes self-realization and His primary aim is to help us achieve our goals in life—would lead us to deny this. But it is true nonetheless. The New Testament reveals that there is indeed a time to sell out.

It all began when Jesus of Nazareth called a small group of ordinary men to an extraordinary destiny. When the Nazarene appointed the twelve by name, they immediately "forsook all, and followed him" (Luke 5:11). Peter left his family and fishing business, James and John forsook their father, Zebedee, and Matthew abandoned his revenue agency and wealthy friends. So strong was their fascination with Jesus that they felt no need of worldly securities. For them the shadow of His wings was sufficient protection. Their sellouts were sudden, all-encompassing, and, in the eyes of unbelievers, fanatical. But because *Christ* had called, their sacrifices were not foolish. On the contrary, they were the height of human wisdom and very natural—creatures responding in loving trust at the summons of their Creator. The twelve were not the only

ones to receive this extraordinary call to abandon all and follow Jesus.

The Lord later challenged a rich young ruler to do the
same. (See Matthew 19:16–22.) One day the preacher who
had no place to lay His head unexpectedly ordered a first-century religious yuppie, "Go and sell what thou hast, and give to
the poor" (19:21). It was a stunning blow, a spiritual bomb-
shell, to this man who, though righteous, fancied a future
filled with the bigger, better and more expensive things of this
world. His theology was shaken to its very core. Jehovah, he
believed, had promised to bless His faithful worshipers with
abundant earthly wealth of every kind. (See Deuteronomy
28:1–14.) Now His Son comes along and asks him to give
away all his possessions. Unexplained, this contradiction left
him bewildered and numb with shock. Thus, with but a few
words, Christ turned the rich young ruler's world upside
down. And Christ's words, ever so plain, simply could not be
misunderstood. Whatever else he questioned, the rich young
ruler knew two facts: Jehovah's Son said, "Sell what thou
hast," and then, "give to the poor."

The late Bible teacher, Walter Beuttler, looking beyond
the letter of this text to its deeper spiritual meaning, taught
that there is a spiritual link between Christ's words "sell" and
"give." Speaking to a group of aspiring ministers he observed:

> We feed the poor only in the measure that we sell out for
> God, and use that to feed them. The proceeds of our
> sale, of our sacrifice, of our consecration, of our leaving
> behind, the proceeds of that [sale] make our ministry to
> the hungry.

Beuttler believed that Jesus was speaking literally when
He referred to selling out, but figuratively when He spoke of
giving out. We "sell what we have" in worldly things, yet we
"give to the poor" in spiritual things. If we sell out in the
natural, God miraculously converts the value of our natural
sacrifice into spiritual resources which we later give out to the
poor. The sellout is the costly personal sacrifice Jesus asks of
us presently; the giving out is the effective ministry He eventually gives us as a result of our sacrifice. And the term "poor"
here speaks of spiritually needy ones, especially Christians. As

the poor are society's dependents, so Christians are God's dependents. The poor subsist on handouts from men, and Christians live by every spiritual blessing God gives them. And, typically, His blessings come to us through ministers who at some point in their pasts have "sold what they had."

Beuttler's insightful observation implies some vital spiritual truths. They are:

- We must sell out to be able to minister to God's people.
- The costliness of our sellout determines the value of our ministry.
- Sellouts are strictly personal sacrifices.
- Sellouts may involve actual or potential possessions.

WE MUST SELL OUT TO BE ABLE TO MINISTER TO GOD'S PEOPLE

When a Spirit-inspired wave of charity swept the early church, many saints sold their excess properties and possessions: "As many as were possessors of lands or houses sold them..." (Acts 4:34). They did this solely to be able to give. To make a monetary donation, they had to first liquidate, or convert their possessions into cash by selling them. The proceeds of their sales were then given to the church: "...and brought the prices of the things that were sold, and laid them down at the apostles' feet..." (4:34–35). The church then passed on these monies to needy believers. Some of these were literally poor, financially and materially needy Judean Christians. Others were foreign Jews who had visited Jerusalem for the feast of Pentecost and had been born again after the Spirit's outpouring and Peter's subsequent preaching. Many of these brethren apparently extended their visits beyond the Jewish feast days that they might feast on the apostles' teaching. Hence, they needed funds for their food and lodging: "...and distribution was made [by the apostles] unto every man according as he had need" (4:35; Acts 2:5, 12, 41). To be able to give to these "poor," the brethren had to sell what they had. If they had refused to sell, they would have had nothing to give.

This was exactly the situation in which the rich young

ruler found himself. Only by selling his possessions would he be able to give to the poor, as Christ requested. Because he refused to "sell what he had," he had no proceeds to donate. In that position, even if he wanted to, he could not "give to the poor." Though "he had great possessions" (Matt. 19:22), that didn't help the poor. They couldn't eat his possessions; they could only eat bread—bread purchased with money generated by his sellout.

The same principle applies today to growing Christian disciples. When Jesus calls on us to "sell what thou hast"—to give up something we value that we may later "give to the poor"—the sellout must be executed. If not, the possibility of fruitful ministry is permanently precluded. Submission is mandatory in this matter. Those who refuse Jesus' call to sell out will never minister anything of lasting value to God's needy ones. Even if they assume ministerial roles, the Spirit will not use them. Like dry river beds, they will be unable to pour out rivers of living water. They will be unable to speak words that nourish, inspire and liberate; or pray prayers that heal, deliver and strengthen; or render counsel that enlightens, corrects and challenges. To be able to give out, disciples must sell out. To minister effectively, we must sell what we have when the Master calls.

THE COSTLINESS OF OUR SELLOUT DETERMINES THE VALUE OF OUR MINISTRY

Simple arithmetic tells us that two plus two equals four. And with the same certainty it dictates that in any sellout, the amount we sell determines the amount we may give. In the example cited above, the first Christians laid at the apostles' feet "the prices of the things that were sold" (Acts 4:34), no more and no less. Therefore, the value of their donation to their brethren was determined by, and limited to, the value of the property they sold. If they sold an inexpensive possession, their gift was small. If they sold a house or a large tract of land, their gift was much greater.

The same principle holds true for us. When Jesus calls us to sacrifice something of worldly importance, as He did the rich young ruler, the value of our sellout—its importance to us, what it means to us—decides precisely how much blessing God will ultimately give others through us. The costliness of

214

our sacrifice fixes the value of our ministry. If we surrender something that means little, our subsequent ministry will help people only a little. But if at the Master's call we give up the dearest, the best, the most valued thing(s) we have, ours will be a truly powerful ministry in due season, provided, of course, that we continue to seek the Lord, abide in Him, and obey Him. If so, our future usefulness to God is a matter of simple arithmetic: The greater the loss in our day of sacrifice, the greater the flow of blessing in our day of ministry. Two plus two equals four.

SELLOUTS ARE STRICTLY PERSONAL SACRIFICES

The essence of a sacrifice is the surrendering of something held dear. And just what that is varies from person to person. Something you prize may mean nothing at all to me, and vice versa. Something I treasure may be worthless to you or to others. The fact that I treasure it, however, makes its loss a sacrifice to me. To whomever a thing is valuable, to that one its loss is significant.

For this reason, when Christ calls a disciple to sell out, the thing He requires is always something that means very much to *that* disciple. This is deliberate, not accidental, because He wants to see whether He, or the thing we value, means more to us. He asked the rich young ruler to sacrifice his possessions because they meant very much to him. Specifically, Christ's words were, "Sell what *thou* hast" (emphasis added). That is, "Sell what you are rich in, give up whatever you consider valuable, surrender the thing that dominates your life. While this may mean nothing to others, to you it will be a sacrifice indeed." A sellout, then, is a strictly personal sacrifice. It is a loss we alone suffer, a wound no one else feels but us.

SELLOUTS MAY INVOLVE
ACTUAL OR POTENTIAL POSSESSIONS

Christ's call to sell "what thou hast" has two applications. First, it refers to actual possessions held, things we currently own or positions we presently occupy. Second, it refers to potential possessions, things we aspire to or seem certain to have in the future. Sellouts, then, may involve actual or potential possessions.

To fulfill their destinies, many disciples have parted with possessions and posts they have long held, such as fortunes, businesses, houses, lands and prominent offices. To please Jesus, Zacchaeus unloaded half of his vast fortune in a single, startling donation to the needy of Jericho. After a long tenure, Matthew resigned his lucrative job as a tax collector to go preach the gospel to the poor. Other sellouts involve surrendering the prospect of great things. Though Moses never occupied Egypt's throne or owned its treasures a single day, tradition says he was next in line to become the Pharaoh. Yet when God called, Moses forfeited his rights to the most coveted office and wealth in the world—choosing instead to do His Lord's will and one day inherit heavenly power and wealth.

~

Jesus' method of feeding the multitudes confirms that we must sell what we have if we hope to give to the poor. Twice when the multitudes were weary, Jesus fed them through His twelve apostles. On both of these occasions, the bread of life passed from His hands to the apostles' hands to the people's hands: "And he … gave the loaves to his disciples [apostles], and the disciples gave them to the multitude" (Matt. 14:19). As stated earlier, the apostles had previously made great sacrifices to follow Jesus. Speaking for the twelve Peter testified, "We have forsaken all, and followed thee" (Matt. 19:27). We see, then, that in the beginning of the Christian era the disciples who had made significant personal sacrifices were the ones Jesus appointed to nourish the multitudes. Those who had sold out were those who gave out Jesus' bread. That He did so on two separately recorded occasions in the gospels (Matt. 14:19; 15:36) reveals that this was not accidental. It was one of His established ways; whenever and wherever He fed the hungry, He did so through disciples who had experienced personal sellouts. This did not cease with His ascension and the advent of the Holy Spirit, and this present Church age, at Pentecost.

After Pentecost, Jesus continued to appoint sold-out servants as prime dispensers of spiritual food. The apostle Paul, a prolific feeder of spiritually hungry souls, testified of his sellout: "Yea doubtless, and *I count all things but loss* for the excellency of the knowledge of Christ … for whom *I have suffered the loss of all things…* " (Phil. 3:8, emphasis added). Early on in his Christian experience Paul heard and obeyed Christ's call to "sell what thou hast, and give to the poor." And because he abandoned his rich Jewish heritage and a promising future in Pharisaism, revelations, visions, epistles, missions and miracles flowed forth from his innermost being to sustain the famishing. And to this day, the Lord's way of feeding the hungry has not changed. He still feeds them through servants who have made substantial sacrifices. Wherever spiritual manna is being steadily fed to God's people, there stands a Joseph who has in some way forsaken all to follow the Lord. To some, this idea of selling out for Jesus sounds very radical.

If for years you have known God only as the supernatural Blesser of your earthly endeavors, it may seem incredible that He would say to you one day, "Sell what thou hast, and give to the poor." Why, He Himself has given you what you have! He "giveth us richly all things to enjoy" (1 Tim. 6:17). He "hath pleasure in the prosperity of his servant" (Ps. 35:27). He wishes above all things that we may prosper, as our souls prosper. (See 3 John 2.) He blessed Abraham and Isaac greatly in worldly goods. For twenty years He steadily increased Jacob's possessions in the way that he went. And He caused others, such as Mordecai and Daniel, to rise to the highest levels of worldly success and power. Surely, the very One who gives us all these blessings would never ask us to give them up. Would He?

The solution to this enigma lies in understanding that there are different seasons in our lives: "To every thing there is a season, and a time to every purpose under the heaven" (Eccl. 3:1). And as summer and winter have very different characteristics, so do the spiritual seasons of our lives. There is a summertime, "a time to get, and…a time to keep" (3:6), in which everything is positive. We are constantly growing, increasing, discovering, rising, prospering and bearing ever more noticeable fruit. And there is also a wintertime, ". . . a time to lose…and a time to cast away" (3:6), in which negative storms visit to test our faith and patience. Daily we face troubles, losses, delays, misunderstandings and enemies, while seeing little fruit on our ministry branches. But the same Lord rules over all the seasons of our lives, both giving blessings and requiring sacrifices.

217

Job summarized this in his immortal words, "The Lord gave, and the [same] Lord hath taken away; blessed be the name of the Lord." (See Job 1:21; 2:10.) Because the Master hasn't yet asked you to sell out doesn't mean that He never will. He may bless you greatly in your worldly calling today, then quietly ask you to leave that calling tomorrow. For forty years God blessed Moses with the highest kind of Egyptian success and prosperity. Then one day He constrained him to lay it all down and go out into a desert, where he began an entirely different season in his life.

Beloved, if the Lord does not call you to sell out, by all means, don't sell out. To throw away one's worldly possessions or prospects without a clear divine mandate profits no one. You lose terribly and God's kingdom gains nothing from your loss. But if the Lord asks you to abandon something for the gospel's sake, don't hold back. Go through with the sacrifice. Whatever He requires—relationships, possessions, prospects, plans, positions, houses or lands—relinquish it: "Whatsoever he saith unto you, do it" (John 2:5). Then follow on to fully know the Lord: "…and come and follow me" (Matt. 19:21). That will guarantee that your sacrifice will bear much fruit.

For as you do so, the Lord will receive your sacrifice and, in a way known only to Him, transform your personal pain into His kingdom's gain. Because of your sellout, the Spirit will open up spiritual granaries within your soul and, as you continue to seek and walk with God, fill them with nourishing spiritual truths. Then, in due season, the Lord will give you a ministry gift and open a door for you to begin feeding the poor: "The Lord God hath given me the tongue of the learned, that I should know how to speak a word in season to him who is weary . . ." (Isaiah 50:4). And in that day, when you least expect it, it will hit you: You are giving to the poor in the same measure you sold out for the Lord.

No, this is not accidental. It is the word of the Lord… the same word that calls you to bear your cross.

Chapter Twenty-one

The Way of
The Cross

"And he said to them all, If any man will come after me, let him deny himself, and take up his cross daily, and follow me."

—LUKE 9:23

In our times the church has hewed out for itself a new religion—cross-less Christianity. It has developed gradually over the latter half of the twentieth century, as more and more Christians insisted on serving God on their terms—and scholars, pastors, writers and singers scrambled to revise the faith to meet popular demand. But Christ's terms of discipleship remain as originally written.

While we may alter our theology, sermons, literature and music to suit ourselves, the Bible cannot be edited to remove its less pleasant truths. It states today, as it did in the first century, that every true Christian must bear the cross. Not simply wear it, but bear it. Not only admire it, but accept it. Not merely study it, but surrender to it. Not just sing about it, but suffer it. Not merely treasure it, but be transformed by it... into the image of the first Cross-bearer. The Bible declares that the troubles and rejections we endure for Christ's sake are "manifest tokens," or clear spiritual indicators, of right standing with God.

Let us, therefore, reflect on suffering—a sure sign...

SUFFERING—
A SURE SIGN

"For unto you it is given in the behalf of Christ, not only
to believe on him but also to suffer for his sake."
—PHILIPPIANS 1:29

Though rarely preached and never popular, this timeless
truth is clearly revealed in the Scriptures:

THOSE WHO LIVE CLOSEST TO GOD
INEVITABLY SUFFER FOR IT

The oft-persecuted apostle Paul taught, "Yea, and all that will
live godly in Christ Jesus shall suffer persecution" (2 Tim.
3:12). Where may we find even one Bible character who was
fully devoted to the Lord and did *not* suffer for it? The list of
righteous sufferers is long.

Some suffered merely because they were right with God.
Abel was hated and eventually killed by Cain just because he
was righteous and Cain was evil. Others suffered because they
obeyed the call of God. To follow the one, true God,
Abraham endured lifelong separation from his idol-serving
kindred and countrymen in Chaldea. Some were persecuted
because God rewarded them with great blessings. After Isaac
received a hundredfold harvest in a single year, his envious
Philistine neighbors asked him to leave their country: "And
Abimelech said unto Isaac, Go from us . . . " (Gen. 26:16).

Others were tribulated because they were established in a

221

spiritually mature lifestyle. Because Job was "perfect and upright," Satan viciously attacked his family, possessions and health for a season. Some were hated because they possessed exceptional spiritual gifts. Joseph, who was unusually suscepti- ble to divine dreams and skilled in their interpretation, soon found himself despised and sold into slavery by his brothers. Others were rejected because they were predestined for lofty service. Divinely selected to be king of Israel, David was envied, slandered, and driven from his home and occupation by his father-in-law, King Saul. And then there were the prophets.

"Take, my brethren, the prophets who have spoken in the name of the Lord, for an example of suffering affliction, and of patience" (James 5:10). Israel's prophets suffered because they lived and spoke for God uncompromisingly. Micaiah was hated and maligned by his king and ostracized by his fellow prophets. For years Elijah was sought for execution throughout his native land, while his only calls for ministry came from other coun- tries. Daniel was falsely accused and incarcerated in a den of lions. Jeremiah suffered reproaches, revilings, beatings, the stocks and cruel imprisonments. And all other true prophets suffered varying degrees of misrepresentation, ridicule, dishon- or and brutality for committing the same "crime"—speaking the truth to people who no longer wanted the truth:

> And what shall I more say? For the time would fail me to tell of...others [who] were tortured...and others [who] had trial of cruel mockings and scourgings, yea, moreover, of bonds and imprisonment; They were stoned, they were sawn asunder, were |tested|, were slain with the sword; they wandered about in sheepskins and goatskins; being destitute, afflicted, tormented...in deserts, and in moun- tains, and in dens and caves of the earth.
>
> —HEBREWS 11:32–38

The last in the line of Israel's inspired spokesmen, John the Baptist, was shunned by the religious authorities and jailed and beheaded by King Herod. But the adversities of God's representatives didn't end with John's death.

Christian witnesses must also suffer. Christ Himself—the first to believe, live and serve in the way of the cross—was disbelieved in His hometown, rejected by His people, denounced by their religious authorities, betrayed by one of His students, condemned by His nation's highest court, and executed as a common criminal. So He forged a path for others to follow. His earliest followers, the apostles, fared no better. As their Lord, they were arrested, threatened, beaten, falsely accused and finally exiled or executed. Others then followed in the apostles' footsteps. In the church's early years, countless Christians were harassed and put to death for their faith, first in Jerusalem and later in Rome. As it passed, time did not change the way of the cross. This trend of trouble continued down through the centuries. The Roman church exhumed and burned John Wycliffe's body more than forty years after his death in 1384. William Tyndale was strangled and burned at the stake in 1536. Martin Luther was excommunicated from the Roman church in 1520 and, after the Diet of Worms in 1521, sought for execution. John Bunyan (1628–1688) was imprisoned for twelve years for preaching without a license. And both George Whitefield (1714–1770) and John Wesley (1703–1791) were banned from Anglican pulpits in England and America and forced to preach in streets and open fields. All these sufferers were of the New Testament era. Hence they are *our* examples, our forerunners in the true Christian faith, walk and service! As unpleasant as they were, their crosses shouldn't shock us. They only confirm the teachings of Christ in the Bible.

Jesus declared that it is "impossible" for Christian disciples to avoid opposition: "It is impossible but that offenses will come..." (Luke 17:1). He prophesied that worldly minded people would "hate" His chosen ones: "If the world hate you, ye know that it hated me before it hated you. If ye were of the world, the world would love its own; but because ye are not of the world, but I have chosen you out of the world, therefore the world hateth you" (John 15:18–19).

He also warned that His true servants would face the same rejection He faced: "The servant is not greater than his lord. If they have persecuted me, they will also persecute you" (John 15:20–21)—and for the same reasons: "All these things will they do unto you for my name's sake, because they know not him that sent me." Even in seasons of fulfillment and prosperity, He assured us, we should expect a measure of Christian suffering; indeed His exhilarating hundredfold recompense brings with it a counterbalancing weight of adversity: "But he shall receive an hundredfold...with persecutions..." (Mark 10:30). So we, too, are destined to suffer for living close to God. In Philippians 1:29, the apostle Paul sounded the keynote of Christian suffering: "For unto you it is given in the behalf of Christ, not only to believe on him but also to suffer for his sake." Now it is up to us to sing along.

If the negative sound of this keynote discourages us, we must remember the truth opened earlier in this book: God never leaves us without hope—strong hope, sure hope, overcoming hope. Accordingly, the New Testament has many uplifting things to say about the way of the cross. In the midst of our inescapable troubles, these truths give us a sure hope, one that motivates us to willingly submit to our share of Christ's sufferings. So motivated was Paul that he exclaimed, "For I reckon that the sufferings of this present time are not worthy to be compared with the glory which shall be revealed in us" (Rom. 8:18). Paul's soaring optimism is all the more amazing when we consider his endless stream of sufferings. He had quite a bit to be negative about!

Amid our negative adversities, then, here are some reasons for optimism.

REASONS FOR OPTIMISM

The right to reign

A common belief among us is that all Christians will rule and reign with Jesus in His millennial kingdom. But nowhere does the New Testament teach this. Instead it states that the right to reign with Jesus is a privilege reserved for overcoming Christian sufferers. We reign with Christ only "if" we endure our share of His sufferings: "*If* we suffer, we shall also reign with him..." (2 Tim. 2:12, emphasis added). By accepting our Christian sufferings, therefore, and enduring to the end of our trials, we win the right to reign with Jesus. If we refuse our share of Christ's sufferings, He denies us our share of His authority: "...if we deny him, he also will deny us." While our right to share Christ's governmental authority is deferred until His return, overcoming sufferers gain *spiritual* authority now in this time.

Currently, we gain power over demons who oppose us, our families, and our works in Christ. When we speak to opposing powers of darkness in Jesus' name and persist in faith they must yield. The apostle Paul possessed and exercised this authority. Because he accepted his Christian sufferings, the very power of Christ rested upon him: "Most gladly, therefore, will I rather glory in my infirmities, that the power of Christ may rest upon me" (2 Cor. 12:9).

Furthermore, our teaching and counsel become authoritative. When we expound God's Word, the Spirit endues our words with power. Like Samuel's utterances, they do not fall to the ground unheeded, but rather impact hearts and change lives eternally. We also rise in authority, or influence, among true believers. Thus we may help encourage, instruct and guide those who are younger in the faith. In all these ways we exert spiritual authority now in this time. We "reign in life by one, Jesus Christ" (Rom. 5:17), ruling over all things by the power of the Spirit, while yet suffering rejection for Jesus' sake. And the more sufferings we endure, the more authority we gain. Every new cross and every fresh surrender wins us more power—spiritual authority now and governmental authority in Christ's coming kingdom. Why? Because we willingly suffer for Jesus' sake.

It's simply a matter of rights. Citizens have rights; property owners have rights; crime victims have rights. And so do overcoming Christian sufferers. They alone have the right to rule and reign with Jesus.

A full inheritance

Scripture directly links our willingness to suffer for righteousness' sake with our inheritance, or rewards, in Christ. We receive our full Christian inheritance "if" we suffer for the Lord. We are "heirs of God, and joint heirs with Christ—*if* so be that we suffer with him..." (Rom. 8:17, emphasis added). So by enduring afflictions we qualify to receive all our rewards in Christ; and by refusing to do so, we forfeit them. And as with our right to reign with Jesus, our rewards are given us both now in this time and in the world to come.

Special fellowship

By accepting our share of "that which is behind of the

225

afflictions of Christ" (Col. 1:24), we qualify for membership in the VSW—the Veterans of Spiritual Warfare. Only good soldiers of Jesus Christ, disciples who have fought the Lord's battles and survived, qualify for the VSW. Because they alone know "the fellowship of his sufferings" (Phil. 3:10), they alone may partake of this special heavenly fellowship. When these suffering servants of Christ sit down to dine at the marriage supper of the Lamb, they'll have true *fellowship* with the other battle-scarred saints and martyrs in attendance, knowing firsthand their grief and agony. As earthly veterans, they will share war stories, recounting victories and comparing wounds and losses. It will be a fellowship non-suffering Christians simply cannot understand.

A Sign of Genuine Faith

Our Christian sufferings openly confirm the genuineness of our Christian faith. When the Thessalonians were troubled by their constant sufferings, Paul comforted them with this truth. He called their sufferings a "manifest token," or clear sign, that they possessed genuine faith and were destined to inherit God's eternal kingdom: "This [your persecution and tribulation] is a *manifest token* of the righteous judgment of God, that ye may be [or are becoming] worthy of the kingdom of God, for which ye also suffer" (2 Thess. 1:5, emphasis added). It was no surprise that Paul used this truth to encourage the Thessalonians. He comforted his own heart with it often, and, when necessary, he used it to authenticate his ministry.

When envious, false apostles slandered Paul, claiming that he was not truly an apostle, the Corinthians began doubting his faith and ministry. At once Paul discerned this was a satanic strategy to ensnare the Corinthians with a lie and thus prevent them from receiving the vital truths Paul taught. To counter this strategy, Paul was forced to prove the genuineness of his apostleship. An extraordinary Christian and minister, Paul could have pointed to any number of signs to verify that he was both called and approved of God. His ministry overflowed with the miraculous power of the Spirit; multitudes were healed, delivered or filled with the Spirit by Paul's prayers alone. Widely traveled, he had established churches and gathered and fed the Lord's sheep in many regions of the world, such as Syria, Pisidia, Galatia, Asia Minor, Macedonia and Italy. He had received a spectacular vision of the risen Christ; Annanias and many other Damascenes could bear witness how the Lord had indeed appeared to Paul in the way. And Paul had since returned to the mountaintop of Christian experience many times; the heavenly revelations he received were too numerous to be contained in any one epistle. He was a gifted orator and a prolific writer; his sermons moved the masses, and the whole church fed upon his writings. And he knew personally the original apostles, Peter and John, who had given him their right hands of fellowship; they would have gladly provided him with letters of recommendation, if he had asked. Any of these tokens of divine approval would have been sufficient to dispel the Corinthians' doubts. But Paul chose none of them.

Instead, and surprisingly, he authenticated his faith and apostleship by citing a single sign—his extraordinary sufferings. In his second epistle to the Corinthians, he listed the numerous and painful hardships he endured (2 Cor. 11:23–33). These sufferings, he declared, resulted from the work of a demon, whom he likened to a "thorn in the flesh" (2 Cor. 12:7). So rich and many were Paul's spiritual revelations (2 Cor. 12:1–7) and the effectiveness of his labors, that Satan appointed a special agent to stir resistance against him constantly—which God conveniently used to keep Paul humble (2 Cor. 12:7). This special resistance was the surest spiritual indicator that he lived near to Christ and that his ministry was the real thing.

~

The foregoing evidence makes an overwhelming case. It is preposterous to think we are going to walk closely with Christ in this Christ-rejecting world without encountering trouble for His sake. Yet that is exactly what many Christians think today. We imagine that suffering is obsolete. We think the cross is a mere relic of religious history; it is a beautiful symbol of our spiritual heritage, but nothing more. We are confident we will never experience the sufferings early Christians faced. They were hated and ostracized and reproached and persecuted— but not us. We have no explanation for the disparity between

227

their struggles and our easy lives. Possibly, they lacked the faith to order away trouble; or they failed to realize they were children of a King and so never took advantage of their privileges; or they never learned the art of compromising to avoid trouble, a skill which our Laodicean generation has perfected. Whatever their deficiency, we feel assured of one thing: We will never suffer as they did. Somehow—by the magic wand of itching-ear teaching and the fairy dust of wishful thinking—we won't have to bear any crosses. Such deluded reasoning ignores the yea of the Bible and the amen of history. And it leads us to rebel against God's will. For when the Lord of suffering sends us a cross by the hand of a Judas, we cry, "It's the devil!" and immediately reject the rejection Jesus wants us to accept.

But when we refuse to take up our crosses and follow Jesus, we oppose ourselves. Christian sufferings are the very means by which God sets us apart as true followers of His Son. They authenticate us as saints and accredit our ministries. They complete our spiritual resume. Without a cross of our own we are left unlike Jesus; our hands bear no semblance to the nail-scarred hands that lead us. Hence, we can never enter the fellowship of Christ's sufferings. Nor will we ever experience the resurrection power of the Holy Spirit that follows the death of self-will. Such is the sad end of cross-less Christians.

Friend, it's time to ask yourself a question. Do you want to know where you stand with the Most High? Then consider not only what your God has suffered for you, but what you are suffering for Him. Look not to your blessings but to your crosses—not troubles caused by foolishness, selfishness or sin, but those that arise from uncompromising loyalty to Jesus' words and the works to which He has called you. They locate you spiritually, and they will determine your crowns. More than anything else, the price you pay for obeying Jesus reflects how closely you are walking with Him and how effectively you are building His kingdom.

And as you endure the way of the cross, hold fast the heavenly vision set before you.

Chapter Twenty-two

The Way of
Vision

". . . I was not disobedient unto the heavenly vision."
—Acts 26:19

In his cerebral essay "Civilization" Emerson advised, "Hitch your wagon to a star." And why not? How else may we mortals keep our humble little life-wagons on the right trail in this dark and perilous world? When plowing, a farmer focuses on a point at the far end of the field. Only then will his furrow be straight. A distance runner holds fast the thought of his final destination. That alone enables him, when exhausted, to keep running and win his race. A mariner fixes his sextant upon the far-flung stars. Only then can he find his position, set his course aright and at last reach safe harbor. These examples show that a correct vision is essential to ultimate success. So it is with every Christian.

To accomplish God's will, we must walk in the way of vision. We do so by setting our hearts on the great goal of Christianity: "I press toward the mark [goal]. . ." (Phil. 3:14). That goal is a vision, the right vision. And the right vision is God's vision—not yours, or mine or anyone else's. Paul laid hold of his vision and never let it go: "I was not disobedient unto the heavenly vision." Hence, he never lost his course in this world, and one day found safe haven above. Only God's vision will set us and keep us on course for glory. Genesis 24 sets before us God's vision—His unchangeable plan for this age. It is our lodestar.

So go ahead and hitch your wagon to a star.
Focus on the mission of the Holy Spirit...

THE MISSION
OF THE HOLY SPIRIT

"Thou shalt take a wife unto my son from there."

—GENESIS 24:7

Genesis 24 contains both history and prophecy. It records past events and foreshadows things to come. Historically, it recalls Abraham's search for a bride worthy of his son Isaac. Prophetically, it is an allegory that describes the Holy Spirit's mission during this church age, telling us why He invaded this world in His fullness at Pentecost and what He has yet to do before the Rapture.

Because this allegory is biblical, it is inspired. And because it is inspired it is infallible—its symbolism is perfect. There is no deviation whatsoever between the symbol and the fulfillment. The allegory tracks reality step for step, and we may count on every detail revealed therein. Everything Abraham's servant did during his search to find and retrieve Rebekah, the Holy Spirit will do—He must do— on His present mission to call and bring home an overcoming people for Christ. By studying Eliezer's mission, therefore, we discover the goals and actions of the Holy Spirit in this dispensation.

The symbolism is as follows: Abraham represents God the Father. Isaac portrays Jesus, God the Son. Abraham's servant, Eliezer (see Genesis 15:2), depicts God the Holy

231

Spirit. And Rebekah, Isaac's bride, represents the true church, the bride of Christ.

THE BRIDE MUST BE BROUGHT TO JESUS, NOT JESUS TO THE BRIDE

Abraham's instructions are explicit and emphatic: The bride must be brought to Isaac, not Isaac to the bride. Twice during his conversation with Eliezer he orders: "Beware thou that thou bring *not* my son there [Haran] again" (Gen. 24:6, emphasis added; 24:8). Clearly, Isaac and his bride will not begin their married life in his bride's country. The aged father's plan is that they should live together with him, where he is.

The heavenly Father has precisely the same plans for His Son. Jesus is now preparing dwellings for His people in His "Father's house," which is heaven: "In my Father's house are many mansions...I go to prepare a place for you" (John 14:2). When Jesus appears, He will not descend and reside with us in this present world. Rather, He will appear in the heavens and *receive* us to His side: "And if I go and prepare a place for you, I will come again, and *receive you unto myself...*" (14:3, emphasis added). The Holy Spirit will then supernaturally transport us to meet the Lord in the air so that we may begin life forevermore with the Lord. The apostle Paul describes this epochal event, commonly known among believers as the Rapture:

> For the Lord himself shall descend from heaven with a shout, with the voice of the archangel, and with the trump of God; and the dead in Christ shall rise first.
>
> Then we who are alive and remain shall be caught up together with them in the clouds, to meet the Lord in the air; and so shall we ever be with the Lord.
>
> —1 THESSALONIANS 4:16–17

Our life with Jesus begins in heaven after the Rapture. For seven years, while the world endures the judgments of the Tribulation period, overcoming Christians will live with Jesus in His Father's kingdom: "...that where I am [heaven], there ye may be also" (John 14:3). At the close of the Tribulation, we will return triumphantly to earth with Jesus at the battle of Armageddon. (See Revelation 19:11–16.) Then we will live and reign with Him on this present earth a thousand years. Elsewhere Scripture confirms the catching away of the saints.

In His high priestly prayer, Jesus requested that His followers might be taken to heaven to behold Him in His eternal glory: "Father, I will that they also, whom thou hast given me, be with me where I am, that they may behold my glory..." (John 17:24). This petition, which must certainly be fulfilled, is the origin of the doctrine of the Rapture. Because Jesus asked the Father to transport His sanctified, unified people to glory, it shall be done. It must be done. The prayer of the Son and the plan of His Father cannot fail. At the beginning of their eternal union, the Christ and His church will live together with the Father, where He is.

THE HOLY SPIRIT'S OATH: THE BRIDE MUST NOT BE WORLDLY— SHE MUST BE WILLING TO LEAVE HER WORLD

Abraham made his servant swear to do exactly as He was told: "And I will make thee swear by the Lord...and the servant put his hand under the thigh of Abraham, his master, and swore to him concerning that matter" (Genesis 24:3, 9). There was nothing light here; this was serious business. Eliezer's oath was irrevocable. If he failed to discharge his obligations, he would be cursed. Eliezer bound himself under three great "musts." They were:

1. The bride must be brought to live with Isaac (Gen. 24:6, 8).

2. The bride must not be a Canaanite (Gen. 24:3).

3. The bride must be willing to leave her homeland (Gen. 24:5, 8).

Since we have already discussed the first of these three requirements, let's examine the latter two.

Not a Canaanite

Canaanites—idol-worshiping sinners who knew not the Lord—symbolize worldlings. Abraham's charge, therefore, forbade Eliezer to bring Isaac a worldly bride: "Thou shalt not take a wife unto my son of the daughters of the Canaanites"

(Gen. 24:3). Abraham knew well that it was his right to command his own home (Gen. 18:19). Though temporarily required to live among Canaanites, he was determined to not bring them and their ways into his own home. No Canaanite girl would marry his son.

Similarly, worldly Christians will not be taken in the Rapture. The Holy Spirit is under oath to exclude them. If we love the world, we love not the Father (1 John 2:15–17); and if we love not the Father, we are not fit for His Son—nor are we fit to live in the Father's home. Though it nauseates Him (Rev. 3:16), God bears with the worldliness of His professing followers in this present Laodicean period, but His mind is set: He will not permit worldliness to enter heaven. Canaanitish Christians—who walk in the lust of the flesh, the lust of the eyes or the pride of life—will not be translated. A God has a right to rule His heaven.

Willing to leave her homeland

Abraham made Eliezer's responsibilities very clear. If the prospective bride was unwilling to leave her homeland—her personal world—Eliezer was not obligated to bring her to Isaac: "And if the woman will not be willing to follow thee, then thou shalt be clear from this my oath..." (Gen. 24:8). At the time she met Eliezer, Rebekah had never seen Isaac. Yet when asked to leave her homeland to marry him, she consented: "And they called Rebekah, and said unto her, Wilt thou go with this man? And she said, I will go" (Gen. 24:58). Soon thereafter Abraham's servant transported Rebekah from Mesopotamia to Canaan. Why was she taken? Because she was willing to abandon her world to live in a better one with Isaac. So it shall be at the Rapture.

To qualify for translation, we must be willing to leave this world. If we are deeply entangled in the things of this world now—ambitiously, commercially, socially, politically— we will be unwilling to leave in the day Jesus appears. That fast-approaching day will find us as we really are. Paramount, then, is our willingness to live without worldliness today. Only those who are living biblically separated lives now will be willing to leave then. If carnal lusts, hunger for money or prideful living mean more to us than knowing and pleasing

Jesus, if we seek the approval of this Christ-rejecting system more than that of our heavenly Father, if our heart-desires and life-goals are earthly and temporal rather than eternal and heavenly, we will not be taken. Why? We are unwilling to leave our world to go to Jesus' world. Therefore, the Holy Spirit is not obligated to take us.

And what's more, because we are still Canaanite in spirit, He is under oath *not* to take us.

THE HOLY SPIRIT TESTS THE BRIDE

When he first saw Rebekah, Eliezer recognized her as a potential bride. So he began to test her, asking questions that forced her to make decisions and take action as he watched and evaluated her performance. If she passed her tests, he would know she was fit for Isaac. If not, he would look elsewhere.

First, he asked for water: "Let me, I pray thee, drink a little water from thy pitcher" (Genesis 24:17). She promptly "gave him drink" (24:18), and so passed her initial test. Then he waited to see whether she would offer to water his camels, as he had prayed (24:14). She did just that: "She said, I will draw water for thy camels also, until they have 'finished' drinking" (24:19). So Eliezer had his second confirmation—and Rebekah cleared her second hurdle. The next test required more time, for Rebekah had volunteered for a big job. Ten camels (each capable of holding a three-day supply) can drink an enormous amount of water. And their arrival late in the day (24:11) implied that they were probably very thirsty. To fill ten *thirsty* camels, Rebekah would have to work hard: drawing water, carrying it to the trough, emptying it and returning to the well for more. And she would have to repeat this process many times. This would require perseverance.

As she "ran again unto the well to draw water" (24:20) for the first camel, Eliezer sat, watched and wondered (24:21). She had vowed to complete the task, but would she? After a while he had his answer. Rebekah, the chosen one, endured to the end: "And she...drew for *all* his camels" (24:20, emphasis added). The next day Eliezer put her to the final test, asking whether she was willing to leave to go live with Isaac. Her immediate response was, "I will go" (24:58). So, having

235

passed all her tests, Rebekah was taken to Isaac: "...and the servant took Rebekah, and went his way" (24:61).

As Eliezer tested Rebekah, so the Holy Spirit tests every Christian, for we are all potential overcomers. Our adversities are more than satanic attacks; they are spiritual examinations sent by God to see whether we are fit to be members of the bride of Christ. No matter how demanding or unfair these tests may seem, the heavenly Father's servant-Spirit is behind them: "This thing is from me" (1 Kings 12:24). He arranges our tests, observes our reactions, and evaluates us. He bids people ask us for help. Will we give to the thirsty? He gives us difficult tasks. Will we willingly work hard? He permits some trials to last a long time. Will we endure to the end? He confronts us with costly choices. Will we take up our crosses and follow Jesus' example of self-denial for the kingdom's sake? By such tests the Spirit probes us to see what is really first in our hearts—our relationship to Jesus or the things of this world. Only one question, then, remains to be asked.

In that awesome moment when Jesus appears, will you be taken? Your response to your trials—your decisions and actions—will determine that. Only those who pass their tests will be ready, and only those who are ready will be taken: "They that were ready went in with him to the marriage; and the door was shut" (Matthew 25:10). So get ready. Give your camels drink—humbly obey—today. If you don't, the Spirit will look for someone else better fit for God's Son.

THE HOLY SPIRIT SPEAKS CONVINCINGLY TO MEN

Rebekah's father was Bethuel. (See Genesis 24:24.) In his appeal to Bethuel, Eliezer first preached the gospel of Abraham and his son (24:34–36). Then he shared his personal experiences (24:37–47). And finally, he testified that he believed the God of Abraham had chosen Rebekah to be Isaac's bride (24:48). A childlike soul, Eliezer was a simple preacher. He used no subtle psychological manipulation or super-smooth salesmanship. His words were frank and his manner forthright. When he finished speaking, he promptly asked for a decision, yes or no: "And now, if ye will deal kindly and truly with my master, tell me; and if not, tell me..." (24:49). So convincing was his sermon that Bethuel immediately believed and accepted Isaac as the new lord of Rebekah's life: "Then Laban and Bethuel answered...The thing proceedeth from the Lord ...Behold, Rebekah is before thee, take her, and go, and let her be thy master's son's wife..." (24:50–51). That Bethuel was so moved so quickly reveals that, though simple, Eliezer's rhetoric was powerful. By all standards, he was a remarkably effective evangelist.

In the same way, the Holy Spirit inspires a compelling witness for Christ. He is the spirit of evangelism. When He inspires Christian witnesses (evangelists, pastors or testifying laymen), their words create faith in the gospel of the heavenly Father and His Son, and predestined hearers promptly surrender to Jesus' lordship. Why? Because it is not the evangelist speaking but the Spirit of God speaking through them (Matt. 10:19–20; Acts 4:8). Let this encourage you to share your faith.

No matter how tongue-tied you may feel, if you have received the fullness of the Spirit you can be an effective evangelist. When God opens doors of utterance before you, simply share the gospel, your experiences and your beliefs about Jesus. You will find that your words will be just as clear, bold and convincing as Eliezer's. Why? Because the most powerful speaker on earth is in you. When He speaks, people listen.

THE HOLY SPIRIT GIVES MANY VALUABLE GIFTS TO THE BRIDE

Acting in Isaac's behalf, Eliezer showered Rebekah with many valuable gifts. First, he gave her a "golden |ring| of half a shekel weight, and two bracelets for her |wrists|" (Gen. 24:22). Later, he bestowed "jewels of silver, and jewels of gold, and raiment" (24:53). These "gifts of the servant" were sent by Isaac as tokens of his love and proofs of his glorious wealth. And they were permanent, not temporary endowments. *Eliezer never took them back.* Rebekah's gifts remained in her possession until she met Isaac.

Similarly, the Holy Spirit has distributed many precious gifts to Christ's bride, the church. These "gifts of the Spirit" are signs of Jesus' love for His people and evidence of His glorious spiritual wealth. They are numerous. To each born-again believer, the Spirit gives a priceless garment, the "robe of righteousness" (Isa. 61:10); purchased by Jesus' blood alone, no one can buy this garment for themselves. To believers who ask, He gives the gift of Himself—the fullness of the Holy Spirit. (See Luke 11:13.) To every Spirit-filled believer, He gives at least one spiritual gift, an operation of the Holy Spirit in their lives that helps build and better the church. (See 1 Corinthians 12.) And to the entire church, He gives the gifted men and women of the five-fold ministry (Eph. 4:8, 11–12). Like the valuable presents Eliezer showered on Rebekah, these precious gifts the Spirit has given the church are permanent. Since Pentecost, God has never retracted them: "For the gifts...of God are without repentance" (Rom. 11:29). They are still possessed and practiced by those who believe.

THE HOLY SPIRIT LEADS THE BRIDE ON HER LONG JOURNEY TO JESUS

Choosing the correct route from Haran to Canaan was very important for Rebekah's safety. In ancient times many dangers—thieves, wild animals, unfordable rivers, treacherous mountains, desert regions—attended lengthy journeys such as this four-hundred-mile trek. (See Ezra 8:21–23.) Wisely, Rebekah did not try to set her own course. Instead, with childlike trust, she followed the path Eliezer chose for her: "Rebekah arose...and followed the man" (Gen. 24:61). Thus Eliezer led her. Not one day, but many days he guided her. In fact, all the remaining days of her epic journey until, at last, she stood face to face with Isaac.

As Eliezer led Rebekah on her journey to Isaac, so the Holy Spirit seeks to lead us on our pilgrimage from here to eternity. He knows well the many dangers—tests, offenses, temptations, deceptions, human enemies, spirit-enemies—that we will meet on our long and perilous journey through this hostile world. Wise Christians trust His wisdom rather than their own. (See Proverbs 3:5–6.) Humbly, Rebekah realized she would find Isaac only with Eliezer's guidance; without it she would perish by the wayside. We do well to follow her example.

It is imperative, not optional, that we seek and follow the leading of the Spirit. Only then are we assured of being translated and wedded to Jesus at last. Only then are we truly "Rebekah"—children-by-covenant of the heavenly Father:

"For as many as are led by the Spirit of God, they [alone] are the [true] sons [children] of God" (Rom. 8:14). Those who do not ask for divine guidance and submit to it when given are not living as God's children. And they're falling by the wayside every day.

THE HOLY SPIRIT HELPS THE BRIDE RECOGNIZE JESUS

When Rebekah first sighted Isaac she did not recognize him. Puzzled, she asked, "What man is this that walketh in the field to meet us?" (Gen. 24:65). Because she had never before seen Isaac, Rebekah didn't know him from any other man. But by Eliezer's long association with Isaac, he knew him—his face, his voice, his ways—and quickly identified him: "It is my master..." This was the highest moment in Rebekah's life, the climax of her long and arduous journey. Yet, though it was a momentous occasion, its setting was very commonplace. Rebekah perceived nothing divine, only an ordinary man in an ordinary field on an ordinary afternoon.

In like manner, the Holy Spirit helps us recognize Jesus in the common rounds of everyday life. We see not our Lord standing before us in the way. We see only the mundane, normal people conducting normal activities as they always do. But the Spirit of God, who knows the Son of God most intimately, always detects Jesus. And He does so quickly. When we least expect it, in the odd moments of the day, the Spirit speaks to our hearts, "It is the Lord; let him do what seemeth to him good" (1 Sam. 3:18). And recognizing Jesus in our circumstances, we discern His purpose and embrace it, taking the line of obedience that pleases Him. So we obey and so we overcome. Why? Because the Spirit has helped us see Jesus in the midst of an everyday situation. This is something you should value.

For one day, one very ordinary day, in a moment, the climax of your Christian pilgrimage will suddenly occur: Your bridegroom will appear and catch you away.

THE HOLY SPIRIT'S MISSION WILL BE SUCCESSFUL

At long last Eliezer introduced Rebekah to Isaac, and the much-anticipated union occurred: "...and she became his wife..." (Gen. 24:67). Thus Eliezer's mission—to find, win, test, endow, guide and retrieve a chosen bride for Abraham's son—ended successfully. To us this is a very significant message.

In this world, success is never guaranteed. In striving to do our will, we fail as often as we succeed. But the kingdom and will of Almighty God are another matter. Unlike Adam's children, God never fails. Success is a divine attribute. Whatever the Trinity wills and speaks ultimately is. On Pentecost Day, God the Father sent God the Spirit into this world to find a chosen people for God the Son. Mark this down: His mission, like Eliezer's, will end successfully! Despite the Laodicean lukewarmness presently prevailing, in the coming days the true church—the overcoming bride of Christ—will be raised up, taught, tested, united and perfected on this earth, and afterwards translated to heaven to be by Jesus' side forever. Jesus shed His blood, not merely to save His people, but ultimately to sanctify and take them unto Himself without spot, wrinkle or blemish. (See Ephesians 5:25–27.) The Holy Spirit has come in power to see that He has that people.

Genesis 24 ends with success, not failure. So will this great church age terminate. The mission of the Holy Spirit will end in glorious triumph.

~

Disciple of Christ, rejoice! Hear the gospel according to Genesis: The aged Father's perfect plan will—it must—prevail. Christ will have His bride, and His bride will have her Christ. And best of all, this will happen soon. Your eyes will see it.

Let this vision inspire you, that you may walk patiently in the way of waiting for God.

Chapter Twenty-three

The Way of
Waiting for God

"But if we hope for that which we see not, then do we with patience wait for it."

—Romans 8:25

I recall hearing a Bible teacher claim that God's favorite word is wait. Though humorous, the comment is also surprisingly accurate. On almost every page the Bible confirms it. David advises, "Wait on the Lord...Wait, I say, on the Lord." Jeremiah observes, "It is good that a man should...quietly wait for the salvation of the Lord," and again, "The Lord is good unto those who wait for him..." Isaiah declares, "Blessed are all they that wait for him," and adds, "Since the beginning of the world men have not heard, nor perceived by the ear, neither hath the eye seen, O God, beside thee, what he hath prepared for him who waiteth for him." Jesus commanded His disciples, "Wait for the promise of the Father..." And the apostle Paul taught that God has called us to "wait for his Son from heaven." But not all waiting is the same.

To wait on, or upon, the Lord is one thing. To wait for Him is another. We wait on God by seeking and soaking in His presence daily. We wait for God by patiently enduring until God fulfills His promises and visions for which we hope.

Consider now the facts of waiting for God...

WAITING FOR GOD

"Wait on the Lord … Wait, I say, on the Lord."

—PSALM 27:14

I n chapter 9 we learned that God places great emphasis on our being led by Him. To live as His children, we must be led by His Spirit: "As many as are led by the Spirit of God, they are the sons of God" (Rom. 8:14). For this—and to await the fulfillment of God's vision—patience is required. We cannot be led by God unless we wait for Him. And to be perfectly led, we must perfectly wait.

This is neither speculation nor opinion but Bible. Thus saith the Scripture: Without exception, God's children wait for Him.

CHILDREN OF GOD WAITING FOR GOD

In both Old and New Testaments, we find children of God waiting patiently for their heavenly Father's signals, messages and interventions. Many are they who kept the word of His patience.

Ruth

Ruth sat still all day while God opened the way for her marriage through Boaz's legal action. (See Ruth 3:18; 4:1–12.)

243

Daniel
Daniel endured a long, tense night in a den of hungry lions before God brought the dawn and deliverance. (See Daniel 6.)

The apostle Peter
Surrounded by guards and bound by chains, Peter waited days in Herod's prison before he was liberated by God's angel. (See Acts 12:1–11.)

Elijah
For months Elijah sat patiently by the drying brook Cherith, looking daily for God's directions for his next assignment. (See 1 Kings 17:7–9.)

Noah
Cramped in the ark with family and "friends," Noah awaited signals from heaven, first that the floodwaters had subsided, and later that it was God's time for him to exit the ark. (See Genesis 8.)

Moses
Moses tarried humbly in Midian forty years, every day tending sheep and listening for God's call to return to Egypt (See Acts 7:29–30.)

The apostle Paul
The apostle Paul (Saul) sojourned a decade in Tarsus, quietly making tents and awaiting his season of ministry to the Gentiles. (See Acts 9:30; 11:25–26.)

Jesus of Nazareth
Jesus worked eighteen years in a carpentry shop, awaiting His appointed time to pursue His "Father's business." (See Luke 2:42, 49, 51–52; 3:23.)

Jeremiah
During Jerusalem's eighteen-month siege the prophet Jeremiah patiently endured prison, aware that only the fall of the city would release him from his bitter yoke. Later he wrote, "It is good that a man should both hope and quietly wait for the salvation of the Lord." (See Lamentations 3:26.)

Joseph

Mary's husband, Joseph, sojourned in Egypt for many days with Mary and young Jesus until advised it was safe to return to Israel. Every day he recalled the divine order, "Be thou there until I bring thee word..." (See Matthew 2:13, 19–20).

David

Pursued relentlessly by King Saul's armies, David occupied himself in the Judean wilderness until God ended Saul's reign. Afterward, he exhorted us to follow his example: *"Wait* on the Lord; be of good courage, and he shall strengthen thine heart. *Wait*, I say, on the Lord" (See Psalms 27:14, emphasis added.)

Joseph

Joseph, son of Jacob, endured Potiphar's prison for over two years, while he waited for God to fulfill the dreams of his youth: "... Joseph ... until the time that his word came; the word of the Lord tested him." (See Psalms 105:17–19.)

The 120 disciples

Having been commanded to "wait for the promise of the Father" (Acts 1:4), 120 of Jesus' disciples waited ten days in unified prayer until He poured the Holy Spirit upon them with power.

A MESSAGE TO US

The examples listed above are more than interesting Bible facts. They convey a strong message from the Spirit to all believers: If we aspire to live as God's children, "conformed to the image of his Son" (Rom. 8:29), we, too, must wait for God. We must learn to keep the word of His patience. For that, our endurance—our faith, patience and self-control—must be developed by testing. Not once, but many times our willingness to wait for God must be tried. Though similar in some aspects, our tests will not be identical. The object, length and conditions of our trials, and therefore their difficulty, will vary, because God requires less of new believers than He does of those who have been long in the faith. Babes in Christ begin with short periods of trial. Only hours or days intervene between their first prayer and their manifest answer. But God will stretch the faith and patience of more experienced believers for months, even years.

Waiting Upon the Lord

When long trials visit, we must learn to wait upon the Lord. To wait upon the Lord means to seek Him, to draw near Him by Bible meditation, prayer and worship. Every time we wait upon the Lord, He strengthens us with a fresh infusion of His own life and power. Only waiting *upon* the Lord enables us to wait *for* the Lord:

> But they that wait upon the Lord shall renew their strength; they shall mount up with wings like eagles; they shall run, and not be weary; and they shall walk, and not faint.
>
> —Isaiah 40:31

Because long trials are exhausting, they force us to seek new strength in God. When expended, our strength must be renewed if we are to continue. In the text above, "renew" really means *"exchange."* Those who wait upon the Lord exchange their strength for His. They learn to no longer depend upon their human strength but on His divine strength, which cannot be exhausted: "Hast thou not known? Hast thou not heard, that the everlasting God, the Lord, the Creator of the ends of the earth, fainteth not, neither is weary?" (Isa. 40:28).

It is this waiting upon God that enables us to wait for God to fulfill His promises. By it we receive new strength every time our strength runs low: "He giveth power to the faint; and to those who have no might he increaseth strength" (40:29). When waiting upon the Lord becomes habitual, a miraculous transformation occurs. We become irrepressibly confident. No matter how long the trial we face, we know God's strength, which we obtain by waiting upon Him, cannot fail. No matter how great our weariness, we know God stands by ready to impart new power. So we become intrepid and indefatigable; we can't be scared and we can't be exhausted. And, as Isaiah foretells, we mount up with wings like eagles, facing new trials with the joyful expectancy of obtaining new blessings by them. We run steadily through grueling marathon trials. And we walk patiently through raging rivers of trouble and intense furnaces of affliction without fainting—without lapses due to discouragement, panic or rebellion.

But those who do not wait upon the Lord cannot so endure. They never learn to renew their strength. So, left to their own strength, they cannot wait for the Lord acceptably. Consequently, in the day of adversity, they faint.

THE AGE OF CONVENIENCE

Since the days of Eden, Adam's fallen children have despised waiting. Yet for ages humanity did little to rid itself of the dreaded duty of tarrying. Life at a slower pace was quietly accepted, if not by choice, then by necessity. Then came the century—the unprecedented, amazing, revolutionizing twentieth century—and modern man decided to do away with his ancient nemesis. Deifying speed and declaring war on delay, he set about to systematically eliminate all forms of tarrying from life, "faster is better" being the universal war cry. The result is the time in which we live, the age of convenience.

During the last one hundred years, the world's collective brain power has gradually made almost every human endeavor less time-consuming. Today, the list of things for which we must wait is growing shorter by the minute. Everything we do—occupation, communication, travel, construction, education, manufacturing, buying and selling, eating, cooking, cleaning—is in a state of perpetual innovation, the chief object of which is to get the job done *faster*. An innumerable host of machines, instruments and computers now help us make decisions, go places and do things quicker. In itself, all this acceleration is not evil. To the contrary, our conveniences are a great blessing, for which we should give thanks. The wise apostle instructs us, "In *everything* give thanks..." (1 Thess. 5:18, emphasis added), and conveniences certainly fall within the scope of "everything." Besides, the result of convenience is leisure—more time to pursue personal interests. This gives us more time for God, if only we will use it.

Nevertheless, this spell of innovation has also affected us adversely. Every indulgence creates a new demand. By having everything now, we have come to expect everything now. "Instantness" has seeped into our spirits and to some degree spoiled all of us. While humanity has never loved waiting, the *now* generation hates it with a special passion. We will do any-thing—pay more, have less, make any compromise—rather than be forced to wait for what we want. Amid this madness, one thing has remained perfectly untouched. It is the way of true New Testament discipleship.

THE WAY OF NEW TESTAMENT DISCIPLESHIP: UNCHANGED

The coming of the church age has not changed God's ways, nor the ways of those who walk with Him. God has not altered His modus operandi to conform to the hasty ways of the age of convenience. Despite our quickened pace of life, He still walks and works at His own pace. So it is with every true disciple of Jesus Christ. As in ages past, children of God still wait for God. If we want to walk with Him at all times, we must wait for Him in all matters. This is God's will for every believer.

The Lord yearns for us to walk in all His ways, including that of waiting for Him: "Oh, that my people had…walked in my ways!" (Ps. 81:13). For this reason the Spirit still instructs us in the ancient art of waiting for God. Waiting is an integral part of true discipleship, which may explain why there are so few serious disciples of Jesus Christ in this age of convenience. We hate waiting. Therefore, we despise any way of life—including God's—that requires us to tarry. There are some biblical facts, however, that compel us to change our attitudes.

APPOINTED TIMES

Waiting for God is essential if we hope to endure trials and receive promises. Why? Because God still acts at appointed times and seasons. While the same God ends all our trials, our trials do not always end for the same reasons.

Some trials end when we show ourselves submissive to God's will. The instant we surrender and obey, deliverance comes. We accept our persecution with thanksgiving and praise, and suddenly an earthquake rocks open every door and looses every band, ending our captivity. We receive the Word into our troubled circumstances, and at once we arrive at the far shore of our test of faith. We stop reasoning and pray the prayer of faith, and that very day our mountainous opposition moves. We confess and forsake the sins that have long beset us, and suddenly long-delayed answers to prayer burst into our lives. In all these instances obedience terminates our tests. But other trials do not end so quickly. They continue until God's appointed time has been reached.

"For the vision is yet for an appointed time..." (Hab. 2:3; see Ps. 102:13). In these trials, God keeps us waiting long after we show ourselves fully and joyfully obedient. Month after month we must wait; again and again we must submit; day after day we must obey. And we wonder, "Why does my trial go on?" It continues because God has set a day for our deliverance and we will not be released until that day arrives: "...but at the end it shall speak, and not lie..." (Hab. 2:3). Even after Joseph fully accepted his lot as a prisoner and believed the vision God gave him, two more years passed before his release. Despite Jesus' immediate and exemplary obedience in the wilderness, Satan continued testing Him until forty days were fulfilled. Though the apostle Peter trusted perfectly and the church prayed ceaselessly, God withheld Peter's angel of deliverance until the evening before his scheduled execution.

Though for years Paul was patient, dutiful and obedient in Tarsus, his vision of apostolic service was not fulfilled until God's salvation of the gentiles began in earnest in Antioch. Though in the coming Tribulation the faithful remnant of Israel will believe God and wait patiently for His help, they will not escape antichrist's tyranny until a time, times and half a time have passed. In these examples, the arrival of God's appointed time terminates His servants' trials, not their submissive obedience. Though they displayed Christ-like surrender and trust, and that for many days, their captivity persisted until the last grain of sand fell from God's hourglass. Though demanding, such delays always serve good purposes.

We always profit spiritually from time spent submissively in trial. The longer we remain in the furnace, the more the bindings of pride and fear are burnt off. The longer we soak in preparation, the more we become saturated with the Spirit of Christ. The longer we are required to trust God, the stronger our trust becomes. The more we are forced to deal with difficult situations and people, the more our ability to overcome is perfected. The longer our trials of affliction, the more fruit of long-suffering we bear. Also, long trials allow time for all the fruits of the Spirit to ripen within us. They alone enable His graces within us, as well as our overall knowledge of God, to mature. Without these seasons of waiting, we cannot minister effectively. The best wine is aged, and the best ministry flows forth from vessels unto honor who have waited long in God's humble winery of tribulation.

Now consider this: If for such purposes God places you in a lengthy trial of faith and sets an appointed time for your deliverance, how will you endure if you refuse to wait for God?

~

Have you been fretting lately because the Lord is requiring you to wait for something you desire, or need, right *now?* Remember, if God delays, He always has His reasons, and they are always for your good. He is constantly working everything together for your good, as long as you continue obeying His Word and His calling.

His good purposes are many. He wants you to walk in His ways. He wants you to ever follow the leading of His Spirit. That He may perfectly lead you, He wants you to be perfectly patient: "But let patience have her perfect work, that ye may be perfect and entire, |lacking| nothing" (James 1:4). He wants you to live as His true child, "disciples indeed" (John 8:31). He wants His graces openly seen in your character. And finally, He wants you to qualify for the Rapture. For that, you must keep the word of His patience—obey Him when doing so requires you to wait long for His help. This patient, enduring faith, which is gained only in long, fiery trials, is "gold tried in the fire." "I counsel thee to buy of me *gold tried in the fire...* " (Rev. 3:18, emphasis added).

This alone will qualify you for the Rapture. Only those who keep the word of His patience are clearly promised exemption from the world's approaching hour of tribulation: *"Because thou hast kept the word of my patience,* I also will keep thee from the hour of temptation, which shall come upon all the world, to try them that dwell upon the earth" (Rev. 3:10, emphasis added). The Lord requires you to wait only that He may do you good in all these ways.

So stop fretting at the Lord and start waiting for Him—patiently, perfectly, praisefully. "Buy" your own gold tried in the fire by keeping His Word and remaining true to His leading in patient confidence, come what may.

Be of good cheer. The way of waiting for God will one day end, and when it ends, the way of fulfillment will begin.

Chapter Twenty-four

The Way of
Fulfillment

"Verily I say unto you, This generation shall not pass, till all these things be fulfilled."

—Matthew 24:34

Fulfillment—there is something majestic, even glorious about that word. Fulfillment is the full possession of desired ends. It is completion, accomplishment, perfection. It speaks of the end of a long, difficult journey and evokes thoughts of permanent rest and joy. To Joseph, fulfillment was an Egyptian throne from which he saved his family and fed the world. To Israel, fulfillment was the land of Canaan in which they lived in peace and from which they will yet enlighten and save the nations. To Paul, fulfillment was an apostolic ministry that enlightened the gentiles and poured out living water on the entire church age. To Jesus, fulfillment is a righteous kingdom that will one day fill the earth with the knowledge of the glory of the Lord as the waters cover the sea.

As these who have gone before us, every Christian is called to walk in the way of fulfillment. Where vision and waiting end, fulfillment begins. And the Bible reveals there is but one way God fulfills His will in our lives.

It is the way of a corn of wheat...

The Way of a
Corn of Wheat

"Except a corn of wheat fall into the ground and die, it abideth alone: but if it die, it bringeth forth much fruit."
—John 12:24, kjv

Jesus taught that God bears eternal fruit through His people in only one way—the way of a corn of wheat: "Except a corn of wheat fall into the ground and die, it abideth alone: but if it die, it bringeth forth much fruit" (John 12:24, kjv). A corn of wheat always passes through death before producing its fruit. So must we. There is no other way to the fulfillment of God's will.

Every time God issues a promise, gives a vision of His purpose, raises up a ministry or sends a revival, we experience the corn of wheat pattern. The promise is first quickened to our hearts, then for a time flatly contradicted, and finally it is performed. The vision or prophecy is given, then obscured in a long valley of impossibilities, but ultimately it is fulfilled in detail. The ministry emerges and bears fruit, then suffers a season of unforeseen barrenness, yet eventually blossoms and bears much fruit. The revival visits with heavenly power and truth, then is hindered and buffeted by strong opposition, only to break free and prevail at last. Always, the work of the Spirit follows the illustration Jesus set forth: It lives, it dies, then it lives again, larger and more effective. It experiences prosperity, then adversity, then greater prosperity. As the

Spirit thus leads us, we experience a pattern of alternating emotions that parallel the up, down, up-again way we trod. We feel hope, then discouragement, and finally ecstasy. We experience confidence, then doubt, but in the end our original confidence is confirmed. We sense expectation, then bafflement, but ultimately the joy of fulfillment. If any purported work of God has come to apparent success without passing through some such death experience, God has not raised it. Remember, not every vision is of God.

If our vision is not God's but our own, God will not fulfill it. All plans born of the flesh—pride, envy, covetousness, self-interest or immature religious zeal—will eventually come to naught. They may prosper for a season due to sheer human effort, and we may mistake their temporary success for God's blessing. But when God's permissive patience ends, these works will fall into the ground and die. And they will remain dead. And no amount of "pumping," whether by labor and advertising or prayer and fasting, will resurrect them. Christ prophesied, "Every plant, which my heavenly Father hath not planted, shall be rooted up" (Matt. 15:13). And Gamaliel pointed out, "If this counsel or this work be of men, it will come to 'nothing'" (Acts 5:38). Undertakings born of God are another matter.

For Gamaliel also taught, "But if it [this counsel or work] be of God, ye cannot overthrow it . . ." (Acts 5:39). If ours is a vision inspired by the Eternal, it is predestined to succeed. That is, if we understand the way of a corn of wheat and submit to it. Sometimes that is a very big "if." Our rebellion, if we persist in it, will cut short God's plans for us.

God's retraction of His promise to Eli's house, the tragic judgment against Samson, the disastrous career of King Saul, the sudden failure of King Josiah, even the aborted ministry of Judas—all these examples prove abundantly that God will cancel heavenly visions if we refuse to walk in His ways. For this reason, the apostle Paul submitted himself very carefully to the way *God* chose to fulfill his ministry vision: "I was not disobedient unto the heavenly vision" (Acts 26:19). "But," you may ask, "why would anyone rebel against a vision from God?"

Many resist because of the way God goes about fulfilling His visions. They desire the end but despise the means—the way of a corn of wheat. That way is a patient, humble way, and initially our pride despises it. We want life, power, fruit-fulness and glory, and we want them now, without the delay, humiliation and sorrow of passing through a death experi-ence. But let us think again. Our Master solemnly emphasized that there is no other way God's Spirit will work:

> *I assure you, most solemnly I tell you,* Unless a grain of wheat falls into the earth and dies, it remains [just one grain; never becomes more but lives] by itself alone. But if it dies, it produces many others and yields a rich harvest.
> —JOHN 12:24, AMP, EMPHASIS ADDED

So it's as simple as that. If we reject the means, we forfeit the end. If we won't have the dying, we can't have the fruit, and we will never rejoice in God's fulfillment. Let's explore in greater detail what Jesus said about the way of a corn of wheat.

"A corn of wheat"
"…Except a corn of wheat…" (John 12:24, KJV).

A "corn" of wheat is a single grain. Being a seed, it speaks of potential. It contains within itself the possibility of increase and inspires a vision of a harvest to come. It is the first stage of the "much fruit" the farmer so earnestly seeks.

Spiritually, the corn of wheat portrays the first phase of God's plan, the original condition of whatever He has called into existence. It represents the promise, vision or ministry before it is miraculously transformed by the process of death and resurrection.

"Fall into the ground and die"
". . . fall into the ground and die . . ." (John 12:24).

When a seed falls into the ground, it "dies" in that it ceases to exist in its former state. No longer visible, it appears inactive, unproductive, and unsuccessful to the agriculturally unlearned. But exactly the opposite is true. In its death, the seed is undergoing a divinely planned transformation, a mir-acle called germination. When the process is finished, new life will come forth from death, and many seeds from one.

Like a grain of wheat, divine promises, inspired visions, and chosen ministries must "fall into the ground and die." The death of a vision occurs when unfavorable circumstances —some form of rejection or trouble for the Word's sake—

temporarily stop its forward progress. After an initial period of success, the work takes a baffling downturn. Evidence of divine favor dwindles. Then the work drops completely out of sight, like a seed during germination, apparently defeated. Habakkuk spoke of these times when our portion from God is, well, *nothing:* "The labor of the olive shall fail, and the fields shall yield no I food I; the flock shall be cut off from the fold, and there shall be no herd in the stalls" (Hab. 3:17). Gradually people lose faith and pronounce the work dead. So unspiritual minds misread the work of the Spirit.

For though it appears dead, the work of the Spirit is not finished. Far from that, it is just preparing to begin. The temporary defeat of the promise is God's appointed pathway to enduring success. As one poet observed:

> Only a grain of wheat,
> So small that folks don't mind it.
> Only a grain of wheat,
> With the power of God behind it.
> There's a harvest in a grain of wheat,
> If given to God in simple trust,
> For though the grain doth turn to dust,
> It cannot die! it lives: it must,
> For the power of God is behind it.*
>
> —Anonymous

In our time "underground," God accomplishes some important works in us.

Chiefly, He crucifies our flesh by forcing us to wait for His help. We die to all dependence on our human wisdom, ways and strength as the Lord gradually opens our eyes to see that our wisdom is ignorance, our ways are errant and our strength is insufficient. Progressively, we learn the great truths of spiritual living, such as:

- God blesses only what He ordains; everything done in independence of Him must at last fail.
- The good is ever the enemy of the best. The best ideas are God's ideas; all others, no matter how

---

*Taken from *Oswald Chambers: An Unbribed Soul,* p.75

good, are merely good.
- Apart from God, we can do nothing acceptable to Him and lasting.
- Submissive obedience and trust, not wheeling and dealing, accomplish God's will.
- Faith and prayer, not reasoning and planning, solve all our problems.
- God can truly do *anything*, including the things we rule out.
- If God does not answer prayer quickly, He will do something better in His time.
- It is better to trust God than man—and wiser to trust the wisdom of the Word rather than the wisdom of our times.
- Our imaginations are untrustworthy. Things never turn out as we think, but as God thinks; and God's thoughts are always better than ours.
- Abiding very closely to Jesus, not frantic working, creates much fruit.
- Success is doing what God wants us to do, even when we appear to be failing.
- Failure is not doing what God wants us to do, no matter how successful we look.
- Only full obedience glorifies God; anything less dishonors Him.
- God alone can fulfill the vision He gives; by trying to help Him, we hinder Him.

As we practice living in truths such as these, turning completely from our old ways, our flesh dies. Only when we are content to pray in faith, pay our vows, wait for God and occupy quietly—not lifting a finger to fulfill the promise, vision or ministry in our own strength—are we truly "dead," for only then are we trusting in God alone. Sometime after we reach this point, God meets us and raises us to new life, power and fulfillment.

Also, while we are underground the Lord humbles us. Humility is another one of His ways, and a most important one. The Book of Proverbs plainly teaches, "Before honor is humility" (Prov. 15:33; 18:12). Invariably, the Lord takes us through valleys of humility before we ascend mounts of honor.

He stated expressly and repeatedly that humility was His objective in taking the Israelites through their wilderness trials: "The Lord thy God led thee these forty years in the wilderness to humble thee..." (Deut. 8:2)—"And he humbled thee..." (8:3)—"...that he might humble thee..." (8:16). Only by living for a time in the wilderness were they prepared to live in the prosperity of Canaan. So it has always been. Only a season of adversity enables us to receive the exhilaration of prosperity without becoming proud. A taste of defeat is vital preparation for all who are destined to dine long at the table of victory. When God does great things for such humbled ones, they are not moved by their flesh. They remain in the Spirit—close to Jesus, thankful, worshipful, sober, steady.

"It abideth alone"

If never planted, a corn of wheat abides alone and unchanged: "...it abideth alone..." (John 12:24).

Thus, it forfeits its glorious potential. Sadly, it will never be anything more than what it is. Sentenced to live forever in its original state, it never experiences the joyful fruitfulness it was created to produce.

This represents believers who refuse to submit to the way of a corn of wheat. When the Lord brings them to the edge of their valley of humiliation, they rebel and go back. Or they obey outwardly, but not inwardly, despising what the Lord requires of them instead of rendering Him willing, thankful obedience. Like seeds that fall into the ground yet stubbornly refuse to die, these refuse to surrender the will of their flesh. And because they refuse to die, they cannot live again. Disqualified, they never experience the Spirit's distinctive work of revived fruitfulness and enlargement. So they are left to themselves, unchanged and unfruitful, and very much alone.

"It bringeth forth much fruit"

After its death, a corn of wheat reproduces itself many times over. From one grain, not few but many new grains spring up: "it bringeth forth much fruit" (John 12:24). Thus its potential is fulfilled.

This describes God's ultimate purpose in our personal lives and in every promise, vision or ministry He calls into existence, which is simply *to bring forth much fruit*. After the death of the promise, God resurrects it by restoring it to a state of visible effectiveness. Then through us He brings forth numerous blessings and good works. As a result, many of His children are saved, filled with the Spirit, delivered from sin, released from error, healed, guided, instructed and set on course for glory. Eventually, the believer who submits to the corn of wheat pattern reproduces his faith many times over in other lives. Thus, many new seeds—potential fruit-bearers—are brought into the world. So, by bringing forth much fruit, the spiritual destiny of the original seed of faith is fulfilled.

"Save me from" or "glorify Thy Name"?

At the time Jesus revealed the corn of wheat process (John 12), He was about to undergo it.

Soon thereafter He "fell into the ground and died" bodily that He might bring forth His holy bride, the church. In no other way could His vision of eternal union with a redeemed people be fulfilled. To bring forth "much fruit," Jesus had to go the way of a corn of wheat. That way is more widely known among us as the way of the cross and the resurrection.

The way of fulfillment through crucifixion was diametrically opposed to Jesus' human self-will and presented Him with a great dilemma. He could not save Himself and also bring forth much fruit. One of the two ends—the will of self or the will of God—had to be sacrificed. Realizing this He said, "What shall I say? Father, *save me from* this hour. But for this cause came I unto this hour, Father, *glorify thy name...*" (John 12:27–28, emphasis added). Paraphrasing, He meant, "Should I ask to be delivered from this death experience, praying 'Father, save me from it'? How then can I bear much fruit and bring glory to My Father, which is the very reason I have come? No, I will rather pray, 'Father, glorify Thy name'...by leading me onward in the way of the cross." With this, the greatest Corn of Wheat, with full understanding and faith, fell into the ground, died, and afterwards bore much fruit. To this day, every new believer is yet another grain of fruit from that first divine planting.

To bear much fruit, every Christian must go the way of the original Corn of Wheat. All the promises, visions and ministries God has given us must fall into the ground and die

before they come to fruition. To enjoy their lasting fulfillment, we must endure their temporary defeat. God must let
His promises be contradicted before He fulfills them. Our
visions must appear false for a season before they are proven
true. God must permit our ministries to be brought low
before raising them high. When the Holy Spirit leads us into
our barren valleys of death, we will relive Christ's dilemma.
What will we choose in that hour? Will we beg our heavenly
Father to remove our adversities before they have finished
their work—"Save me from!"—and forfeit the purpose of
God? Or will we accept our difficulties as the necessary
preparation for fruitfulness and glory, and with this understanding pray, "Father, glorify Thy Name..."? Foreseeing
this, the dilemma of every lesser corn of wheat, Jesus calls,
counsels and consoles us.

He calls us to follow His example: "If any man serve me,
let him follow me [in the way of a corn of wheat, the way of the
cross and the resurrection]..." (John 12:26). Then He counsels
us to obtain lasting blessing by putting the eternal will of God
before the temporal will of self, as He did: "He that loveth his
life shall lose it; and he that hateth his life in this world shall
keep it unto life eternal" (John 12:25). And finally, He consoles
us by promising that His Father will honor all who honor Him
by submitting to the corn of wheat pattern: "If any man serve
me [by following me in the way of a corn of wheat], him will
my Father honor" (John 12:26; 1 Samuel 2:30).

SPIRITUAL MOVEMENTS

As stated previously, spiritual movements, or revivals, also follow the pattern of a corn of wheat.

For instance, the successive ministries of John the
Baptist and Jesus constituted a single movement of the Spirit
in Israel. John came first, preaching repentance to prepare the
people's hearts for Christ's message. The people recognized
God's hand upon John and rejoiced: "...all men counted
John, that he was a prophet indeed" (Mark 11:32). At long last
God had visited His people in fulfillment of His promise!
Revival was underway!

Then, suddenly, a terrible contradiction visited. Without
warning, King Herod imprisoned John and his inspired words

and inspiring baptisms ceased. The people gasped as John's ministry fell from public view, inactive, silent, unfruitful. While John languished in Herod's prison, the people feared and wondered, "Is the movement dead? Has persecution permanently halted the work of God?" Mercifully, God did not keep them waiting long for an answer.

After Herod bound John, the heavenly Father released His Son to run His course: "Now when Jesus had heard that John was cast into prison,...leaving Nazareth, he came and dwelt in Capernaum...From that time Jesus began to preach..." (Matt. 4:12–17). Not many days hence, new spiritual growth appeared as Jesus began preaching and teaching throughout the land. And the people breathed a sigh of relief: The revival was not dead; the baptist had fallen, but a greater One than he had risen. And much more fruit was abounding.

For in every way Christ's outreach exceeded John's. Jesus' ministry endured longer than John's ministry; it lasted not one, but three years. It covered a greater territory; it reached not merely the Jordan valley, but also Galilee, Judea, Samaria, Decapolis, and the borders of Tyre and Sidon. More truth was spoken; there was not only a call to repentance, but also a great sowing of priceless principles, parables and revelations. More converts were made; even the most notorious sinners, such as the woman at Jacob's well, Zacchaeus, and the thief on the cross, were reached. More captives were released; indeed hopeless cases, like the demon-possessed boy and the wild man of Gadara, were liberated by the Master's touch. And more spiritual power was manifested; John's words were with power, but Jesus' words and works were *dunamis!*

In that amazing visitation that stretched from Cana to Calvary, the supernatural became natural, as miracles flowed daily. Truly, Jesus' revival brought days of heaven upon earth. What was the explanation of it all?

John's ministry had gone the way of a corn of wheat. In a surprising and unexplained twist, the spirit that possessed Herod sensed what God had done. Seeing similarities between John's and Jesus' outreaches, Herod described Jesus' ministry as an extension of John's: "John the Baptist was risen from the dead, and therefore mighty works do show forth themselves in him" (Mark 6:14). Though not literally true, Herod's words were spiritually accurate. Not John, but his ministry had fallen into the earth and had died; then the irrepressible Spirit that inspired it rose again to bring forth much more fruit through Jesus' ministry. Thus, John's and Jesus' ministries were really one continuous work of the Spirit of God, a spiritual movement that lived, and died, and lived again.

~

Friend, has God not yet fulfilled His promise to you? Does the vision He gave long ago seem only to lie? Is the ministry in which you labor presently fruitless? Has the movement of His Spirit in your church, denomination, city or nation been hindered by opposition? Then do not despair. If God has inspired your vision, your faith is not errant and your labor is not in vain. You have not been wrong to confess faith in the promise, to hope for the vision, to give yourself to the ministry, or to believe for the revival. "For surely there is an end, and thine expectation shall not be cut off" (Prov. 23:18). The reason for your present trial is simple: The Spirit is leading you in the way of a corn of wheat.

And as the death of a corn of wheat, your present trouble is a part of God's plan. You have fallen into the ground, just as Jesus said you would. So now be a good corn of wheat and die. That is, finish your spiritual germination. Fully surrender to the will of God and accept the humble circumstances in which He has placed you. Do not be offended with the Lord because your way is long and difficult. If you rebel and turn aside to sin, you will only make things worse. Disobedience prevents God from completing the corn of wheat pattern. He raises up only the upright. So stay faithful to the vision. Keep sowing the precious seed of God's Word in your heart and in other lives, and believe that God will resurrect what you have committed to Him. If you do so, you will doubtless bear much fruit one day.

> They that sow in tears shall reap in joy. He that goeth forth and weepeth, bearing precious seed, shall doubtless come again with rejoicing, bringing his sheaves with him.
> —PSALM 126:5–6

At His appointed time, the Husbandman will raise you to a new and enduring plain of authority and fruitfulness, for all His ways lead to and end in the way of fulfillment. So hold steady. Your day of fulfillment will come.

> For the vision is yet for an appointed time, but at the end it shall speak, and not lie; though it tarry, wait for it, because it will surely come, it will not tarry.
>
> —HABAKKUK 2:3

ABOUT THIS MINISTRY...

Mission Statement:

Greg Hinnant is called to help train believers to walk in New Testament discipleship by teaching the timeless, priceless, and unfailing principles of the Word of God. It is this ministry's earnest hope that in this way we may help prepare the body of Christ worldwide for, and so hasten, the appearing of our Lord Jesus Christ.

"Prepare ye the way of the Lord" (Isa. 40:3).

Other Ministries Available:

Brother Greg offers a tri-weekly Bible message to interested believers. Pastors, and others in Christian ministry, are particularly encouraged to take advantage of this mailing. Foreign readers are gladly served, with emphasis given to missionaries and others in the ministry.

The Lord has given Greg many biblical messages, similar in length and style to the chapters in this book. These pieces are electronically stored and available for publication or distribution free of charge to interested Christian magazines, ministries and individuals.

Also, if you are interested in having Greg come share God's Word with your church, conference, or Bible school, please do not hesitate to contact us.

To contact this ministry please write, call, fax or e-mail:

GREG HINNANT
P. O. Box 788
High Point, N.C. 27261

Telephone: (336) 882-1645
Fax: (336) 886-7227
E-mail: rghinnant@aol.com

Other books by the author:
Spiritual Truths for Overcoming Adversity